Nietzsc[...]
Phenomenology

Nietzsche and Phenomenology

Edited by

Andrea Rehberg

Cambridge
Scholars
Publishing

Nietzsche and Phenomenology

Edited by Andrea Rehberg

This book first published 2011. The present binding first published 2018.

Cambridge Scholars Publishing

Lady Stephenson Library, Newcastle upon Tyne, NE6 2PA, UK

British Library Cataloguing in Publication Data
A catalogue record for this book is available from the British Library

ISBN (10): 1-5275-1405-6
ISBN (13): 978-1-5275-1405-8

TABLE OF CONTENTS

ABBREVIATIONS OF NIETZSCHE'S WORKS

BGE   *Beyond Good and Evil*, trans. R. J. Hollingdale. Harmondsworth: Penguin, 1973.

BoT   *The Birth of Tragedy*, trans. Ronald Spier. Cambridge: Cambridge University Press, 1999.

BT   *The Birth of Tragedy*, trans. Walter Kaufmann. New York: Vintage Books, 1967.

EH   *Ecce Homo*, trans. Walter Kaufmann. New York: Vintage Books, 1969.

EHC   *Ecce Homo*, trans. Judith Norman. Cambridge: Cambridge University Press, 2005.

GM   *On the Genealogy of Morality*, trans. Maudemarie Clark and Alan Swenson. Indianapolis: Hackett, 1998.

GoM   *On the Genealogy of Morals*, trans. Walter Kaufmann. New York: Vintage Books, 1969.

GS   *The Gay Science*, trans. Walter Kaufmann. New York: Vintage Books, 1974.

GSc   *The Gay Science*, trans. Josefine Nauckhoff. Cambridge: Cambridge University Press, 2001.

HAH   *Human, All Too Human: A Book for Free Spirits*, trans. R. J. Hollingdale. Cambridge: Cambridge University Press, 1996.

HH   *Human, All Too Human: A Book for Free Spirits*, trans. Marion Faber and Stephen Lehmann. London: Penguin Books, 1994.

KSA   *Sämtliche Werke: Kritische Studienausgabe in 15 Bänden*, eds.
        Giorgio Colli and Mazzino Montinari. Berlin and New York:
        dtv/de Gruyter, 1967-1977.

KSB   *Sämtliche Briefe*: *Kritische Studienausgabe in 8 Bänden*, eds.
        Giorgio Colli and Mazzino Montinari. Berlin and New York:
        dtv/de Gruyter, 1975-1984.

TI   *Twilight of the Idols*, trans. R. J. Hollingdale. London: Penguin
        Books, 1990.

TIC   *Twilight of the Idols*, trans. Judith Norman. Cambridge:
        Cambridge University Press, 2005.

TIO   *Twilight of the Idols*, trans. Duncan Large. Oxford: Oxford
        University Press, 1998.

TSZ   *Thus Spoke Zarathustra*, trans. R. J. Hollingdale. London:
        Penguin Books, 1969.

TZ   *Thus Spoke Zarathustra*, trans. Graham Parkes. Oxford: Oxford
        University Press, 2005.

UM   *Untimely Meditations*, trans. R. J. Hollingdale. Cambridge:
        Cambridge University Press, 1997.

WEN   *Writings from the Early Notebooks*, trans. Ladislaus Löb.
        Cambridge: Cambridge University Press, 2009.

WLN   *Writings from the Late Notebooks*, trans. Kate Sturge. Cambridge:
        Cambridge University Press, 2005.

WM   *Der Wille zur Macht*, Stuttgart: Kröner Verlag, 1964.

WP   *The Will to Power*, trans. Walter Kaufmann and R. J. Hollingdale.
        New York: Vintage Books, 1967

WS   "The Wanderer and His Shadow", in *Human, All Too Human: A
        Book for Free Spirits*, Vol. II, Part 2, trans. R. J. Hollingdale.
        Cambridge: Cambridge University Press, 1996.

PREFACE

A few years ago Tony O'Connor, formerly of University College Cork, and I were invited by the executive of the British Society for Phenomenology to organise the annual conference of the Society on the theme of "Nietzsche and Phenomenology", a task we accepted with great pleasure. In the Spring of 2009 this conference took place and was, by common consent, a great success. At about the same time we were asked by Cambridge Scholars Publishing to edit the papers for publication. Unfortunately, soon afterwards Tony O'Connor had to withdraw from the project for a number of extrinsic reasons. I would like to take this opportunity to express the great debt this collection nevertheless owes to him, for without his work in helping to organise the conference this collection too would not have come into existence. I would also like to thank Carol Koulikourdi and Amanda Millar of CSP for all their swift and efficient work and for their support throughout the project. Special thanks are also due to Selma Aydın Bayram for her unstinting technical support.

Thinking back to the above-mentioned conference, as is in the nature of these things no prior arrangements were made to determine the specific topics to be addressed within the general area of "Nietzsche and Phenomenology", and so the astonishing variety of papers it produced is all the more remarkable. To my mind this indicates, above all else, the philosophical wealth inherent in this area, and the contributors' great acuity in attending to and presenting it.

Even though most of the contributors to this volume have provided their own translations of German, French and other foreign-language texts and terms, and – if they have done so – have therefore not given references to existing translations, I have provided, as appropriate, chapter, section, or page references, so that the reader who is less at ease in other languages can nevertheless find the texts quoted. When a contributor has provided their own translations, this is indicated in their first endnote; t.m. means "translation modified".

References to Nietzsche works are to the *Kritische Studienausgabe Sämtliche Werke* (*KSA*) and *Sämtliche Briefe* (*KSB*). Bibliographical details for these and the translations used can be found on the Abbreviations page. *KSA* volumes 1-6 contain Nietzsche's published or finished works. References to these volumes are therefore given as volume number, followed by page number, so that, for instance, *KSA* 5:257 refers to the first page of the main text of *Zur Genealogie der Moral*. *KSA* volumes 7-13, by contrast, contain Nietzsche's famous *Nachlass*, the unpublished, posthumous notes and fragments. References to these are given by volume number, followed by the numbers of the notebook and the note, e.g., *KSA* 10:7 [212], without page numbers, except in cases where a note continues for a considerable number of pages, so that finding the reference without the page number would be unnecessarily time-consuming. *KSA* volumes 14 and 15 contain the text-critical apparatus. All *KSB* references give detailed information as to where a letter can be found, again starting from volume numbers.

Given the large number of different English translations of Nietzsche's works that are available, and in order to avoid any possible confusion between page numbers, section numbers, chapter numbers etc., I have aimed for maximum explicitness in the references, in the hope that this will be considered a boon, rather than a burden, for the reading experience. But with all due respect for all translators of Nietzsche's works – and the utmost respect is due to anyone who takes on such a formidable task – Nietzsche's thought takes place in German, it is an event in the German language, just as the thought of any essential thinker is an event in the language that articulates it. Ultimately, then, in order to hear and to appreciate the tremendous subtlety and complexity of Nietzsche's thought, as that of any significant philosopher, it has to be read in the language in which it was written, in which it thinks.

INTRODUCTION

ANDREA REHBERG

I. Heterogeneities: Phenomenology and Nietzsche

"Nietzsche and Phenomenology"? This title above all suggests a series of questions[1] – questions which do not admit of straightforward answers, in fact questions that do not demand answers at all, but rather a series of exacerbations of the initial conundrum. The papers in this collection carry out exactly such exacerbations, that is, they practice the type of philosophical investigation associated both with Nietzsche and with phenomenology, i.e., one that eschews simplification and instead complicates and differentiates to the greatest possible degree. Towards the end of this introduction a brief overview of the essays will be provided, but to begin with it may be helpful to outline some of the questions which seem to subtend the title of this collection, and to suggest – even if as yet only very broadly – some of the ways in which Nietzsche's thought and phenomenology at times converge, at others diverge, depending on the perspective from which this conjunction is being viewed.

One of the questions surrounding our title is surely what is meant by phenomenology here. As has been said many times, but perhaps most decisively by Heidegger when he stated that "there is no such thing as *the one* phenomenology"[2], no single, definitive, final answer to that question is possible, and the reasons for this are legion. To begin with, phenomenology is nothing like a system of philosophy, or a unified school, with a set of shared doctrines, or anything like an agreed programme. In a sense, then, there is no such easily delimitable phenomenon which could be called "phenomenology", but at most a certain continuity of concerns between different phenomenologists, although even these concerns may be conceived in very different ways, and according to very different styles of thinking, by different practitioners of the philosophical "genre" of phenomenology. But despite these caveats, the general characteristics of phenomenology – or at least the three most pre-eminent of them – can preliminarily be outlined in the following terms.

1) It is first and foremost a philosophical *method*, and specifically a method which enables pure descriptions of phenomena cleared of all extraneous impositions. Hence, although to speak of the phenomenological method is in one sense a tautology (phenomenology is, or is supposed to be, *nothing but* a method), this expression may be used in order to emphasise this central feature of phenomenology. One of the key distinguishing features of this method is that it aims to reject all prior constructions, or "doxa", surrounding and distorting phenomena – summarised by Husserl as the "principle of freedom from presuppositions"[3], or "freedom from prejudice" (*Vorurteilslosigkeit*[4]), so that we may "see" the phenomena under investigation as they are given to consciousness, without any of our habitual pre-given assumptions, constructions or theories intruding into our investigations. This is what is expressed in Husserl's famous demand that "we must go back to the 'things themselves'"[5]. Foremost among these prior, extrinsic ways of approaching phenomena could be named a) modern science (with its proclivity to quantify phenomena and thereby to make them calculable); b) so-called common sense (which claims to look at phenomena in an unbiased way but is instead the repository of self-naturalising and highly problematic ideologies); and, of course, c) traditional philosophical approaches.

On the one hand, then, it can be said that Nietzsche and phenomenology share this understanding of philosophy, according to which its first task is to dismantle the doxa – in the case of phenomenology, so that phenomena are allowed to show themselves from themselves uninterruptedly; in the case of Nietzsche, so that the soothing, comforting reassurances of our doxic convictions may be interrupted. It is obvious from the outset, then, that Nietzsche and phenomenology share suspicions about scientific, commonsensical, and traditional philosophical constructions, and indeed about any other means (such as religion, morality, politics, society, etc.) of "framing" phenomena before they have been allowed to show themselves. But, on the other hand, it should immediately be emphasised that in Nietzsche's thought this aspect of the "method" is complicated by the complex mode of enquiry into these constructions that is genealogy. One of the numerous implications of this is that, for Nietzsche, the idea of presuppositionless access to phenomena requires abstraction from the very forces which the genealogical enquiry is intended to investigate, in other words, that this idea is itself idealist.

Without going into the subtleties of the seminal exposition of this, namely Foucault's analysis of Nietzschean genealogy[6], it can briefly be said that genealogy is more than a method in the strict sense. Not only does it absorb the genealogist herself into the maelstrom of its destabilising forces, but it transforms the phenomena it investigates, literally, beyond recognition. As Foucault puts it, Nietzsche challenges the search for pure origins because,

> ...it is an attempt to capture the exact essence of things, their purest possibilities, and their carefully protected identities, because this search assumes the existence of immobile forms that precede the external world...what is found at the...beginning of things is not the inviolable identity of their origin; it is the dissension of other things. It is disparity[7].

In other words, the assumed identities both of the practitioner of genealogy and of the phenomena submitted to its disruptions are subjected to extensive practical revaluations, such that the latter – at the very least – take on entirely new aspects and, as happens for instance everywhere in the *Genealogy of Morals*, surrender their apparent goodness and innocence to reveal the subterranean web of their sinister, nihilistic provenance.

2) As is well known, and here merely restated by way of reminder, in contrast to the above-mentioned ways of categorising phenomena beforehand, the phenomenological manner of doing philosophy aims to let the phenomena under investigation show themselves as they are given in intuition, i.e., without first subsuming them under any conceptual schema, model, or theory. So prior to the customary problems dominating the traditional branches of philosophy (e.g., ontology, metaphysics, epistemology, ethics, etc.), phenomenology "only" aims to describe phenomena as they are given in experience, as opposed to theorising about them.

Phenomenology thereby draws attention to the fabric of experience itself, i.e., to those features of experience that had tended to fall between the conceptual cracks of traditional philosophy, with its inclination to universalise, to subsume under larger concepts and, more generally, to privilege the abstract constructions of thought over descriptions of the concrete ways in which the multiple, often ineffable, aspects of life are experienced. In this respect, the same can be said about Nietzsche, who pays careful attention to the very phenomena and aspects of phenomena that escape the blunt instrument of the concept, the category, the idea, etc., which above all operate by "making equal" (*ausgleichen, gleichmachen*, etc.[8]) all that in fact tends towards increasing differentiation and complexification[9].

The self-understanding of phenomenology, whereby it investigates the subtle phenomena that escape traditional philosophy, inevitably leads to questions about a) where the experience of phenomena registers with us, b) how it registers, how it becomes meaningful, and c) whether there are privileged phenomena, the experience of which is especially important for us[10]. Here only the first of these questions need to concern us. Heeding only that question, then, we can remind ourselves of Husserl's dictum that "phenomenology has to do with 'consciousness', with all types of lived experiences, acts and act-correlates"[11]. By contrast, when Nietzsche turns his attention to the phenomena of consciousness, and to consciousness as a phenomenon, he is struck by its capacity for falsification under the reign of herd values[12]. For Nietzsche, what registers with us on the level of consciousness is merely froth, the latest outcome of the struggle between different forces, a struggle which takes place in the unconscious and – it should be stressed – entirely impersonal realm he calls the will to power[13]. Although it would go a long way beyond the scope of this Introduction to pursue this here, one of the most fascinating – or symptomatic – texts to consider in the context of this respective privileging of consciousness or the unconscious as the primary "site" of experience is surely "Appendix VIII", on "the Problem of the 'Unconscious'"[14] – penned by Eugen Fink – to Husserl's *Crisis*. In lieu of a detailed discussion, I will confine myself to quoting one especially telling sentence from its concluding paragraph, where it is stated programmatically that, "only after an explicit analysis of consciousness [i.e., by transcendental phenomenology] can the problem of the unconscious be *posed* at all" (387, emphasis added).

3) I would suggest that perhaps the most lasting and important feature of all forms of phenomenology, bestowed on it by Brentano (in Husserl's words "my one and only teacher in philosophy"[15]), was what Brentano called the "intentional inexistence" of an object in mental experience, or "immanent objectivity". Summarised briefly, this refers to the object's being-in (being immanent to) the mind, in the same way that an *accident* (property, characteristic) necessarily is in, belongs to, a substance, according to Aristotelian and Scholastic philosophy[16]. What Brentano uncovered in the notion of intentionality was the ineluctable directedness of each and every mental act to an object which is nonetheless qualitatively distinct from it. Leaving aside all questions about such an object's real existence or actuality, Brentano saw that in all of its activity, the mind is inevitably concerned with and related to something (an "object") which, although somehow given to it, is at the same time profoundly different from it. It is thus a central structural (or dynamic)

feature of the mind that it necessarily goes beyond itself in order to carry out its most essential activities and, it should be emphasised, such directedness or relationality is a feature considered to be absent from all phenomena other than the mind. Brentano's early key statement of this was,

> Every mental phenomenon includes something as object within itself, although [not all mental phenomena] do so in the same way. In presentation something is presented, in judgement something is affirmed or denied, in love loved, in hate hated, in desire desired and so on[17].

What makes the issue of intentionality so momentous for phenomenology is that it establishes two of its most productive convictions, namely 1) the fundamental relationality between so-called "mental acts" and the phenomena they are concerned with, the fact that experience is always the experience *of* something, whether that something is real or not; and 2) the "givenness" of phenomena, including the mysterious ways in which they present or show themselves to experience. Both of these features were taken up and adapted, if in significantly different ways, by post-Husserlian phenomenologists. The first, an originary relationality – albeit purged of its mentalist bias – can be seen to re-emerge, for example, as the notion of being-in and its equiprimordial extensions (being-in-the-world, etc., being-towards-death) in *Being and Time*, or as a certain understanding of our corporeal being in Merleau-Ponty's later works. The second arguably gives rise variously to Heidegger's notion of the "*es gibt*", to Levinas' "*il y'a*", as well as to Derrida's notion of "the gift", and thereby to core concepts of the later phenomenological tradition.

Although intentionality (both as a central feature of early phenomenology and of its later adaptations) could be juxtaposed with many different aspects of Nietzsche's thought, I propose a "Nietzschean" rejoinder to it which points only in one particular direction. For it could be pointed out that, from a Nietzschean perspective, the early phenomenological understanding of the intrinsic relatedness of mental acts to their objects, although on the one hand showing the mind[18] to be essentially directed beyond itself[19], at the same time enshrines an anthropocentric bias at the core of classic phenomenology. But such a bias presents for Nietzsche the greatest obstacle, not only to thought, but to the affirmation of life itself. From his earliest works (e.g., *The Birth of Tragedy*, "On Truth and Lie in an Extra-Moral Sense") to the final notes of 1888, Nietzsche maintains that human being – if not an altogether illusory fixed point – is no more than a node in a perpetual if discontinuous material becoming, the core aspects of which are will to power, eternal recurrence and physiology. To elevate and valorise this nodal point into a privileged, unique perspective represents to Nietzsche's thinking a type of delusional phantasy[20].

The centrality of the descriptive method to phenomenology in comparison to the tenets of Nietzschean genealogy; the position, and the value placed on consciousness in early phenomenology and in Nietzsche's thought, respectively; the core phenomenological concept of intentionality in contrast to Nietzsche's critique of anthropocentric conceptuality – do these points not lead us inevitably to conclude that the connections between Nietzsche and phenomenology are so few and so tenuous as to doom from the very beginning any attempt to pursue, develop and intensify them? Although the foregoing, adopting the position of devil's advocate, seems to suggest so, this impression can swiftly but decisively be countered by the simple reminder that phenomenology, despite tracing its inception to that phase, is by no means reducible to its Husserlian instantiation[21]. In fact, several of the papers presented here carry out subtle readings of the texts of Nietzsche by – broadly – phenomenological means and others, conversely, enhance our understanding of phenomenological issues by engaging with the thought of Nietzsche. What we see in them, then, is a kind of cross-fertilisation between apparently very heterogeneous types of thought. This is very far from the appropriation of one to the other, and rather in the nature of a series of mutual enhancements, of reciprocal elaborations and challenges, in each case sensitive to the textures of thought and the complexities of texts attended to.

II. Convergences: Nietzsche's Readers

Continuing our gradual approach to the matter of thought in these essays, allow me to outline in broad terms the history of the reception of Nietzsche over the past century or so, at least as it presents itself to us today. This may help to set the scene for some of the following papers, and to indicate some of the issues and discussions which form part of their background.

It is possible to distinguish three important events or incisive points in the history of Nietzsche interpretation, firstly, Heidegger's seminal (if not unproblematic) mid-1930s to mid-1940s readings, which unfolded Nietzsche's texts in serious philosophical terms for the first time[22]; secondly, the French readings of and responses to Nietzsche of the second half of the twentieth century, above all, those of Deleuze, Foucault,

Bataille, Klossowski, Kofman, Derrida, Irigary, and Blanchot[23]; and thirdly, the continuation and mediation of both of these highpoints of Nietzsche interpretation to a predominantly anglophone audience, above all in such ground-breaking volumes such as *The New Nietzsche* and *Exceedingly Nietzsche*, to name but two[24].

In his sustained, if not univocal, confrontation (*Aus-einander-setzung*) with Nietzsche[25], Heidegger drew out many of the central themes of Nietzsche's thought – will to power, eternal recurrence, the overman, nihilism, justice, Platonism, revaluation of all values – which still occupy our attempts at reading Nietzsche today, and eventually (in 1940) drew them together into the quasi-systematic whole of what he then called Nietzsche's metaphysics[26]. Put all too swiftly, according to Heidegger, Nietzsche's thought must at least in large part be understood as a continuation of the concerns, structure, language and, above all, of the internal logic of occidental metaphysics, although at the same time he finds Nietzsche in the ambiguous position of the "consummation" (*Vollendung*) of metaphysics. What is therefore Heidegger's greatest achievement vis-à-vis previous readings of Nietzsche, namely the demonstration of the internal coherence of his thought, as of its continuity with the central themes of Western metaphysics, presents itself at the same time – from the vantage point of more than half a century and innumerable subtle Nietzsche readings later – as the problem of the over-systematisation of a thought which has been shown essentially to escape such regimentation. Needless to say, the details and complexities of Heidegger's confrontation with Nietzsche lie beyond what can be considered here. Suffice it to say that Heidegger's *Nietzsche* volumes – regardless of the degree of explicitness with which they enter into the discussions in this volume – form something like their more or less distant background. That is to say, they are simultaneously "condition of possibility" and something from which differentiation is necessary in order for new readings to be able to emerge.

Much the same could also be said of the second wave of European Nietzsche interpretations, namely by a variety of French thinkers, in that they too – albeit to different degrees and in different ways – found it necessary to put a distance between Heidegger's hermeneutic-phenomenological and *seinsgeschichtliche* reading of Nietzsche and their own understanding of his thought. Although it is – fortunately – impossible to unify these French readings under any one heading, certain tendencies traversing them can be pointed out, although these too finally escape homogenisation. So the following points are in the nature of general indications, rather than precise definitions.

I would suggest that two broad, but by no means mutually exclusive, orientations can be discerned among the French interpretations of Nietzsche. The first may be characterised as displaying a great sensitivity to the nuances of the text, of its fluctuating rhythms, its variegated tones, its subtle modulations of language, both in Nietzsche's writings and in those of the French authors themselves. No less philosophically serious than the most literal-minded, technically rigorous treatises, these readings incorporate as their starting point one of Nietzsche's most profound insights, namely that thinking is itself a matter of desire flows, of the body and the senses, with which it is entirely continuous, rather than being dualistically opposed to these libidinal-material streams. They thereby celebrate the *jouissance* of the body, of the differential play of language, and of the sensuous textures of textuality, in the full knowledge that concepts – if they have any force at all – are not abstractions but signs and symptoms.

The second orientation, although by no means devoid of these insights, may perhaps be said to tend more towards philosophical analysis and the creation of concepts with which the complex structures of Nietzsche's thought can be approached, for example, by exploring this thought via new and revealing conjunctions with other thinkers or modes of thought[27].

I would furthermore maintain that both orientations are driven – if to different degrees – by what must finally be understood as a political motivation, even though the thinkers' conceptions of the political, of the interconnections between philosophy and the political, and of their relative priority, tend to differ significantly from one another. Nevertheless, it should be remembered that Nietzsche's incisive analyses of the conceptual machinery of what has become known as the metaphysics of presence, and his thorough dissections of the herd mentality and other forms of slavishness, are not only philosophically revolutionary, but are also capable of constituting powerful instruments of political transformation, in thought and deed[28].

It should be remembered that the English-speaking reader had to wait (especially in some cases[29]) an inordinately long time for translations of the major works of the French Nietzsche reception to be made available. Given this situation, it can easily be appreciated why the 1977 collection of essays, *The New Nietzsche*, edited by David B. Allison, and containing selections from the works of many of the major exponents of the "French Nietzsche", was so influential. It was followed (in some cases after an interval) by a flurry of books, essays, and collections of essays written in English, such as *Exceedingly Nietzsche*, edited by Krell and Wood. We are most fortunate in being able to include original essays by two of the main figures of the third, English-language, wave of Nietzsche interpretation, namely David Krell and John Sallis[30], in this collection.

These three waves, then, provide some of the context – although not of course exclusively so – for the essays presented here. But I would like to emphasise that the convergences of the section heading equally apply to these essay themselves, in that different perspectives, concerns, tones, voices, etc. converge here, not to coincide or to harmonise, but so that the plurivocity and exuberant wealth of contemporary readings of the issues surrounding Nietzsche *and* phenomenology can be heard again.

III. The Phenomena of Thought

The following papers have been grouped according to whether a thematic approach or a "comparative" approach – that is, in each case the staging of an encounter between Nietzsche and an important figure in twentieth-century thought – has been the relatively more dominant organising principle. Before going into this in more detail, it should be pointed out though that a number of alternative groupings would have been possible. One alternative way in which papers could have been arranged is according to whether they pursue the question implied in the title "Nietzsche and Phenomenology" in a more "classical" manner, that is, by addressing themes or figures commonly associated with phenomenological concerns, or in what might be termed a more "ex-centric" way, opening up new and perhaps unexpected avenues of enquiry. The chief virtue of the former group surely lies in their deepening and enhancing our understanding of issues that have variously occupied both phenomenology and studies of Nietzsche; whereas the latter group extend or expand our ideas about what can at all fall into the purview of an investigation of the nexus "Nietzsche and Phenomenology". In the former group fall the papers by Sallis, McNeill, Haase, Krell, and myself; in the latter those by Burnham/Jesinghausen, Kirkland, Marsden, Parkes, and Urpeth.

Above I say "relatively more dominant" organising principle because some of the thematic approaches, such as for instance in Jill Marsden's paper, also have a comparative element – in that case between Leibniz and Nietzsche. Conversely, as is the case for instance in Jim Urpeth's essay on Nietzsche and Bergson, the comparative approach is tempered by the thematic focus, namely, as the title of his paper indicates, on what he calls "natural religion". So the division between Parts One and Two is not a rigid or absolute one. Similarly, a number of cross-groupings could be seen to be at work within and across the two parts of the collection. For instance, the challenge of immanentism (or what is called "life" by Nietzsche) is addressed and/or confronted in several of the papers, especially in those by Sallis, Marsden, Urpeth, and myself. In a related vein, Kirkland, Parkes, and Urpeth explore the task of affirmation and its implications. And so one could continue to point out several other sub-divisions that undermine the thematic-comparative division, some of which will resonate more with certain readers than with others.

Having pointed out some of the potential alternative ways in which continuities between these papers might be conceived, let us now turn to the papers in their actuality, and try to tease out some of the issues, concerns, texts, and figures they deal with. In the opening paper of the collection, "Shining in Perspective: Nietzsche and Beyond", John Sallis addresses what may be thought of as *the* underlying issue connecting Nietzsche and phenomenology, namely the central meaning of appearance, "shining", i.e., the entire register of terms surrounding the German *Schein*, *Erscheinung*, *scheinbar*, etc. More concretely, this paper explores the consequences of Nietzsche's inversion of Platonism and it shows how this inversion, if radically carried out, opens upon phenomenology and how, in the late fragments concerning shining and the perspectival, Nietzsche already inaugurates the task proper to phenomenology.

Albeit it in an entirely different vein and manner, Douglas Burnham and Martin Jesinghausen continue this theme by enquiring into the fate of the figure of Apollo, associated with "beautiful appearance" (*der schöne Schein*), in Nietzsche's writings. The paper begins with a discussion of the curious, gradual disappearance of the figure of Apollo from the text of Nietzsche's *The Birth of Tragedy*. The interpretation of Nietzsche's strategy centres upon the metaphor that in Socratism the Apollinian pupates and cocoons itself away (*sich verpuppt*). The cocoon not only covers over what is within it and hides it from view, but it also protects and preserves what is within, and it thus creates the "space" for transfiguration. At the end of *The Birth of Tragedy*, the Apollinian re-emerges in glory. According to the authors, this involves two initial tasks: first, to enquire into the phenomenological structure of the cocoon as a double hiding; second, to ask how this structure fits into Nietzsche's understanding of art in the book. The second half of the paper outlines how this double-hiding function reappears in Nietzsche's middle-period and later works as the theme of the mask, in turn showing that the duality of Apollo and Dionysus that is essential to *The Birth of Tragedy* is not dropped by Nietzsche in favour of mono-pole key ideals, but continues in a modified form.

In "Zarathustra and Redeeming the Past", Sean Kirkland thinks through the temporal aspects of the philosophical persona of Zarathustra and their implications for the self-understanding of human being. Specifically, the essay concerns an aspect of Nietzsche's project in *Thus Spoke Zarathustra* that is usually overlooked – our relation to the past. Given the explicitly "prophetic" mode of Zarathustra's discourse, the temporal mode on which interpreters usually (and rightly) focus is the future. However, if this occurs at the expense of Zarathustra's remarks about the proper relation to the past, his project will be misinterpreted. After first considering the "causal" function of the overman, as an essentially futural figure, the discussion shifts to Zarathustra's call for an "*Erlösung*" or "Redemption" of our past. Kirkland argues that "redeeming" our past with Zarathustra entails a setting free of the multiple, dynamic, non-self-identical origin still active there, and, in this creative act, a bringing into proximity of the disavowed, anti-metaphysical, past source and an open, unanticipatable future.

In her paper on "The Immeasurable Fineness of Things", Jill Marsden tackles one of the thorniest issues in phenomenology, namely the role and the understanding of the workings of consciousness, and plays it through a broad register of Nietzschean reflections on the issue. She reminds us that, according to Nietzsche, the psychologists' chief error is to take the indistinct idea to be a lower species of idea than the luminous one. To this Nietzsche opposes the thought that "what moves away from our consciousness and thus *becomes obscure* may yet be perfectly clear in itself". Via the highly original route of Leibniz's suggestive propositions on the issue of perception, Marsden discusses the ways in which Nietzsche, as part of a broader fascination with elusive forms of awareness and anomalous perceptions, insists upon the existence of a vast array of perceptual and affective phenomena which are only sensed at thresholds beyond empirical representation. In a gesture akin to peripheral vision, she

explores how in certain estranging moments something unassimilable for
consciousness is fleetingly apprehended.

Another paper that significantly broadens our sense of the possible
ambit of any enquiry into Nietzsche and phenomenology is that by
Graham Parkes. By way of staging an encounter between Nietzsche's
thought and that of classical East-Asian thinkers, he reflects on our
relation to the phenomena of nature and asks whether there is any way of
getting back to "the things themselves" when they are the things of nature.
In response to this Parkes discusses the variety of ways, suggested in
Nietzsche's texts, in which we might come to experience a "de-
anthropomorphised", "de-divinised", and "newly redeemed" nature.
Assuming we attempt to pursue these paths, and do so successfully, he
asks what we would then encounter, if – perhaps – no longer our own
selves.

Each of the papers in the second part of the collection, as I mentioned
above, is chiefly concerned with staging an encounter between Nietzsche
and one of the influential figures of twentieth-century phenomenology,
although in each case they do so in order to allow a specific philosophical
issue to emerge. William McNeill and Ullrich Haase both explore the
Nietzsche-Heidegger connection, albeit in rather different ways; the
differences being not least due to the different texts by Heidegger, on the
basis of which each examines the famous *Auseinandersetzung*. Both
McNeill and Haase eschew discussions of Heidegger's *Nietzsche* volumes
in favour of less obvious – but therefore perhaps all the more telling –
textual sites of the encounter.

McNeill explores the trope of the "descent" of philosophy and, by
linking it to genealogy, he uncovers a largely hidden legacy of
Nietzschean thought, and not just in Heidegger's work of the 30s and 40s.
The "other" Nietzsche whom he discovers makes his appearance much
earlier, namely in *Being and Time* in 1927. McNeill shows how this early,
phenomenological work is also intensively concerned with the
genealogical issue of descent, despite what might appear to be a
metaphysical or transcendental concern with origins. By broaching this
genealogical dimension of Heidegger's phenomenology, McNeill's paper
does not merely reveal a common ground between Heidegger and
Nietzsche, but demonstrates that the Heidegger of *Being and Time* was
already decisively influenced by Nietzsche.

Ullrich Haase's paper on history and life in Heidegger and Nietzsche provides a neat continuation of McNeill's investigation of the Nietzschean legacy in *Being and Time* by choosing as its main textual foci what is now widely considered to be Heidegger's second magnum opus, i.e., *Beiträge zur Philosophie (Vom Ereignis)*, and the first of the group of texts that continue its concerns, namely *Besinnung*. By concentrating on the issues of history and life, but also on a host of related issues, such as, importantly, justice, Haase is able to carry out a multi-facetted investigation of the Nietzschean elements of Heidegger's works surrounding the famous Turn (*die Kehre*).

In my paper I discuss the nexus of issues surrounding Nietzsche's key concept of physiology, arguably one of the richest and most complex notions in his thinking. In the first part the textual and thinkerly effects of the concept of physiology are being chiselled out to discover, not so much what Nietzsche means by it, but how it works in his texts. I then turn to an examination of the most important and sustained phenomenological work on the body, that of Maurice Merleau-Ponty. Here his late text "The Intertwining – The Chiasm" from *The Visible and the Invisible* is examined and its notion of flesh is placed alongside Nietzsche's thoughts on the body and on physiology. One of the chief questions motivating this enquiry is whether it is Nietzsche or Merleau-Ponty who can be read to make a more radical and far-reaching contribution to our understanding of our "own" physicality.

In his essay on "Nietzsche in Derrida's *Politics of Friendship*", David Farrell Krell first of all provides a brief but incisive analysis of the textual sources and key theses of each of the ten chapters of Derrida's text. He then turns to a more nuanced consideration of the role or roles Nietzsche plays in *Politics of Friendship*. He subtly interweaves Nietzsche's and Derrida's with his own reflections on the challenges and difficulties, the aporias, of friendship between mortals (especially if they are of different genders), and thereby also draws out the implications of this for a genuine democracy, for a *politics* of friendship.

Finally, Jim Urpeth discusses some themes in what he terms the "philosophical biologies" of Nietzsche and Bergson that bear upon the articulation of a philosophical naturalism which offers a non-reductive account of the origin and nature of religion on the basis that the real is "religious" in essence. He reads both of them as advocates of the view that ultimately religion has a reality irreducible to and distinct from anthropomorphic projection, psycho-physiological illness, ideological conflict, etc. Implicitly, an alternative is thereby proposed to the approaches and presuppositions of the "theological turn" in contemporary phenomenology.

What all these essays in their great variety demonstrate, then, is that both the thought of Nietzsche and that of phenomenology are essentially unfixable and unsubsumable to one organising principle, term, or word, and that they both, singly and in conjunction, continue to challenge readers to ever more incisive and, perchance, daring interpretations of their texts. Not for this reason alone readers will continue to feel that they have not done with these texts, which perpetually engage, provoke and productively confound us in equal measure.

Notes

[1] In this respect I wholeheartedly agree with David Farrell Krell, who also takes his essay's point of departure from this insight or intuition.

[2] "*Die* Phänomenologie gibt es nicht". Martin Heidegger, *Die Grundprobleme der Phänomenologie*. Gesamtausgabe Bd. 24. Frankfurt a.M.: Klostermann, 1989, 467. *The Basic Problems of Phenomenology*, trans. Albert Hofstadter. Bloomington, IN: Indiana University Press, 1982, 328.

[3] Edmund Husserl, *Logical Investigations*, vol. 1, trans. J.N. Findlay. London: Routledge, 2001, hereafter *LI* 1, 177.

[4] Edmund Husserl, *Cartesian Meditations – An Introduction to Phenomenology*, trans. Dorion Cairns. The Hague: Martinus Nijhoff, 1960, §15, 35f.

[5] *LI* 1, 168.

[6] See Michel Foucault, "Nietzsche, Genealogy, History", in Donald Bouchard (ed.), *Language, Counter-Memory, Practice: Selected Essays and Interviews*. New York: Cornell University Press, 1988, hereafter NGH. See also the papers by Sean Kirkland and William McNeill, which touch on this text.

[7] NGH 142.

[8] Cf., for instance, "Jeder Begriff entsteht durch Gleichsetzen des Nicht-Gleichen", "Ueber Wahrheit und Lüge im aussermoralischen Sinne", hereafter WL, in *KSA* 1:880; "Every concept emerges through the positing-as-equal of the non-equal", m.t.

[9] These points are being developed in greater detail especially in the papers by Jill Marsden and myself.

[10] Needless to say, disagreement about the answers to these questions is precisely one of the factors by which practitioners of phenomenology can be distinguished.

[11] Edmund Husserl, *Ideas Pertaining to a Pure Phenomenology and to a Phenomenological Philosophy, First Book*, trans. Fred Kersten. Dordrecht: Kluwer, 1998, hereafter *Ideas* I; XIX, t.m.

[12] See, for instance, "On Truth and Lie in an Extra-Moral Sense", as well as innumerable sections of *The Will to Power*.
[13] Several of the papers either discuss this in some detail or at least touch upon it in passing, e.g., Marsden, Parkes, Rehberg, and Urpeth.
[14] Edmund Husserl, *The Crisis of European Sciences and Transcendental Phenomenology*, trans. David Carr. Evanston, IL: Northwestern University Press, 1970.
[15] Quoted in Herbert Spiegelberg, with Karl Schuhmann, *The Phenomenological Movement – A Historical Introduction*, 3rd ed. The Hague: Martinus Nijhoff, 1982, 27.
[16] Franz Brentano, *Psychology from an Empirical Standpoint*, trans. Antos Rancurello, D.B. Terrell and Linda McAlister. London and New York: Routledge, 1995, hereafter *PES*, 88.
[17] *Ibid.*
[18] Or even human being as a structural whole, Dasein, to be always already beyond itself, cf. Martin Heidegger, *Being and Time*, trans. John Macquarrie and Edward Robinson. Oxford: Blackwell, 1987, hereafter *BT*.
[19] In Heidegger's understanding of this relationality Dasein becomes "out-standing", "ecstatic", and "futural", cf. *BT*.
[20] See, for instance, the opening pages of WL, *KSA* 1:875-7, or *Twilight of the Idols*.
[21] In this regard too I agree with points made by Krell in the opening remarks of his essay.
[22] Martin Heidegger, *Nietzsche*, 4 vols., trans. Joan Stambaugh, David Farrell Krell and Frank Capuzzi. San Francisco: HarperCollins, 1987, hereafter *N*. See David Krell's nuanced and highly informative account of the pre-history of Heidegger's *Nietzsche* volumes, *N* 1, "Contexts", especially 238-45.
[23] Gilles Deleuze, *Nietzsche and Philosophy*, trans. Hugh Tomlinson. London: Athlone, 1983; Michel Foucault, "Nietzsche, Genealogy, History" (cf. n. 6 above); Georges Bataille, *On Nietzsche*, trans. Bruce Boone. New York: Paragon House, 1992; Pierre Klossowski, *Nietzsche and the Vicious Circle*, trans. Daniel Smith. London: Athlone, 1997; Sarah Kofman, *Nietzsche and Metaphor*, trans. Duncan Large. London: Athlone, 1993; Jacques Derrida, *Spurs – Nietzsche's Styles*, trans. Barbara Harlow. Chicago and London: University of Chicago Press, 1979; Luce Irigaray, *Marine Lover – Of Friedrich Nietzsche*, trans. Gillian Gill. New York: Columbia University Press, 1991; Maurice Blanchot, *The Infinite Conversation*, trans. Susan Hanson. Minneapolis and London: University of Minnesota Press, 1993. This is by no means an exhaustive list, in that all of the above have other texts on Nietzsche. Nor, needless to say, is this list of authors in any way final. It is merely meant to give a snapshot of seminal French readings of Nietzsche in the second half of the twentieth century. For a detailed account of the key texts that mark the spread of the "New Nietzsche" in France, especially after 1961, see, for instance, Duncan Large's "Translator's Introduction" to his translation of Sarah Kofman, *Nietzsche and Metaphor*, especially x-xxi.
[24] David Allison (ed.), *The New Nietzsche – Contemporary Styles of Interpretation*. Cambridge, MA: MIT Press, 1986; David Farrell Krell and David Wood (eds.),

Exceedingly Nietzsche – Aspects of Contemporary Nietzsche Interpretation.
London and New York: Routledge, 1988. In the same breath such influential
English-language works on Nietzsche as those by David Krell and John Sallis
should be mentioned. See, for instance, David Farrell Krell, *Infectious Nietzsche.*
Bloomington and Indianapolis: Indiana University Press, 1996; and John Sallis,
Crossings: Nietzsche and the Space of Tragedy. Chicago and London: University
of Chicago Press, 1991.

[25] Martin Heidegger, *Nietzsche*, 2 vols.. Pfullingen: Neske, 1961, hereafter *Nie*, 9.
See also David Krell's enormously illuminating Introductions, Notes, and
Analyses to the four volumes in English of Heidegger's *Nietzsche.*

[26] *N* vol. 3, 185-251.

[27] Here Deleuze's understanding, in *Nietzsche and Philosophy*, of Nietzsche's
genealogy as a radicalisation of Kantian critique in general, and his path-breaking
analyses of Nietzsche and Kant on the problem of paralogistic thinking in
particular, could be mentioned.

[28] The most obvious exponents of this conviction are, I would claim, Deleuze,
Foucault, and Irigaray, albeit in markedly different ways.

[29] Both in the case of *Nietzsche and Philosophy* and of *Nietzsche and Metaphor*,
twenty-one years, incredible to say.

[30] Both are not just enormously influential writers on Nietzsche but of course also
tremendously important readers of Heidegger and of the broader (post-)
phenomenological movement. In addition, Krell edited and co-translated the four
volumes of Heidegger's *Nietzsche* into English. Sallis is the author of too many
essays and books to mention here.

PART ONE:

THEMATIC APPROACHES

SHINING IN PERSPECTIVE: NIETZSCHE AND BEYOND

JOHN SALLIS

For Nietzsche, as for phenomenology, Platonism never ceases to be a provocation. Never, despite all the gestures in this direction, is Platonism made to settle into a well-defined form and thus brought under control; never, despite all the effort expended, is it consigned once and for all to a pre-ordained place in the history of thought in such a way as to guarantee that it will not return to haunt thinking in the very turn to another beginning. While expressing his deep mistrust of Plato, branding him as an aberration from the basic instincts of the Greeks, as pre-existently Christian, Nietzsche describes him, at the opposite extreme, as an artist who preferred appearance (*Schein*) to being. It is hardly otherwise with Heidegger: on the one hand, it is through Plato that, with the ascendancy of the idea, the older Greek sense of truth is lost, and yet, on the other hand, it is precisely the *Republic* that, in its concluding myth, is said to name in its essence the *lethe* of *aletheia*[1].

Yet most often, for Nietzsche, Platonism assumes the guise of something to be overcome; as subsequently, for Heidegger too, Platonism, identified with metaphysics, is to be surpassed in and through the overcoming of metaphysics. For Nietzsche, in particular, this overcoming is to be an overturning, an inverting, of Platonism. This figure of inversion remains effective throughout the entire course of Nietzsche's thought, from the time of *The Birth of Tragedy* up through his final creative year. It is already explicit in one of the sketches made as Nietzsche was preparing *The Birth of Tragedy*. In the sketch he writes, "My philosophy an *inverted Platonism*: the further removed from true being, the purer, the more beautiful, the better it is. Living in *Schein* as goal"[2]. There is perhaps no other passage that anticipates so perfectly and at such an early date the inversion that will come more and more to structure Nietzsche's thought as a whole.

The terms of this inversion are first taken up thematically in the initial volume of *Human, All Too Human*, published in 1878. What in the early sketch was called "true being" is now designated as "the metaphysical world", this designation serving as the title of the aphorism addressed to this theme[3]. Nietzsche begins with what has the appearance of a concession, "It is true, there could be a metaphysical world; the absolute possibility of it is hardly to be disputed". This possibility is, however, of the emptiest, most abstract sort, and Nietzsche characterizes it as "a purely scientific problem", one not likely to be much of a bother to anyone. But then, with a sudden injection of genealogy, Nietzsche completely recasts the problem; for what he declares to lie behind the belief in metaphysical assumptions, prompting this belief, begetting these assumptions, is passion, error, and self-deception. He concludes, "When one has disclosed these methods" – in effect, these non-methods – "as the foundation of all extant religions and metaphysical systems, one has refuted them!". Nietzsche grants that even after this refutation the empty possibility of a metaphysical world remains; and yet, he adds, "one can do absolutely nothing with it, not to speak of letting happiness, salvation, and life depend on the spiderwebs of such a possibility". Nothing could even be said of this world except that it is other, that it is inaccessible and incomprehensible. Even if, against all likelihood, the existence of such a world could somehow be demonstrated and if knowledge could be had of it, this knowledge would be utterly useless, even more useless than knowledge of the chemical composition of water would be to a sailor endangered by a storm at sea. Short of such a most unlikely demonstration, there is nothing to motivate positing such a metaphysical world as existing, granted that the passion and lies that otherwise supported it have been exposed as such.

In this aphorism a shift is detectable, a shift from the metaphysical world in general to the thing-in-itself specifically. Another aphorism[4], entitled "Appearance and Thing-in-itself", stages the problem dramatically. Philosophers are portrayed as stationing themselves before the so-called world of appearance as though it were a painting depicting a scene; their task is to interpret this scene so as to draw a conclusion about the nature of the thing-in-itself, which is regarded as the ground of this world. While some venture such conclusions, other philosophers contend that there is no connection, that from the world of appearance no conclusion can be drawn regarding the thing-in-itself. Against both parties, against both those who affirm and those who deny such a connection, Nietzsche poses another alternative: that the character of the world of appearances has, in its becoming, been determined, not by the thing-in-itself, but by a human, all too human process. Here is how Nietzsche describes it, "Because we have for millennia made moral, aesthetic, religious claims, looked upon the world with blind desire, passion, or fear, and abandoned ourselves to the bad habits of illogical thinking, this world has gradually *become* so wondrously variegated, frightful, meaningful, soulful, it has acquired color – but we have been the colorists: it is the human intellect that has let appearance appear and transported [*hineingetragen*] its erroneous basic conceptions into things". Thus, just as, according to the earlier aphorism, passion and lies produced the metaphysical world and thus the thing-in-itself, so likewise it is human desire, passion, and misconception that have colored the world of appearance, that have brought it to appear as it does. And yet, exposing the true nature of such appearance requires that the appearing be interrupted; it requires, says Nietzsche, a rigorous science (*strenge Wissenschaft*) capable of detaching us, a discipline that can "lift us up out of the entire process". It is no doubt in aiming at such detachment from the human, all too human process of appearing that the book *Human, All Too Human* is, as its subtitle declares, a book for free spirits.

These analyses bear significantly on the inversion of Platonism at which Nietzsche aims. The metaphysical world – in Platonic terms, the intelligible, *to noeton* – is shown to be so vacuous, so innocuous, so utterly irrelevant, that even if it were to remain as an empty possibility, the full weight of what is called reality would still be shifted to the world of appearance. Hence, the inversion would in effect be carried out, primacy now being given to – in Platonic terms – the sensible, *to aistheton*, while the intelligible becomes, at most, only secondary. Furthermore, with this inversion, the terms themselves do not go unaltered, do not merely exchange places in the schema, the lower becoming the higher, and conversely. Not only does the alleged ground of being get reconstrued as empty possibility but also the world of appearance, previously construed in relation to this ground, is now referred instead to the genealogy of subjectivity, to the human, all too human process by which misconceptions are carried over into things so as to appear – or reappear – as the character of the things.

The figure of the inversion of Platonism remains operative in the works of the 1880s, for instance, in the injunction, repeatedly sounded and echoed in *Thus Spoke Zarathustra*, to remain true to the earth. Yet it is only in his final year, primarily in *Twilight of the Idols* that this figure is fully developed and its most extreme consequences are drawn out.

One of the very remarkable features of the text *Twilight of the Idols* is its use of modifying punctuation, quotation marks set around certain words in order to indicate a double meaning, or rather a shift from the traditional sense to its effacement and replacement, this shift corresponding precisely to the inversion of Platonism that the text effects. Thus, when Nietzsche writes of reason in philosophy, using this phrase as a section title[5], he sets the word *reason* in quotation marks so as to represent graphically what the text itself declares: that what has been called by this name, what has been taken as reason, is now exposed as a power of dissimulation that has led us to falsify the testimony of the senses and to add to the apparent world the lie of a true world. The name of this true world that has been exposed as a lie, the expression "true world", thus also appears in quotation marks. Even in writing that "the 'apparent' world is the only one", such modifying or doubling punctuation must come to mark the word *apparent* (*scheinbare*); for as soon as it is recognized as the only world (*die einzige*), the designation of it as apparent begins to lose its appropriateness, and it becomes necessary to mark a shift, a certain effacement, of the designation. In these as well as numerous other passages, Nietzsche proves to be a superb master of punctuation.

In *Twilight of the Idols* the figure of the inversion of Platonism receives its most concentrated expression in the section entitled "How the 'True World' Finally Became a Fable". Here, in barely more than one page, Nietzsche recounts the history of philosophy precisely as the series of positions by which the inversion of Platonism has come about. Beginning with the true world of Plato – *true world* written without quotation marks – Nietzsche tells of the six stages by which this true world – acquiring quotation marks in the course of the story – finally came to be exposed as an error, how its history, the history told here, proved to be, as the section subtitle says, the history of an error.

This compact history of the inversion of Platonism has been repeatedly interpreted by Heidegger, Derrida, and others, interpretation layered upon interpretation to the point that its outcome has become almost paradigmatic of the task that imposes itself on our time. Against this background, let it suffice, first, merely to recall the penultimate stage, that of the pandemonium (*Teufelslärm*) of all free spirits, thus the stage enacted in *Human, All Too Human* where the "true world" – with quotation marks

– proves useless, superfluous, and so is to be abolished. And then, second, let us reread once more Nietzsche's account of the final stage, the stage that this very text enacts. It reads, "The true world we have abolished: what world has remained? The apparent one perhaps?...But no! *With the true world we have also abolished the apparent one!*"[6].

This enactment, the completion of the inversion of Platonism, Nietzsche marks as noon, the moment of the shortest shadow. It is the moment of escape from the long shadow cast by Platonism, the moment of liberation that comes only with the end of this longest error. It is also the moment of dissolution in which the future becomes sheer possibility, the opening of a new era for mankind (*Menschheit*), indeed the high point of mankind opening beyond mankind. It is the moment in which the stage is set for Zarathustra's first speech to the people, the speech that begins, "*I teach you the overman. Man is something that is to be overcome*"[7]. It is a moment that Nietzsche thus marks with the indication, INCIPIT ZARATHUSTRA.

What remains, then, in this moment? In a sense nothing remains. The true world has been abolished, and now the apparent world also is abolished, is recognized as having already been abolished with the abolition of the true world. Nothing remains, neither the intelligible, metaphysical world nor the apparent, sensible world. Yet the sense of the abolition is not the same in both cases. The intelligible world is abolished in the sense that it is no longer regarded as existing, is no longer accorded even the empty possibility that was still granted it in *Human, All Too Human*. It is this abolition that is expressed when Zarathustra, just before coming to speak for the first time to the people, muses that perhaps the old hermit he has met in the forest has not yet heard that God is dead. What is said here in terms of Christianity – identified by Nietzsche as "Platonism for the people"[8] – means that the intelligible world has vanished with an absoluteness comparable to that of death.

This is, most decidedly, not the sense in which the sensible world has been abolished. For – it need hardly be said – no matter how thoroughly one has detached oneself from belief in an intelligible world, the sensible world does not disappear and cannot be made to disappear, cannot in this sense be abolished. Indeed it is not even conceivable what it would mean for the sensible world as such to disappear, for this world is the very scene of all appearing and disappearing, is the precondition of all appearing and disappearing. No matter how thoroughly one relinquishes belief in the intelligible world, the things of the sensible world, things as they unfold before our senses, continue stubbornly to appear; they persist in showing themselves. In what sense, then, can it be said – as Nietzsche does – that with the true world we have also abolished the apparent one? What has been abolished is not the world that hitherto has been taken as apparent but only its character *as apparent*. What now, with the abolition of the true world, is excluded is the possibility of understanding it in this way. Once the true world has been abolished, once it has been exposed as an error that can be allowed to drift into oblivion, then the sensible can no longer be understood by reference to this allegedly true world. It can no longer be taken as a realm of remote images through which the true world appears, albeit faintly, from a great distance, concealedly – that is, it can no longer be understood *as apparent*. As an apparent world it will have been abolished along with that which was alleged to appear through it; yet as unfolding before our senses, as constituting the very scene of all appearing, it will persist no less assuredly than ever.

Thus, the effect of the inversion of Platonism, once it is fully carried out to the point of this final abolition, is neither simply to invert the terms nor even, once they are inverted, to institute a new hierarchy, a new ordering structure (as Heidegger proposes in his interpretation). Fully and decisively twisting free of Platonism – to use David Krell's wonderful translation of *Herausdrehung* – requires letting go of the intelligible world and hence of all ordering of it with respect to the sensible. The effect of the inversion of Platonism is to constrain thinking entirely to the sensible and thus finally to efface its very character as inversion.

If things – that is, sensible things – are not to be understood by reference to intelligibles that they would image, if, in venturing to understand things, thought is constrained to the region of these things themselves, then what is required is that they be understood *from themselves*. To understand them from themselves requires, in turn, that they be apprehended as they show themselves or as they can be brought to show themselves; and it requires that thinking bind itself to the self-showing of things. The directive that thus emerges in the move beyond the inversion of Platonism is nothing other than the imperative *zu den Sachen selbst*. What opens beyond the inversion of Platonism is phenomenology.

If, in this connection, sensible things can still be called appearances, what this designates is their own appearing, their own self-showing, not that they serve for the appearing of something else that exceeds the world of appearance. Yet even granted this restriction, there would still seem to be a basic difference between what Nietzsche declares regarding appearances and what phenomenology envisions in its imperative. For, according to the analysis in *Human, All Too Human*, appearances, though not determined by things-in-themselves, are determined by a human, all too human process. Things appear as they do because we have colored them, because, in more rigorous terms, we – here the "we" means: the genesis of subjectivity – carry misconceptions over to things, transport them there in such a way that they then reappear as characters of the appearing things. Thus, by this analysis, things do not show themselves *as themselves* but rather as having a character, a coloring, that has been transported to them from and by subjectivity.

And yet, this very analysis demonstrates in deed, in its being carried out, that it is possible for us to interrupt such appearing and thereby to disengage from it those characters that have their source in subjectivity rather than in the things themselves. As noted already, Nietzsche even alludes to the rigorous science that, detaching us from the process, would make it possible to disengage those apparent characters that, alien to the things themselves, only distort, falsify, conceal the things. Such rigorous science could be conceived as carrying out a series of reductions aimed at bringing the things themselves to show themselves as themselves. Putting aside the conception of phenomenology as naive, immediate beholding, Heidegger stresses that wresting the phenomena from concealment is integral to phenomenology. As he succinctly expresses it, "Precisely because the phenomena are, at first and for the most part, *not* given, there is need for phenomenology"[9].

Suppose, then, a thinking that would take up the inversion of Platonism and, carrying it through, would open into phenomenology. It might readily be assumed that such thinking would have as its task peeling away, as it were, the layers of misconceptions covering the things themselves; thereby the things would be freed from everything subjective and brought to stand forth in what could properly be called their pure, transparent objectivity. And yet, matters are not nearly so simple, nor the task manifestly so straightforward. In particular, this assumption overlooks two crucial considerations, two possibilities that pose complications, the consequences of which are virtually unlimited.

The first consideration is that even if everything subjectively imposed upon things could be disengaged and set apart, there would still be no necessity that things show themselves transparently, that they come fully to light as themselves. While they would indeed show themselves as themselves and from themselves, there remains the possibility that things also offer resistance to showing themselves, that in that very showing they also withhold themselves. Indeed the most elementary circumstance of perception offers support for this possibility: that in the perception of an object, one has present to one's vision only certain faces of the object, while others remain unseen. In the Preface to *The Gay Science* Nietzsche puts it more dramatically, "We no longer believe that truth remains truth when the veils are withdrawn from it...Today we consider it a matter of decency not to wish to see everything naked"[10].

The second consideration is that the process of transporting subjective conceptions into the object may, if properly conceived, prove to be not an obstacle to but rather an essential element in the self-showing of things. This is a possibility that one can see developed in Heidegger, perhaps most distinctly in *Contributions to Philosophy* and indeed on the basis of the radical mutation to which such concepts as subject and object are exposed in this text. The development requires that subjectivity be thought more fundamentally as Dasein and that the process of letting certain conceptions appear to frame things be rethought as the very opening of the *there*, of the space of self-showing, that is, as what Heidegger explicates as *Ereignis*. More minimally and aside from the Heideggerian instance, it is a matter of rethinking the process, no longer as a transporting of subjective into objective, but as the way in which we, by our relation to the space in which things show themselves, contribute to letting self-showing as such take place[11].

In any case, for a thinking that would follow through the inversion of Platonism, the imperative remains that sensible things be understood from themselves and not as mere images of alleged intelligibles. Thus, whatever the complications and whatever possibilities must at least be left open to further consideration, what is required is a new interpretation of the sensible. This interpretation must be such that the sensible is understood, not through its opposition to the intelligible, but from itself, that is, as it unfolds before the senses and for an apprehension geared to the senses.

Nietzsche took a first step in this direction, drawing the consequences of the inversion of Platonism out towards a new beginning. In certain of his texts and fragments from the mid- and late-1880s, the outline of a new interpretation of the sensible can be discerned. This interpretation can be summed up in two words: The first of these is *perspective* or *perspectival*. In the Preface to *Beyond Good and Evil*, dated 1885, Nietzsche links the question of perspective directly with Platonism. He refers to Plato's invention of the pure spirit and the good as such, characterizing it as "the most dangerous of all errors so far" and celebrating both the fact that this error is now overcome and that we – presumably the free spirits of the time – are heirs to the strength gained in the long struggle against this error. Then he identifies the fundamental error that was at the core of Plato's invention of pure spirit and the good, "To be sure, it meant standing truth on its head and denying the *perspectival*, the basic condition of all life, to speak of spirit and the good as Plato did"[12]. The figure coheres perfectly with that of the inversion of Platonism: to invert Platonism, now that this error is overcome, amounts to standing truth back on its feet and affirming the perspectival as the basic condition of life.

In a fragment from early 1888, Nietzsche explains precisely how the moment of perspective, of the perspectival, belongs constitutively to the sensible, to the apparent world (*die scheinbare Welt*), as he calls it both in the fragment and in the contemporaneous text *Twilight of the Idols*. According to Nietzsche's account, the apparent world is the world as seen from the viewpoint of utility in the preservation and enhancement of the power of a certain species of animal. As Nietzsche expresses it, more generally, "Every center of force adopts a perspective towards the entire remainder". It is this viewpoint, this perspective, that determines how the world appears. Nietzsche writes, "The perspective therefore decides the character of the 'apparentness' [*giebt den Charakter der 'Scheinbarkeit' ab*]!"[13]. Furthermore, Nietzsche insists that it is not as though a world would remain intact if one deducted the perspective, not as though the perspectival character of the world were a mere overlay that could be removed. Rather, this perspectival character belongs constitutively to the sensible, determining how it appears as such.

The second of the two words that sum up Nietzsche's new interpretation of the sensible is *Schein*. If, in hopes of retaining somewhat the unity of the word, we translate it as *shining*, it is imperative to bear in mind the broad range of senses the word commands: shining, shine, appearance, semblance, illusion. Equally important is its affinity with *Erscheinung* (appearance – less ambiguously) and with *scheinbar* (apparent), as in *die scheinbare Welt* (the apparent world). Although Nietzsche grants that *Erscheinung* is one of those "fateful words that appear to express knowledge but that in truth hinder it"[14], and though

Heidegger raises doubts whether Nietzsche became "master of the fate entrenched in that word"[15], the fact remains that in *The Birth of Tragedy*, specifically in the analysis of the Apollinian, Nietzsche went quite far towards renewing the polysemic force of the word *Schein*[16].

It is only in a few late fragments that Nietzsche gives some positive indications as to how shining belongs to the character of the sensible. In every case Nietzsche's intent is to undercut the usual distinction between reality and shining, that is, between the reality that would belong to things as such and the shining forth by which they would appear, by which they would become apparent. Over against this distinction, this simple opposition, Nietzsche maintains that the character of apparentness belongs to the very reality of things. Thus, in a fragment from early 1888, which begins by dismissing the so-called true – as opposed to apparent – world as a mere fiction, Nietzsche continues, "Apparentness [*Scheinbarkeit*] itself belongs to reality: it is a form of its being, that is, in a world where there is no being, a certain calculable world of *identical* cases must first be created through *shining*"[17]. In other words, since there is no being, there is only appearing; or rather, appearing is the being of things, the way in which they *are*. Because things are not simply present, because they would not remain intact after the deduction of the perspectives in which they appear, their very occurrence must be their appearing, their shining forth in such a way as to become apparent. Because they are nothing beyond their perspectives, they are nothing outside their shining appearance.

Thus, in another fragment, dated 1885, Nietzsche is explicit about the identification of shining with reality. He writes, "Shining as I understand it is the actual and sole reality of things". It is not as though things simply were – or could be – without shining and appearing; rather, they *are* – they are real – only as shining forth so as to appear. Hence, Nietzsche continues, "Thus I do not posit 'shining' in opposition to 'reality' but on the contrary take shining as the reality that resists transformation into an imaginative 'world of truth'"[18]. Shining is the very reality of things, and it is their shining, rather than some inert state of being, that bestows on them their resistance, their resistance to being transformed into something merely imagined (so, reality in distinction from phantasy) and their resistance to being assimilated, as in Platonism, to an alleged true world. Rather, as they shine forth in their perspectives, things persist in their apparentness, in their sensibleness.

In Nietzsche's interpretation of the sensible as perspectival shining, as shining in perspective, the proximity of his later thought to phenomenology is evident. In the fragments cited, together with *Twilight of the Idols*, one can discern how the inversion of Platonism, carried through to its ultimate consequences, opens onto phenomenology. To be sure, carrying out the transition to phenomenology would require that the human, all too human process by which, according to Nietzsche, subjectivity transports conceptions into the object be interrogated in a more rigorous way. Yet, in referring to the rigorous science that could lift us up out of the entire process, Nietzsche acknowledges – as the coherence of his own text requires – the possibility of a rigorous analysis of this process and, above all, of the concepts that Nietzsche's account of it takes for granted, most notably, those of subject and object. The introduction, for instance, of the concept of intentionality would have profound and indeed subversive consequences for the transpositional schema that Nietzsche takes to be operative. This concept and its phenomenological elaboration would allow a precise differentiation to be established between a perceptually engaged act of consciousness, capable of intuitive fulfillment, and an act of phantasy in which consciousness would bring something before itself in a way that could not be fulfilled in sense intuition.

Yet clearly Nietzsche's conception of the perspectival character of appearances, if detached from Nietzsche's residual metaphysics of force and then developed in a more descriptive manner, leads directly to the phenomenological problematic of horizonality. Most notably – though not by any means exclusively – this character links up with what Husserl calls the inner horizon, or, as it has also been called, the lateral horizon. By this is meant the ordered totality of other profiles or faces of an object that is cointended when an object is – as always – seen from a particular perspective. The problem that phenomenology takes up is to render a descriptive account of just how it is that objects, appearing to a particular perspective, show themselves within a lateral horizon, which bestows on them the depth and density of the real.

As to shining, Nietzsche's account would need to be taken much further towards differentiating between shining (*Schein*) and appearing (*Erscheinung*). In the fragments cited, the character of shining expresses for the most part simply the apparent character of things, the fact that they occur only in appearing. Thus, in Nietzsche's account, shining is not determined as a positive character belonging to the appearing or, more precisely, to the self-showing of things. In the one passage in the fragments where Nietzsche does propose a determinate name meant to characterize reality, that is, shining, from within, he resorts to saying that it is will to power[19]. If, on the other hand, one insists on stopping short of the metaphysics of the will to power, if, instead of installing the will to power as an inner core of things withdrawn from their appearing, one persists – more insistently than Nietzsche himself – with the identification of reality with appearing, then one will need to ask about the character that, within appearing, shining assumes. What, one must ask, must be the character of shining such that things can come to show themselves precisely by shining in perspective, by shining within the complex of horizons that belong to the scene of self-showing? What does it mean to shine? Or is shining an occurrence so delicate that it escapes – or appears to escape – meaning? As the brilliant red of a male cardinal, seen across a woodland path, shines against the glistening snow. Even as, with a drastic reduction of horizons, a natural reduction, the deep blue of a cloudless sky shines forth in a manner so singular that it seems to escape, to exceed, even the word with which we would pretend to name it.

Notes

[1] On Nietzsche's relation to Platonism, see *Platonic Legacies*. Albany: SUNY Press, 2004, ch. 1. On Heidegger's relation to Platonism, see *Delimitations: Phenomenology and the End of Metaphysics*, 2nd ed. Bloomington: Indiana University Press, 1995, ch. 14; and *The Verge of Philosophy*. Chicago: University of Chicago Press, 2008, ch. 1. All translations are mine.

[2] *KSA* 7:7 [156].

[3] *HAH* I, sec. 9, *KSA* 2:29.

[4] *HAH* I, sec. 16, *KSA* 2:36.

[5] *TI* "'Reason' in Philosophy", sec. 1, *KSA* 6:74.

[6] *KSA* 6:80f.

[7] *KSA* 4:14.

[8] *BGE* Preface, "Christenthum ist Platonismus für's 'Volk'", *KSA* 5:12.

[9] Martin Heidegger, *Sein und Zeit*. Tübingen: Max Niemeyer, 1960, 36.

[10] *GS* Preface, sec. 4, *KSA* 3:352.

[11] I am referring here to the analysis in *Force of Imagination: The Sense of the Elemental*. Bloomington: Indiana University Press, 2000, 197-99.

[12] *KSA* 5:12.

[13] *KSA* 13:14 [184].

[14] *KSA* 11:40 [53].

[15] Martin Heidegger, *Nietzsche* I. Pfullingen: Neske, 1961, 248. There is a discrepancy between the passage as Heidegger cites it and as it is given in the Colli-Montinari edition: in the former, two examples of such words are given, *Schein* and *Erscheinung*, whereas in the latter only *Erscheinung* is given.

[16] See my discussion in *Crossings: Nietzsche and the Space of Tragedy*. Chicago: University of Chicago Press, 1991, ch. 1.

[17] *KSA* 13:14 [93].

[18] *KSA* 11:40 [53].

[19] "A determinate name for this reality would be 'the will to power', namely, designated from within and not in terms of its ungraspable, flowing Prometheus-nature" (*ibid.*). The contrast with sheer becoming serves to reveal that in effect Nietzsche is simply installing being (by another name) behind the appearing, behind the shining in perspective.

OF BUTTERFLIES AND MASKS: THE TRANSFIGURATIONS OF APOLLO IN NIETZSCHE'S EARLY TO LATER WRITINGS

DOUGLAS BURNHAM AND MARTIN JESINGHAUSEN

Nietzsche's first published book, *The Birth of Tragedy,* introduces a pair of "drives" whose achievements or struggles permit the understanding of both the production and meaning of art. For a concept that is one half of a partnership fundamental to any healthy culture, however, the Apollinian seems rather poorly done by. The Dionysian gets all the attention in later Nietzsche, and explicit discussions of Apollo dry up almost entirely. (Indeed, the discussions dry up even within the text of *The Birth of Tragedy*.) Why should this be, we ask, and by that we mean, what philosophical or strategic decisions lie behind the change? One tempting answer is that the dualist conception of the early work is discarded as either creating too many problems, or being too Hegelian (or both), and replaced by something akin to a monism: will to power. But this would be simplistic, and fail to capture how the later Nietzsche understands the dynamism and internal conflicts of modes of will to power. Our analyses in this paper suggest that reports of the death of Apollo are premature, and that a suitably revised conception of the Apollinian, considered now as an *aspect* of the total Dionysian, plays a vital role in Nietzsche's later thought. The paper is in three parts. First, we look briefly at *The Birth of Tragedy* to get our bearings. Then, we look at the very few occasions when Apollo or the Apollinian are explicitly discussed in Nietzsche's work after the mid-1870s. Finally, we focus primarily on a few key moments of *Thus Spoke Zarathustra* in order to identify the "suitably revised conception" alluded to above.

1. Apollo's Vanishing Act in *The Birth of Tragedy*

Halfway through *The Birth of Tragedy*, the figure of Apollo virtually disappears. "Apollo" or the "Apollinian" occur only a few times in the text (and those few are clearly summaries of earlier discussions), until making their reappearance in the last sections. Since this is a book whose topics are roughly chronological, and since the disappearance corresponds roughly to the introduction of the figure of Socrates, it is an easy mistake to confuse Apollo and Socrates. That is, to interpret Nietzsche as asserting that Socratism is a diseased or degenerate Apollinian drive. The result of this mistake is an overly Hegelian reading of Nietzsche's early philosophy[1]. On such a reading, tragedy is viewed as a synthesis of two antithetical art drives; while in Socratism, this dialectical logic has become constipated, incapable of reaching resolution.

Nietzsche himself employs this misreading strategically, as a hyperbolic correction of the early text, in the "Attempt at Self-Criticism". A main point of Nietzsche's self-critique is that in those youthful days he was not yet fully equipped to follow the imperatives of the instinctive maenadic voice that had already gripped him and was trying to speak through him[2]. To be sure, Nietzsche's position changed in part because he recognised that the early configuration of drives resembled the Hegelian model. But as we will see, the "Attempt" ignores the fact that Nietzsche's account in *The Birth of Tragedy* is already anti-Hegelian; and moreover, it exaggerates by playing down the productive possibilities of *The Birth of Tragedy*'s complex juggling of positions, and thus over-simplifies Nietzsche's mature conception of the Apollinian (and thus also of the Dionysian)[3].

Let us try first to restore the balance from within *The Birth of Tragedy*. Nietzsche does discuss what happens if the Apollinian does not make clear its appearance-status: the "effect" is "pathological". But that is quite different from an assertion that the Apollinian itself is ever pathological. Thus, we should not be surprised when Nietzsche writes unequivocally that Socrates is "an altogether newborn daemon" (*The Birth of Tragedy*, sec. 12[4], *KSA* 1:83). He even considers this point significant enough to include it in his brief summary of the book written much later in 1885-6 (see *KSA*, 12:2 [110]; and see also the corresponding discussion in *Ecce Homo* – both of these passages will be discussed in detail below). Socratism, then, is a third cultural drive, neither Apollinian nor Dionysian, gradually taking hold of Greek sensibility from Sophocles onwards. The defining feature of Apollo is appearance that knows itself as appearance (the dream that wishes to carry on dreaming). That is, a cultural drive to create forms that understands these forms as objectifications of, and constituted from out of, the underlying fluid surge of will. If you will, the

Apollinian is a phenomenological rather than a naïve natural attitude[5]. Apollo is thus not the antithesis of Dionysus. The defining feature of the Socratic drive, however, is that it is intrinsically incapable of such an attitude; it defines itself and its world such as to render such an awareness rigorously impossible. Now, all drives are intrinsically relational (that is, in struggle vis-à-vis other drives, or obstacles). However, the Socratic drive is both endlessly optimistic (recognising no obstacle) and also demands that it be recognised as universal (recognising no other drives – indeed, not recognising itself as a drive and its products as cultural forms). Although incapable of internalising the fact, Socratism as a drive nevertheless remains relational, and in fact must work with respect to the materials (that is, the cultural forms) at hand. It must then involve a misinterpretation of the existing metaphysics of art: so, Dionysus-like cultural forms are interpreted simply as emotion; Apollo-like cultural forms are interpreted as logic. And, indeed, that is precisely what Nietzsche says.

Historically, Nietzsche argues, both the art drives are either marginalised or repressed. Dionysus becomes the property of cults. Apollo's fate is worse; the Apollinian drive suffers a kind of living death, only allowed to appear if it can successfully masquerade as something else. Nietzsche's metaphor for this is particularly striking. Under conditions of the dominance of Socratism, the Apollinian has *"sich verpuppt"* (*BoT* sec. 14, *KSA* 1:94) – it cocoons itself away. The cocoon is a shield of Apollo, and a refuge in the face of Socratic culture – it is womb, coffin, fortress, disguise. Mention of the Apollinian then virtually disappears from the text of *The Birth of Tragedy* until near the end as, encased, Apollo prepares himself for a future transfiguration, for an emergence under conditions of modernity. The resurgence of the Dionysian drive (described at the end of the book) does not rescue Apollo, but rather is conditional upon the latter, too, having (first or already) emerged from its long pupation. Thus, in the last section of *The Birth of Tragedy* (sec. 25), Nietzsche argues that if in the present day we are seeing in the works of Wagner a rebirth of tragic culture then "Apollo, too, must already have descended amongst us, concealed in a cloud..." (*BoT* sec. 25, *KSA* 1:155). The descent from clouds is an extraordinary triple allusion: first to the *deus ex machina* – a plot and stage contrivance that Nietzsche had already criticised Euripides for employing; second to Aristophanes' play, which lampoons Socrates; and finally to the emergence of Apollo from the cocoon. The triumph of modernity that Nietzsche predicts, then, is the reincorporation of the Socratic drive into productive and self-knowing relations. Thus, earlier, we had the figures of the music-making Socrates, or science realising itself as art.

A proper understanding of the relationship between the Apollinian and the Socratic helps clear up the mystery of Apollo's disappearance from the text of *The Birth of Tragedy*. It also prepares the ground for our main topic: the trace of the Apollinian in Nietzsche's mature works.

2. Apollo in Later Nietzsche

Still more remarkable than the protracted disappearing act of Apollo in *The Birth of Tragedy* is the paucity of discussions of Apollo or the Apollinian in Nietzsche's writings after the early 1870s. In the notebook entries and unpublished manuscripts from the period of Nietzsche's first book, discussion of Apollo is frequent and is broadly in agreement with the discussion in *The Birth of Tragedy* itself. However, shortly thereafter, matters change dramatically. While of course the figure of Dionysus remains important – and indeed becomes absolutely central after the end of the 1870s – Apollo is dropped almost entirely. Of the four most substantial discussions, three are explicit reflections back to *The Birth of Tragedy* (*Twilight of the Idols*, "Skirmishes" 10-11; *Ecce Homo*, "Why I Write Such Good Books", "The Birth of Tragedy", *KSA* 12:2 [110]); the fourth implicitly so (*The Gay Science* sec. 84[6]). It is as though Nietzsche made a strategic decision to drop any new discussion of Apollo, as a marker of the distance he felt from his first book with its overt Schopenhauerian and Wagnerian influences. Even the "Attempt at Self-Criticism", added to the new edition of *The Birth of Tragedy*, avoids naming Apollo. Of course, themes associated with Apollo in *The Birth of Tragedy*, such as dreams, individuation, form and above all appearance, remain important Nietzschean topics. It is thus clear that Nietzsche has not simply dropped the concept (or the set of problems the concept was intended to encapsulate and elucidate) as abruptly and completely as he has dropped the name. Rather, the concept has changed in a complex trajectory accompanying the changes in the notion of the Dionysian and the Socratic. Here, we will attempt a partial outline of the changes that the concept of the Apollinian undergoes, together with some discussion of the significance of those changes.

To accomplish this, we will first look carefully at the four passages mentioned above where, directly or indirectly, the later Nietzsche is looking back to and appraising his early work. Then, we will focus on several passages and image patterns in *Thus Spoke Zarathustra* that seem to elaborate Nietzsche's new concept.

The Gay Science section 84 is part of a series of sections on art, poetry and the Greeks. This series begins around section 77 and extends to the end of Book Two. The series serves as a brief recasting of ideas from *The Birth of Tragedy*. Section 78, for example, returns to the notion of the transfiguration of the audience; the unnaturalness of tragedy is the subject of section 80; the logic of the Greeks in section 82; in section 107 he claims that to art's healing qualities we owe our "ultimate gratitude" (*KSA* 3:464). Section 84 entertains the idea of the origin of poetry as a utility (in a cultural evolutionary sense), particularly the utility of rhythmic speech. Just as humans feel themselves transfixed, compelled to dance, or purged of strong emotions by rhythm in music so, Nietzsche reasons, early humans believed that rhythmic speech or singing would make the spirits or gods happy, and so allow humans thereby to "exercise power" over the gods, to make them "tools" (*KSA* 3:440). Poetry begins as an attempt by humans to have dominion over gods. However, about two thirds of the way through the passage, there is a subtle change of emphasis, not marked by a change in tone or a new paragraph but rather by a change of topic: Nietzsche here turns to the oracles. The argument seems the same: in asking for a prophecy,

> one thought one could force the future by gaining Apollo's favour – he who according to the oldest views is much more than a god of foresight. The way the formula is pronounced, with literal and rhythmic precision, is how it binds the future; the formula, however, is the invention of Apollo, who as god of rhythm can also bind the goddesses of fate. (*GSc* sec. 84, *KSA* 3:441f.)

The most important thing about these two sentences is also the most obvious: Apollo is not among the "compelled" or bound gods. Rather, Apollo is the one who binds the future, acting for those whom he *favours*. Apollo is in a middle role, having invented and supplied human beings with the means of influencing the gods. Apollo is – surprisingly – cast in the role of Prometheus, offering humanity something much more valuable than fire[7]. This middle role, though, has a clear affinity to the middle world of dream images described in *The Birth of Tragedy* (see e.g., sec. 7). We should also notice the words "literal" and "precision". These words link back to the passages, early in the *Gay Science* passage, that concern rhythm as organising all the "atoms of a sentence" and bidding "one to select one's words". Nietzsche intends that we associate this idea of rhythm with the notions of logic and proof in *GSc* sections 81 and 82. However, there is an important difference also. Logic and proof are described in terms of attaining to a truth or correctness that is a correspondence with an existing state of affairs – in other words, they are characteristic of science in the broadest sense. Rhythmic speech and music, however, become true by transcending the "flat" ontology of Socratic science and bringing about in the future that to which they could then be said to correspond. In other words, poetry – taken as a statement about something – is false by this scientific standard. Indeed, section 84 ends with a discussion of just this falsehood. Just as in *The Birth of Tragedy*, then, there is a superficial resemblance between the strategies of Apollinian art (beautiful order or form) and the discourse characteristic of Socratic culture (logic). This resemblance is such that many would not notice the sleight of hand that substitutes the latter for the former in later Greek culture, and such that Apollo could be said to have cocooned itself away in logic. That superficial resemblance, however, disguises the fact that the Socratic culture has lost this middle world – its link to the transcendence of appearance and, indeed, it has lost art as such – a fact that Nietzsche here in *The Gay Science* emphasises over and over in speaking of the beneficent falseness of art.

In 1886, Nietzsche prepared a new edition of *The Birth of Tragedy*, adding the famous "Attempt at Self-Criticism". There is a notebook entry (*KSA* 12:2 [110][8]) from this period where he summarises for his own use what he now sees as the basic achievements of his early book, using a few words and phrases that will make their way into the "Attempt" (e.g., "romantic" or the "metaphysics of the artiste" (*Artisten-Metaphysik*)). Despite this, the tone of the note is much less hostile towards his earlier self. Nietzsche here claims that the book already amounted to a critique of Schopenhauer, first in that it focused on the urge to create in the experience of the artist rather than on that of the "recipient". Also, he claims to have identified a distinctive tragic pleasure, and indeed also a "voluptuousness" (*Wollust*) of Dionysian creation, rather than Schopenhauer's resignation. Similarly, Nietzsche credits his earlier self with an important critique of Wagner vis-à-vis the means-end relationship of music and drama. Nietzsche writes,

> Becoming, felt and interpreted from within, would be continual creating by someone dissatisfied [*eines Unbefriedigten*], over-wealthy [*Überreichen*], endlessly tense and endlessly under pressure, by a god whose only means of overcoming the torment of being is constant transformation and exchange [*beständiges Verwandeln und Wechseln*]: – illusion as its temporary

redemption achieved in every moment; the world as the succession of divine visions and redemptions in illusion. (*KSA* 12:2 [110])

A fascinating sentence! The whole note is a mixture of young and older Nietzsche, and this mixture achieves its focus in that sentence. Here we find fused Nietzsche's portrayal of Dionysian truth in *The Birth of Tragedy* with the later account of the Dionysian found, for example, in *Thus Spoke Zarathustra*. To be sure, here Nietzsche employs *Schein* (translated as "illusion") and *Erlösung* ("redemption") in much the same way as in the earlier work. However, *überreich* occurs in *The Birth of Tragedy* (in adjectival form), but never in the sense used here, which is the same as on the first page of *Zarathustra* ("*du überreiches Gestirn!*", *KSA* 4:11). Similarly with *beständiges Verwandeln*, transformation is a key notion in *The Birth of Tragedy*, but in the sense of a metamorphosis of one being into another (e.g., chorus into Satyrs, dramatist into character). By contrast, the Protean and beyond-Protean sense of the term in which Nietzsche is using it here belongs, again, to the late 1870s or early 1880s. Furthermore, there is now no temptation to see the Apollinian as the antithesis of the Dionysian (as in the Hegelian interpretation discussed above) nor, metaphysically, to see being as the antithesis of becoming. Rather, in each case the former is an aspect or mode of the latter. Becoming is essentially the realisation and destruction of form. The "tormented" and "dissatisfied" becoming is *also* characterised by being over-rich and voluptuous (the latter is another word important in *Zarathustra* but used only twice and, in an entirely different sense, in *The Birth of Tragedy*). Thus, there is no longer anything special about tragedy as the unique place where a reconciliation of Apollo and Dionysus occurs. For, in the above passage there is no mention of tragedy or art at all: this way of expressing the artiste's metaphysics takes it out of the hands of the artiste as a specific type of cultural agent. Thus, a few notebook entries later, Nietzsche can write "The world as a work of art giving birth to itself –" (*KSA* 12:2 [114][9]). Remarkably, Nietzsche is using a hybrid conceptual language which is in part made up of that from his first book, in order to describe nothing less than the will to power.

The significance of this becomes clearer when we compare this *Nachlass* passage with the last section of the "Attempt at Self-Criticism". There, Nietzsche's accusations against his younger self reach their climax. He is accused of harbouring an early to mid-19th-century Romantic hatred of the present, of a pessimism that is already akin to a nihilist's rage of destruction, or still more of plotting a specifically Christian escape. These accusations are directed against the idea of tragic art as metaphysical solace. "No", he writes,

> you should in the first instance [*vorerst*] learn the art of comfort *in this world*, you should learn to *laugh*, if you are really determined to remain pessimists. Perhaps then, as those who laugh, you will some day send all attempts at metaphysical solace to Hell – with metaphysics the first to go! (*BoT*, "Attempt", sec. 7, *KSA* 1:22)

Nietzsche then quotes his own (i.e., Zarathustra's) injunction to laughter and dancing. As always, the precise phrasing needs our attention. In contrast to the unconditional prophetic tone of the *Zarathustra* passage, what Nietzsche just wrote seems tentative, "in the first instance", "if", "perhaps", "some day". This serves to emphasise the gap between Nietzsche's "own" philosophical voice and that of the "Dionysian fiend" (*Unhold*) that is Zarathustra. The tentativeness is not just rhetorical, however, nor does it display a lack of certainty. Rather, it stands for Nietzsche's anti-Romanticism, essential to this passage and to Nietzsche more generally. He cannot accuse himself of a hatred of the present and of "modern ideas" in one sentence and then, shortly thereafter, dispense altogether and all at once with them. Zarathustra is deliberately free-floating historically, geographically and to some extent even psychologically, so as to display *possibilities* of human thought and action. By contrast, as the historical specificity of the rest of "Attempt" section 7 shows, Nietzsche's untimeliness departs from *within* his modernity. Thus "this world" not only means the immanence to itself of the field of will to power, as contrasted with metaphysical or theological beliefs; "this world" also refers to the immersion within the specific historical human condition of the late 19th century. Thus, earlier in the "Attempt", Nietzsche accuses himself of having thrown the philological baby out with the late Socratic bathwater. He writes that everything is "still there" to be discovered through the science of philology, the cowl of that historically specific mode of academic scholarship. This may be a far-too-late attempt to ingratiate himself again with former colleagues, but it also shows how important to Nietzsche is the historical sense of "this world" and the proper employment of the possibilities of analysis that it offers. This observation will prove vital later in understanding Nietzsche's 1880s concept of the Apollinian.

Let us turn to the discussion of the Apollinian in *Twilight of the Idols*[10]. As in *The Gay Science* we find here in "Skirmishes" sections 8-11 a miniature treatise on the grounds of art, and thus on themes related (though here much more distantly) to *The Birth of Tragedy*. The issue at hand is "intoxication" (*Rausch*). "The essential thing about intoxication is the feeling of increasing power and fullness " ("Skirmishes", sec. 8, *KSA* 6:116, t.m.); the artist then releases or forces him- or herself on to things, making them into enriched or perfect versions of what they are (Nietzsche calls this "idealisation") and also mirrors of his or her power. Nietzsche provides an extensive inventory of types of intoxication, including sexual excitement; post-coital ("in the wake of") intoxication (compare *Thus Spoke Zarathustra* II, sec. 10, *KSA* 4:139-41); and the intoxication of the "glutted and swollen" will, which in "Skirmishes", section 11, is exemplified as architecture (*KSA* 6:118f.). Having said "finally" before the last in his list in section 8, Nietzsche proceeds in section 10 to add two more: Apollinian and Dionysian. The former is described in terms akin to *The Birth of Tragedy*; that is, what is stimulated, feels full and rich and imposes itself upon its field is the eye, and thus the artist's range of expressivity concentrates on vision and visionary seeing. The latter, however, receives a different emphasis. The Dionysian is the simultaneous stimulation of all the systems of affects, and thus also the simultaneous employment of all the modes of expressivity. (Nietzsche critically modifies but never entirely gives up on the Wagnerian idea of the *Gesamtkunstwerk*.) Music, along with acting, dancing and lyric poetry, are all specialisations of this root Dionysian state. The comprehensive and simultaneous affectivity and expressivity have been narrowed or channelled, Nietzsche claims, to this or that affective sub-system or mode of expression.

This latter claim, however, seems to contradict the original description of Apollinian and Dionysian as types of intoxication: the former involved stimulation of the eye, the latter a comprehensive stimulation. What prevents us from classifying the Apollinian as another specialisation of the root Dionysian intoxication, one channelled into vision? Now, in a broad sense, this is precisely what we argue Nietzsche does in the later thought: the Apollinian (newly recast) must be seen as an intrinsic, necessary moment of Dionysian becoming. Thus, this passage in *Twilight of the Idols* gives us an important clue, to which we will return below. However, this specialisation or narrowing down argument is too simplistic as it stands. For Nietzsche, in his characterisation of the Dionysian state, does not stop at what we just called "comprehensive stimulation". Rather, he continues, "The essential thing [in the case of the Dionysian] is the ease of metamorphosis, the inability *not* to react...He enters into any skin, into any affect: he constantly transforms himself [*er verwandelt sich beständig*]" – notice the echo of the *Nachlass* entry we discussed above, "constantly transforms" (*TI* "Skirmishes", sec. 10, *KSA* 6:118). The Dionysian is in a sense "raw", turned inside out and utterly open and infinitely sensitive to his or her exterior. This is Nietzsche's new description of the Dionysian ecstatic dissolution of individuality as it was originally found in *The Birth of Tragedy*. But this utter openness is also transformative of the exterior, for it discharges itself again as art. The Dionysian is thus the conduit through which, to use the phrase we mentioned above, the world is "a work of art giving birth to itself –" (*KSA* 12:2 [114]).

Here, we want to draw attention to phrases like "the inability *not* to react" or "it is impossible for a Dionysian to...miss any affective signal". This suggests that our characterisation of this state as a conduit through which the world as exterior realises itself as art is accurate. There is here a certain blindness, compulsion, or lack of control. Again, this agrees broadly with Nietzsche's account fifteen years earlier in *The Birth of Tragedy*. But such features are identified by Nietzsche as precisely what distinguishes the Dionysian from the Apollinian. The Apollinian, then, cannot be a total stimulation that has been narrowed or specialised to the field of vision, it cannot be simply a truncated Dionysian – because the Apollinian is not originally open to its exterior, not "turned inside out" as we put it above. It keeps its distance – echoing the discussion in *The Birth of Tragedy* of the Apollinian as calm and characterised by clear boundaries. This distance is more than just affective and physical. It borders on the metaphysical because of the relation to Schopenhauer's principle of individuation. As we suggested earlier, though, it stops short of the metaphysical because the Apollinian knows itself as appearance and does not get caught up in appearance. Its vision is *phenomenological*. Here in *Twilight*, then, we have a hint that the phenomenological understanding of the Apollinian has been in some way carried forward into the later Nietzsche. However, precisely what this idea now looks like is not yet clear.

Our final Apollo/Apollinian passage is in *Ecce Homo*, not surprisingly in the survey Nietzsche gives of his published writings (*EHC*, "Why I Write Such Good Books", "The Birth of Tragedy"[11]). Nietzsche's appraisal is more akin to the *Nachlass* passage we discussed than the "Attempt". To be sure, the discussion begins with a few self-accusations, above all his having let the hymn to Wagner overshadow the more general and important analysis of the art drives and the Greek overcoming of pessimism; but also the presence of the offensive smells of Hegel and Schopenhauer. (Both of these points were also made in the "Attempt".) Nevertheless, Nietzsche seems to dismiss these as superficial defects, for in what follows he credits himself with original insights of epochal significance. Again, as so often before, the treatment of the Apollinian is brief and what little is there closely resembles *The Birth of Tragedy*. However, there are a few unusual features in Nietzsche's discussion which are quite telling. The summary he provides of the early book includes, "One 'idea' – the opposition between Dionysian and Apollinian – translated into metaphysics; history itself as the development of this 'idea'; the opposition sublated into a unity in tragedy..." (*EHC,* "Why I Write Such Good Books", "The Birth of Tragedy", sec. 1, *KSA* 6:310) After a few more elements are added to this list of consequences of the "one 'idea'", Nietzsche continues, "The two decisive *innovations* [*Neuerungen*] of the book are, first, the understanding of the Dionysian phenomenon among the Greeks ... it sees it as the single root of the whole of Greek art. The other innovation is the understanding of Socratism..." (*ibid.*, t.m.).

Now, the mention of history as the development of an idea and of sublation are Nietzsche's explicit pointing out the precise moments of what he earlier termed the offensive smell of Hegel. The concept of sublation is indeed used in *The Birth of Tragedy*, but the young Nietzsche rather wickedly (or self-defensively) puts it in the mouth of Wagner (*BoT* sec. 7). We have argued elsewhere that the passage in question from *The Birth of Tragedy* contains at least as much of a *critique* of Hegel as it contains naïve Hegelianism[12]. Much more interesting to us here are the inverted commas that Nietzsche puts around "idea" in *Ecce Homo*. This only serves to exacerbate the sharp edge of the distinction between the "idea" and the "innovations". The first part of the passage is written as straightforward paraphrase of the earlier book – the clue is the explicit Hegelian language. The second part of the passage, on the other hand, is in Nietzsche's voice of 1888, putting the book's defects well behind him though accepting his former self as himself. Notice that the analysis of Socratism is not part of the paraphrase Nietzsche gives, for it is not part of the unfolding of the one "idea". Again, Socrates is a third cultural force, as we argued above, and as Nietzsche here confirms a few sentences later in calling the phenomenon "neither Apollinian nor Dionysian" (*ibid.*). Moreover, Socrates enters from the outside of the intellectual structure of the one "idea"; if history is the unfolding of that "idea" then Socrates literally interrupts history (and the text of *The Birth of Tragedy*) itself. It is an alien history and an alien understanding of history. This gives rise to the curious hope found in *The Birth of Tragedy* and of which Nietzsche here, in *Ecce Homo*, says "I have no reason to take back my hope" (*EHC*, "Why I Write Such Good Books", "The Birth of Tragedy", sec. 4, *KSA* 6:313). Notice that the one "idea" becomes, in contemporary interpretation, two "innovations". But only part of the "idea" is an innovation, namely, the Dionysian. In contrast, the Apollinian is left out only to return negatively as *not* the Socratic. The other innovation (Socratism) enters from outside. This radical interruption from outside of the dialectical course of history, and the complex play of ones and twos, comprise an elaborate joke at Hegel's expense.

All of which leaves unanswered our central question of what happens to the Apollinian in the later Nietzsche. The *Ecce Homo* passage suggests that Nietzsche feels the Apollinian is not an innovation, or is at least not "decisive" (*entscheidend*). Or, more precisely, it suggests rather that Nietzsche has come to take seriously the oneness of his original "idea" – the idea of a dynamic *relationship* and not of two "things" called Apollinian and Dionysian. That is, he has come to see the Apollinian as an intrinsic moment of the Dionysian. Only this interpretation allows us to understand how Nietzsche could say that the Dionysian is "the single root of the whole of Greek art". Taken at face value that statement flatly contradicts what Nietzsche had said as recently as *Twilight of the Idols* (see above); the contradiction disappears upon our hypothesis.

However, is the Apollinian only alluded to indirectly, or are the specific characteristics of the Apollinian still at work in this *Ecce Homo* passage? The last of those sections in *Ecce Homo* on *The Birth of Tragedy* appears to be primarily a discussion of "Wagner in Bayreuth", fourth of the *Untimely Meditations*. This essay, Nietzsche here claims, was never about "Wagnerian reality", Bayreuth, or "the whole pathetic little German spectacle" (*KSA* 6:314). One could replace the name "Wagner" with "Nietzsche" or "Zarathustra" throughout. (Nietzsche says something very similar about "Schopenhauer as Educator" a few pages later in the sections of *Ecce Homo* explicitly devoted to the *Untimely Meditations*.) Instead, he writes, that "German spectacle" was a "cloud in which an infinite *fata morgana* reflects the future" (*ibid.*). A *fata morgana* is a type of mirage in which a series of air layers at different temperatures not only refract light up and around the curvature of the earth but also elongate or otherwise exaggerate the image. The name comes from the Italian translation of "Morgan le Fey", of Arthurian legend. Now, as one might expect, *fata morgana* (like "mirage") is used in both German and English primarily to stand for an insubstantial, thoroughly deceptive illusion[13]. Clearly, however, this meaning cannot be what Nietzsche has in mind here, for that which is the basis of the "illusion" (Nietzsche's mature notion of the Dionysian philosopher and artist) is the most real thing under discussion. What is illusory, then, is that we take the "illusion" (what appears; here, the historical situation of German politics and culture) as an inescapable, primary reality, and do not realise that it is the distorted and displaced image of something quite other. And this realisation, of course, is precisely what distinguishes the structure of appearance ascribed to the Apollinian in *The Birth of Tragedy*. Moreover, other than being an atmospheric phenomenon, a *fata morgana* has nothing whatsoever to do with clouds. That Nietzsche should unexpectedly say "cloud" here at the end of those sections which are still under the heading of *The Birth of Tragedy*, must be an echo of the reappearance of Apollo escaping the cocoon in the last section of *The Birth of Tragedy*. The whole extraordinarily rich metaphor here reintroduces the full notion of the Apollinian.

What these passages all have in common is a recasting of the Apollinian not only as an aspect of the Dionysian but specifically as akin to the idea of the *mask*. A mask, in Nietzsche's texts, is a historically specific discourse, method or role, a means to an end, a mode of engagement with one's contemporaries, or a process of development. It is something never simply put on deliberately (a fully conscious strategy or lucid deception belonging to a transcendent subject), nor something that could simply be taken off (thus removing oneself from historical conditions, again a transcendence). Removing the mask means overcoming the situation within which the mask became necessary. Thus, it is neither strictly speaking a true nor a false appearance, the mask is the vanishingly thin structurally embedded concern for itself as *having a surface constituted by relations* (on the theme of the mask see especially *Beyond Good and Evil* sec. 4). Still in *Ecce Homo*, only a few paragraphs later, Nietzsche confirms our reading of the Apollinian as mask. He writes, "It is clever of me to have been many things and to many places so I can become one thing, – can come to one thing. For a long time I even *had to* be a scholar" (*EHC*, "Why I Write Such Good Books", "Untimely Meditations", sec. 3, *KSA* 6:321). This "cleverness" is not the cleverness of calculation but rather the historical and cultural sensitivity that generates masks.

What have we learned from this sustained reading of four passages in the texts of the later Nietzsche where the notion of Apollo or the

Apollinian is explicitly discussed? There appear to be three aspects to Nietzsche's mature conception of the Apollinian. Firstly, there are suggestions that the Apollinian, rather than being the other side of a dynamic relationship of drives, as in *The Birth of Tragedy*, is now considered a moment of the Dionysian as the most fundamental characterisation of, and response to, the will to power. Secondly, something like the original Apollinian notion of an appearance aware of its appearance remains, for example, in Apollo as the middle ground of prophecy or in the theme of masks. Thirdly, and similarly, the Apollinian seems to stand for the historically concrete situation, or *type*, of human life which, if overcoming is called for, must overcome itself from within.

3. The Concept of the Apollinian in *Zarathustra*

In order to further pursue the question of what happens to the concept of the Apollinian in later Nietzsche, we now wish to turn our attention to relevant passages that are not explicitly about Apollo or the Apollinian. From here on we will focus mainly upon *Thus Spoke Zarathustra*[14]. This is partly because otherwise the field of study would be too open, and partly because we suggest that it is in *Zarathustra* that Nietzsche provides his most complete solution to the problem of the philosophical meaning of the Apollinian in his mature philosophy. *Zarathustra* represents a breakthrough, its author thinks. For the first time in his career he has managed to cast his ideas in a literary form adequate to their expression. Zarathustra's is a Dionysian philosophy of dance; the text translates the invitations to dance as its compositional imperatives. The text itself is the dancing and also struggling body of ideas. Part of our meaning in saying that *Zarathustra* offers a "more complete solution" is that it *enacts* Nietzsche's new ideas about the dynamism of modes of will to power. It is to a few key moments of this enactment that we will turn in completing our account of the Apollinian.

In a text almost entirely devoid of historical proper names, it is not surprising that the presence of Apollo in *Zarathustra* is indirect; mainly, it occurs through his emblem, the *Leier* (lyre). On two occasions, Nietzsche uses the image of a lyre: In Part III, section 13, "The Convalescent" and IV, section 19, "The Drunken-Song". In "The Convalescent", Zarathustra repeats the compound "*Leier-Lied*" several times in addressing his animals' account of eternal recurrence (*TZ* "The Convalescent", sec. 2 , *KSA* 4:273). Since a few lines earlier he says also barrel organ, "*Drehorgel*" (*ibid.*), "hurdy-gurdy song" is an appropriate translation. The emphasis is on a song that is comforting in its gaiety, child-like, but also mechanically produced (the *dreh* of the hand-crank is of course a reference to eternal recurrence) and superficial. Zarathustra in his convalescence welcomes this song; it does him good. Nor indeed are the animals deceived by their own song, "how well you know", Zarathustra tells them. And, at the end of the section, Zarathustra recovered from the seven days of illness, the animals respect his healthy silence as he converses with his soul. His animals are thus performing the Apollinian function perfectly. In the meantime, Zarathustra has reflected on anything *but* eternal recurrence directly: on the nature of language as individuating, and on cruelty ("for the human its most evil is necessary for its best–", *TZ* "The Convalescent", sec. 2, *KSA* 4:274). Both of these topics are, in fact, discussions of the Apollinian. On the first topic, Apollinian "chatter" is contrasted with that reality, and especially Dionysian reality, that it purports is its object. "[H]ow could there be an outside-me?" (*ibid.*), the Dionysian monster that is Zarathustra says, reflecting the theme of the Dionysian as essentially and comprehensively de-individuated as *exterior*. On the second topic, cruelty is praised as the necessary incorporation of the Apollinian moment into the Dionysian, for the animals had to choose the right moment to intervene in Zarathustra's long recovery, and that involved a "cruel" (and knowing) watching and waiting.

The "convalescent" should be compared with two other passages. First, consider III, section 7, "On Passing By" – here Zarathustra nearing a city is warned away by "Zarathustra's ape" – a man who manages to imitate "something of the phrasing and cadences" of Zarathustra and even some of the wisdom (*KSA* 4:222). After listening to "the frothing fool" for some time, Zarathustra shuts him up, accusing him of the spirit of revenge. Significantly, though, Zarathustra does indeed not visit the city, saying to the man, "[Y]our fool's words harm *me*, even when you are right!" The man does not inhabit Zarathustra's words and wisdom, only "apes" them (*KSA* 4:225). Similarly, at III, section 2, "The Vision and Riddle", the dwarf spirit of gravity also gets eternal recurrence "wrong" by making it too easy. But there is no "lightness" or "refreshment" here. Importantly, the dwarf was carried along the path, and then sits on a rock next to it, and is thus never *on it* – the dwarf exists as a deluded transcendence from which the shape of time viewed from outside (appearing as a circle) would be visible. Apollinian language is not necessarily any more "correct" or "accurate" in its account in contrast to Zarathustra's ape or the dwarf, but is a spiritualisation or objectification *from within* and *serves* Dionysian life. That is, it neither leaves the immanence of will to power as being (it is only the appearance of being) nor as transcendent knowledge (Apollinian awareness of its status as appearance is not an *idea*).

At IV, section 19, "The Drunken Song", the lyre returns. This passage is a sustained poetic *tour de force*, with six long lines for each of the short lines from the "Other Dance-Song", weaving together dozens of different image patterns from earlier in the book. The poem is precipitated by the sound of a midnight bell. In stanza 6, the sound of the bell signalling midnight is transformed both into a "toad croak" and into the "sweetest lyre" (*TZ* "The Drunken Song", sec. 6, *KSA* 4:399). Specifically, the lyre signals the world become ripe "as golden autumn" (*ibid.*). A perfection has been reached ("Did my world not just now become perfect?", *TZ* "The Drunken Song", sec. 7, *KSA* 4:400). The Apollinian is the moment of achievement of life – its beautiful new forms, its approximations of stillness and being, its sustaining virtues and increasing strength, its linguistic formulations both in poetry and philosophy – but as "gold autumn" it is also the moment of harvesting, death, destruction and new growth ("blessed be the vintner's knife!", *TZ* "The Drunken Song", sec. 9, *KSA* 4:401). The symbol of the lyre, then, is symbol of one half of a never-disconnected totality: woe and joy meet in the thought of eternal recurrence and in the notion of the Dionysian. Joy "wants *herself*, she bites into *herself*" (*TZ* "The Drunken Song", sec. 11, *KSA* 4:403).

One key metaphor, and one that has been key since the beginning of Nietzsche's career, is the *butterfly*. Interestingly, there are at least four distinguishable, though related, meanings to butterfly imagery running through Nietzsche's work. Let us catalogue these. The first, conventionally enough, is of ephemerality combined with superficiality and dizzy aimlessness. The only time the word butterfly is used in *The Birth of Tragedy* is in section 20, and it is of this type. Nietzsche is speaking of higher education, and the tendency among academics to "adopt the diction of the journalists". As always, when Nietzsche talks of journalism, the emphasis is on thinking and writing for the day, for the moment, and not beyond. The image is used similarly at *TZ* III, section 9 and, with different emphasis, at *TZ* IV, section 9. The second type of butterfly image is as a stand-in for nature when Nietzsche wants to talk about having an unmediated and unconceptualised (we could perhaps say "instinctive") relationship to natural forms and processes. Generally, this usage goes hand in hand with Nietzsche's symbolic praise of childhood and is contrasted with adult science, conceptualisation and utility; likewise, it is often associated with poetry or music. This is not far from a standard

Romantic trope. Good examples can be found in the 4th lecture of "On the Future of our Educational Institutions" (*KSA* 1:716); *Human All Too Human*, section 207 and *The Wanderer and His Shadow*, section 51.

The third way Nietzsche uses the image of the butterfly is related to the second. Here, the butterfly represents a valid, *positive* mode of life (we say "positive" here to contrast with the first meaning, which is always based upon cutting one's self off from something, and ultimately founded on the reactive will to power), but one nevertheless characterised by ephemerality and lightness. Excellent examples are to be found at *Daybreak* section 553 and at *TZ* I, section 7. The *Daybreak* passage is particularly interesting. Nietzsche meditates on the possibility that philosophy is nothing but an idiosyncratic drive, a desire for that particular diet, climate and company that suits one, spiritualised as intellectual quest[15]. It leads him to look anew at a butterfly, "unconcerned that it has but one day more to live". The butterfly too may have a philosophy that is the root drive of its mode of life spiritualised. This passage is often over-read as a clear contrast and evidence for Nietzsche's moral naturalism – but Nietzsche's description of himself and the butterfly is very close; both lives are solitary, simple, near the sea, among southern vegetation, have "fleeting meals" and seem unconcerned. Notice Nietzsche writes "unconcerned" (*unbekümmert*), not "oblivious to" or "blissfully unaware of" (*KSA* 3:324). Thus, we cannot read the butterfly as a kind of random example of an "alien" mode of life; rather, the butterfly is posited as different but akin. The careful grammar of Nietzsche's last phrase signals both difference and possible proximity, the butterfly has its philosophy "even if it may not be possible to call it mine". The butterfly here represents something of an ideal of lightness, laughter, dance and happiness – a mode of life that humanity, transformed so as to align itself with the Dionysian, might approach.

The fourth meaning of butterfly imagery in Nietzsche, again, follows on from the previous one. This fourth meaning encapsulates the full structure of the Apollinian. Our first example, then, must be the properly Apollinian image that we saw in *The Birth of Tragedy*. Recall that Apollo there is the butterfly both in the sense of it cocooning itself away from the metaphysical misinterpretation of its form in Socratism, and then also a butterfly as newly emergent form capable of providing modern mythic structures, and thus struggling productively once again with the Dionysian. Nietzsche uses the image in this way again in *Human, All Too Human*, section 107. The "bitterest draught" is knowledge of determination at the level of action and evaluating. But this bitterness has a "consolation", it is a "birth pang" into "freedom" and the insight that "everything is in flux, it is true: – but *everything is also flooding forward*: towards *one* goal". This "birth-pang" is described as follows, "The butterfly wants to get out of its cocoon, it strains against it, it tears it open" (*KSA* 2:104f., t.m.) The metaphor of a new form of humanity is here marvellously combined with the Apollinian butterfly image from *The Birth of Tragedy*. Here, again, the Apollinian encapsulates both the pain and struggle of its emergence and also the lightness and joy of emergent form, together with knowledge of the *basis* of that form.

Let us now have a look at one of *Zarathustra*'s most extraordinary passages – II, section19, "The Soothsayer" – where this fourth meaning of the butterfly reappears. The Soothsayer's Schopenhauerian prophecy leads a troubled Zarathustra to have a dream at once gothic and symbolist in tone. He is "night- and grave-watchman" in the castle of death; three knocks sound at the gate, which is then torn open and a storm leaves a black coffin; the coffin opens and "from out of a thousand grotesque masks [*tausend Fratzen*] of children, angels, owls, fools, and child-sized butterflies, it laughed and jeered and roared at me" (*KSA* 4:173f., t.m.) Again, the coffin is the cocoon, the transformed form violently emerging from a kind of death into new life. However, the dream also rewrites the myth of Pandora's box. Now, in different ancient versions of the myth this is a box (or urn) of sorrows that are allowed to escape and torment mankind, or alternatively a box/urn of blessings allowed to slip away[16], in either version leaving only "hope". The Pandora myth should be compared to *Iliad* 24.527 where a similar doubleness is asserted. Finally, note a corresponding ambiguity in the name "Pandora": either the one to which all gifts have been given (the better, on Zeus' plan, for the first woman to seduce man), or the one who gives all gifts *to* mankind. Now, the dynamic moments of the will to power are symbolically *gendered*. There was already an attempt in *The Birth of Tragedy* to apply a masculine/feminine symbolic framework to the Apollinian/Dionysian distinction (see sections 1 and 5 especially), with the Dionysian a revelation of the "mothers of being". However, there is clear evidence of Nietzsche's dissatisfaction with this framework[17]. Although there are any number of well-documented problems with Nietzsche's treatment of symbolic, social and biological gender, it is certainly the case that the symbolic framework employed in the later work – and especially in *Thus Spoke Zarathustra* – is both more worked out and more philosophically interesting than the early version. The masculine and feminine moments in the text enter into a literal dialogue, aspects of Zarathustra debating or struggling. For our purposes, one key passage for exploring the link between this apparatus of symbolic genders and the Apollinian would be Part Four, "At Noon", with its internal dialogue among gendered aspects of Zarathustra's manifold self, and its refrain "Did not the world become perfect?". A treatment of the Apollinian is incomplete without a full discussion of its relation to this framework; unfortunately, this is impossible here, but we have made a start elsewhere[18].

Through these various complex symbolic references, the Pandora's box-as-cocoon-and-coffin image asserts the inexhaustible resurgence of forms of life yet to be overcome, against the Soothsayer's entropic pessimism. This resurgence is violent, manifold, unpredictable and both beautiful and horrible. The imagery here correlates then with the fourth meaning of the butterfly.

This last passage condenses all the observations we have made above about Nietzsche's new understanding of the Apollinian in a brief symbolist evocation. The Apollinian is a function of the broader Dionysian inner character of life as will to power. If the Dionysian is the restless cycle of the creation and destruction of forms (of life, culture, thought or whatever), then the Apollinian more specifically comes to represent the function of having-arrived-at new form, together with what it takes for that form to exist and to be sustained under these particular, concrete historical conditions; knowledge of the constitution of form from objectifications of underlying will to power; and foreknowledge of the necessary destruction of form. The Apollinian thus resists, in a sense, the Dionysian – or rather, again, is a moment of self-resistance within the Dionysian – the better to reveal it within that which appears and to serve it. The naïve dualism of Apollinian and Dionsyian posited in *The Birth of Tragedy*, which then gives rise to the danger of an Hegelian reappropriation of that text, is supplanted. What takes its place though is not a simple monism that is opposed only to misunderstood or diseased versions of itself. Rather, Nietzsche's mature concept of the Apollinian is part of his sophisticated treatment of the moments of life as the dynamic of will to power, particularly but not exclusively in its Dionysian health.

Notes

[1] Heidegger is among the most prominent interpreters who appear to fall into this trap.

[2] See "Attempt", 3.

[3] The irony is that *The Birth of Tragedy*, despite whatever sweeping or subtle reservations Nietzsche may have had about it, had at least as much impact on late 19th- and 20th-century modernism as anything else he wrote.

[4] Friedrich Nietzsche, *The Birth of Tragedy*, trans. Ronald Spier. Cambridge: Cambridge University Press, 1999, t.m.

[5] See also John Sallis, *Crossings: Nietzsche and the Space of Tragedy*. Chicago: University of Chicago Press, 1991.

[6] Friedrich Nietzsche, *The Gay Science*, trans. Josefine Nauckhoff. Cambridge: Cambridge University Press, 2001.

[7] It would be interesting to link this transfiguration of the art-god with a reading of early Goethe's eponymous *Sturm und Drang* poem. J. W. Goethe, *Werke Hamburger Ausgabe in 14 Bänden*. vol. 1, 44–6. München: C. H. Beck, 1999.

[8] Friedrich Nietzsche, *Writings from the Late Notebooks*, trans. Kate Sturge. Cambridge: Cambridge University Press, 2003.

[9] See also *WP* no. 796.

[10] Friedrich Nietzsche, *Twilight of the Idols*, trans. Judith Norman. Cambridge: Cambridge University Press, 2005, t.m.

[11] Friedrich Nietzsche, *Ecce Homo*, trans. Judith Norman. Cambridge: Cambridge University Press, 2005, t.m.

[12] See Douglas Burnham and Martin Jesinghausen, *Nietzsche's* The Birth of Tragedy. London: Continuum, 2010.

[13] For example, Friedrich Georg Jünger uses the phrase in this sense when discussing the illusion of a moral God in his *Nietzsche*. Frankfurt a.M.: Klostermann, 1949, 139.

[14] Friedrich Nietzsche, *Thus Spoke Zarathustra*, trans. Graham Parkes. Oxford: Oxford University Press, 2005, t.m.

[15] For a slightly different reading of this passage, see Keith Ansell-Pearson, "On the Sublime in *Dawn*". *The Agonist*, issue 3, 2009.

[16] A standard view of mid- to late-19th-century classicists. See William Smith (ed.), *Dictionary of Greek and Roman Biography and Mythology*. Boston: Little, Brown and Company, 1870, see vol. 3, 111.

[17] See Douglas Burnham and Martin Jesinghausen, *Nietzsche's* The Birth of Tragedy. London: Continuum, 2010.

[18] See Douglas Burnham and Martin Jesinghausen, *Nietzsche's* Thus Spoke Zarathustra. Edinburgh: Edinburgh University Press, 2010. On this gender symbolism and its relationship to the dramatic structure of *Zarathustra* and Nietzsche's notes from the period, see especially David B. Allison, *Reading the New Nietzsche*. Lanham, MD: Rowan & Littlefield. 2001, 159ff.; and David Farrell Krell, *Postponements: Woman, Sensuality and Death in Nietzsche*. Bloomington: Indiana University Press, 1986.

ZARATHUSTRA AND REDEEMING THE PAST

SEAN D. KIRKLAND

Nietzsche's *Thus Spoke Zarathustra* presents itself first and foremost as a prophetic work, even if simultaneously as a parody of prophetic works[1]. Zarathustra does indeed have an evangel to proclaim and the problem that largely drives the book's narrative is that of how and to whom this evangel is to be communicated. Moreover, the parody of the prophetic mode is here internal and necessary, for the peculiar "divine truth" that this prophet brings is neither true nor divine in any traditional sense. In place of God's coming, Zarathustra reports His death, the loss of that fundamental reality in which not only our moral codes have been grounded, but which also acts as the source and guarantor of all being and truth. In place of salvation and transcendence, Zarathustra suggests we imagine the inescapable immanence of the eternal return. And it is in place of any commandments or laws of conduct that Zarathustra teaches his central "doctrine", the *Übermensch* or "overman".

The Overman as Lightning and Madness

Prophets are those who *pro-phanai*, literally, "speak for" or "speak ahead of" what remains hidden, enveloped in the future, withheld there and not yet present. Although quite traditional in this, for he heralds the *approach* of the overman, one aspect of Zarathustra's radicalization and parody of the prophetic mode is the fact that his overman is an *essentially futural* figure. That is to say, the overman will never arrive, never present himself, but *is* properly in his approach.

Looking back in 1888, in *Ecce Homo*, Nietzsche says the following about *Thus Spoke Zarathustra*, "Here at every moment the human is overcome; the concept 'overman' became here the highest reality [*höchste Realität*]" (*EH* "Why I Write Such Good Books", "Thus Spoke Zarathustra", sec. 6, *KSA* 6:344). That is, this book in which the overman is announced but never himself appears, this book that situates Zarathustra (along with the "last human" and the "higher humans") in the liminal space between the human and the overman, here this withheld figure becomes the "highest reality". But this is so precisely and only in the futural mode indicated by the human overcoming that is to be provoked "at every moment" by Zarathustra's simultaneously destructive and hortatory teaching.

It is crucial to note, however, that Zarathustra's overman is not therefore to be understood as some kind of *regulative ideal*. It must be opposed to, for example, the notion of "humanity in its complete perfection", which Kant in the *Critique of Pure Reason* also presents as, *qua ideal*, unrealizable, but which nonetheless positively determines and delimits our actions by providing our reason with a standard of completeness against which all instances of the human might be measured in their inevitable incompleteness (*KrV* A568-71/B596-99).

No, Zarathustra's overman is intended to name no such end point in a development, no such completion, and no such fixed idea. In *Ecce Home*, Nietzsche remarks,

> The word 'overman' as a designation for a most well-accomplished type [*eines Typus höchster Wohlgerathenheit*], as opposed to 'modern' humans, to 'good' humans, to Christians, and to other nihilists – a word that in the mouth of a Zarathustra, the annihilator of the moral, becomes a thought-provoking word – this has been understood almost everywhere in utterly naïve innocence under the meaning of those values that are the very opposite of what was brought to light in the figure of Zarathustra. That is, [the 'overman' has been misunderstood] as an 'idealistic' type of a higher kind of human being [*als 'idealistischer' Typus einer höheren Art Mensch*], half 'holy man', half 'genius'. (*EH* "Why I Write Such Good Books", sec. 1, *KSA* 6:300)

Rather than any such "ideal", the overman must be understood, as the name indicates, as having its *being* only within the *Untergang* or "going-under" of each of us qua human being, insofar as this is an *Übergang* or "going-over" to something else, something other (see *TSZ* "Zarathustra's Prologue", sec. 4, *KSA* 4:17). The overman exists then if at all only at or as the futural edge of the site of self-transformation. But as such, this figure changes us in its very appearance, exposes us, undermines the comforting, settled certainty and necessity (but also the suffocating constraint and shame) we have experienced previously with regard to our human identity and its moral imperatives. Strictly speaking, there will never "be" an overman, for in overcoming ourselves as human "*beings*", we open up on to another mode of relating to our world and to one another, something other than the persisting self-identity of an autonomous and morally responsible subject, something instead utterly at the mercy of and immersed in the dynamism, the emergence and destruction that is, for Nietzsche, nature or life. The overman only ever *becomes* the overman, but never *is*. Indeed, given this departure from an ontology of presence, given that the overman is properly in coming-to-be rather than merely absent but one day to be present, the very distinction between Zarathustra and the overman breaks down. Already in being and living *towards* the overman, one *is* in a certain sense the coming-to-be overman.

Zarathustra will later pose the question, "Who is Zarathustra to us?" He responds, "having given questions for answers", that he is, "A seer, a willer, a creator, a future himself and a bridge to the future – and oh, also still at the same time a cripple at this bridge – all that is Zarathustra" (*TSZ* II, "Of Redemption", *KSA* 4:179). This captures the human comportment towards the future that the overman should provoke, not simply achieving a new full presence, completion, and settled identity in some present moment to come (i.e., crossing the bridge), but instead coming to exist as relentlessly open, torn open, towards the future, and in this already "arriving" in the future but *qua* future, *qua* "not yet" (the cripple at the bridge). This is nothing other than the peculiar mode of coming to be that we humans might take on in living *towards* the overman. It is in the context of this central teaching that Zarathustra calls on you to "let the future and the farthest be the cause of your today" (*TSZ* I, "Of Love of One's Neighbor", *KSA* 4:78)[2].

But how precisely should the overman act as this essentially futural *cause*, if not as an ideal, a *telos*, an end-point? Zarathustra tells us already in the "Prologue",

> Your contentment [*Genügsamkeit*] screams to high heaven, your stinginess even in sinning screams to high heaven!
> Where is the lightning that licks you with its tongue? Where is the madness [*Wahnsinn*], with which you would have to be inoculated?
> Look, I teach you the overman: he is this lightning, he is this madness!
> (*TSZ* , "Zarathustra's Prologue", sec. 3, *KSA* 4:16)[3]

In becoming suspicious and malcontent with what has made us human, our reason, our consciousness, our moral character, our national identity, our culture, our body, our history, in revealing each of these to be questionworthy, we become ready for the overman. Ready for him to act upon us in his proper mode, which is as "lightning" and "madness". Immersing ourselves in our previously unremarked or only dimly sensed *Noth*, our "distress" or "need", we are ready to be what Archilochus,

Nietzsche's paradigmatically Dionysian poet, refers to as "thunder-smashed [*sunkeraunôtheis*]"[4].

Consider the phenomenon that comes into view here. It is a condition that may be encouraged, but not anticipated (much less engineered), for no anticipation can prepare us for a lightning strike. When it explodes into view, tearing open the sky, it transfigures not just this or that thing or region of things, but everything. It creates a new, violently illuminated and charged world. It is not experienced as one event, then, among others, caught in a causal series within a fixed horizon of appearance, a world. Rather, it is always an event of radical, unpredictable, and total transformation.

And madness is likewise all-transforming. True madness is not a momentary and specific lapse in one's reasoning or one's self-control with respect to this or that entity or context. In *The Gay Science*, the two editions of which in 1882 and 1887 act as bookends for the publication of the four parts of *Zarathustra* from 1883 to 1885, Nietzsche explains precisely how he understands madness. He writes,

> The greatest danger that has hovered over and still hovers over [humanity] is the outbreak of madness [*Irrsinn*] – that is, the outbreak of an arbitrariness [*Beliebens*] of feeling, seeing, and hearing, the enjoyment of the head's lack of discipline, the joy in human-non-understanding [*Menschen-Unverstande*]. The opposite of the madman's world is not truth and certainty, but the universality and universally binding character of believing; in short, it is the opposite of the non-arbitrary in judgment. (*GS* sec. 76, *KSA* 3:431)

Notice that Nietzsche speaks here of the opposition between the "madman's world" and the world of those who are not mad, indicating that what is at stake in becoming "mad" is an utterly global transformation. Having engaged with Zarathustra in shaking our most basic concepts and values, we wait for the appearance of the overman, the flash of lightning and the madness that will transfigure everything. The overman appears along with, or more properly *is* this menacing and liberating, in short affecting, illumination of our world and ourselves, which overtakes[5] us and exposes us like a raw nerve, bringing us to suffer a world stripped of the universally binding character of our categories and structures of experience and understanding. And then the overman *draws us into* the "madman's world", a world where the arbitrariness, which is to say, the non-necessitated and thus "aesthetic" production, of these categories is undertaken with pleasure and joy.

And yet, even in rightly emphasizing the radicality of this transfiguration, we are in danger here of seeing the future that Zarathustra prophecies as a complete and total break from the past. That is, we are in danger of seeing the overman as a lever that frees the will not only from the gratuitous suffering of past realities and morals, but from any past at all, imagining ourselves in the overman's light as perfectly free, unhinged, spontaneous movements, masters of an "artiste's metaphysics" (*BT*, "Attempt at Self-Criticism", sec. 2, *KSA* 1:13)[6] creating new values and realities *ex abrupto*. This is, however, not the case.

Motley with Signs of the Past

Rather, even in the "willful lust for future ones [*die Wollust der Zukünftigen*]" (*TSZ* III, "Of the Great Longing", *KSA* 4:278), which Zarathustra as prophet attempts to stir up, there is no simple and decisive break with the past, with history. Quite to the contrary, Zarathustra again and again insists on the "redemption [*Erlösung*]" of the past. He demands in the section, "Of Old and New Tablets",

> In your children you should make good on being the children of your fathers; thus you should redeem [*erlösen*] all that is past! This new tablet I place above you! (*TSZ* III, "Of Old and New Tablets", sec. 12, *KSA* 4:255, see also 177-82)

And in "On Poets", Zarathustra fends off the worship of a too-faithful disciple, saying, "I am of today and of the past…but there is something in me that is of tomorrow and of the day after tomorrow and of time to come" (*TSZ* II, *KSA* 4:165). Zarathustra thereby indicates that, although he is the prophet of the overman and the one perhaps most able to let this future act as the kind of radical "cause" discussed above, he *remains* nevertheless "of today and of the past". Our question, then, must be what Zarathustra's "redemption" of this past entails.

We can say, at least, that the task to which Zarathustra calls us is in no way the simple weeding out of what in us remains of our today and of our past. It cannot be, for as we learn, we are constituted by *nothing other than* this residue of history. Listen to Zarathustra's description of us "present ones [*Gegenwärtigen*]",

> Truly, you could not wear a better mask, you present ones [*Gegewärtigen*], than your own face [*eigenes Gesicht*]! Who could recognize you?

> Completely inscribed with the signs of the past [*Vollgeschrieben mit den Zeichen der Vergangenheit*], and these signs painted over also with new signs: thus you have hidden yourselves from all sign-interpreters...
> Motley, all times and peoples peek from your veils; motley, all morals and beliefs speak from your gestures. (*TSZ* II, "Of the Land of Culture", *KSA* 4:153f.)

Notice first that our "own face" is itself declared a mask, and this is then described as a surface *vollgeschrieben* or "completely inscibed" with the "signs of the past". That is, there is no true face of a true self, a *hupokeimenon*, a real *subjectum* that might be understood simply to don the mask of historical categories, concepts, and values, and which might then be revealed as it truly "is", finally, in the creative and free production of new values and realities in the light and madness of the overman. Rather, we "are" only in the appropriation of these masks, in the play of these veils and in the meanings and values that arise through that play.

We cannot be called upon simply to cast aside these masks and veils, identities grounded in our historically contingent concepts, structures of thought, and values, for we would be left with nothing. Instead, we are asked to *erlösen* or "redeem" them. That is, we are asked to treat them *as the "signs" they are*, even *as symptoms*, which must be understood to hold within them more than they are, to refer beyond themselves. They must therefore be interpreted and diagnosed, in order to read them *along with their disavowed origins*.

Zarathustra indicates how this might occur when he asks his own soul, "Where would future and past be nearer to one another than with you [*Wo wäre Zukunft und Vergangenes näher beisammen als bei dir*]?" (*TSZ* III, "Of the Great Longing", *KSA* 4:279). This is to say, we redeem our past by bringing it into an extreme *nearness* with our future, with the violently illuminating flash of lightning and madness that is the futural overman. But how is this nearness accomplished and what does it entail, precisely?[7]

History and Exposure to an Excessive Origin

The illumination that is the first aspect of the overman's appearance is accomplished through that critical examination of our past, which Nietzsche practices from *The Birth of Tragedy* on as a highly unorthodox form of philology, and later gives the name "genealogy". Genealogy is always an *archeology*, a tracing of a given concept, value, or term back to its hidden *archê* or "origin, source, beginning"[8]. Simply in undertaking such a study, any claim that concepts and values might make to universality, timelessness, or ahistoricality is called into question, staging these instead as contingent products of specific circumstances passed down to us through specific historical developments. However, genealogy is *not* concerned with the excavation of *actual* historical events, that is, with history understood as a temporally ordered set of objectively present realities located in past time. Rather, it is concerned with *our* history, the history that is still active and vital (even if pre-cognitively) in our thought and actions today. Genealogy works on the history *of the present*, not on history as such. As Nietzsche writes of historical method already in 1881's *Dawn*, "*Facta!* Yes, *Facta ficta!* – A writer of history does not have to do with that which actually happened [*mit dem, was wirklich geschehn ist*], but rather with the supposed events [*mit den vermeintlichen Ereignissen*]: for only these have had an effect [*haben gewirkt*]" (*D* sec. 307, *KSA* 3:224f.).

However, in rejecting the *objective past reality* that the scientific study of history would aim to uncover, Nietzsche's earlier "philological" and later "genealogical" project[9] should not therefore be viewed as settling for a wholly fictional past, a merely illusory and invented, purely *subjective image* of the past[10]. All of these categories, fiction/fact, subjective/objective, and most fundamentally appearance/reality or being, have been radicalized. Indeed, Nietzsche's project (and then Zarathustra's redemption of the past as well) must be seen as a proto-phenomenological approach to history, for it concerns what 1873's "On the Use and Disadvantage of History for Life" terms a "historical phenomenon" (II. UM sec. 1, 67, *KSA* 1:257), the affective phenomenality or appearing *of our past to us*. In taking up and redeeming the past, we address ourselves to that which appears in its appearances to us, treating these neither as secondary to the objective being of that past nor as merely subjective and potentially wholly disconnected from that past reality. Appearance is in this context addressed *qua* phenomenon as the legitimate appearance of "what is to be thought", or of "what is". As Nietzsche writes in *The Gay Science*, in the section entitled, "Consciousness of Appearance [*Das Bewusstsein vom Scheine*]",

> What is 'appearance' ['*Schein*'] to me now! Truly not the opposite of an essence [*eines Wesens*] – what do I know to say of any essence except only the predicates of its appearance! Clearly it is not a dead mask, that one could place upon an unknown 'x', and also take it off! Appearance is for me the active and living itself [*das Wirkende und Lebende*]. (*GS* sec. 54, *KSA* 3:417)

For Nietzsche, in accomplishing a proper relation to our past, we are no longer called upon at the outset to strip away its suspicious and always potentially groundless initial appearing to us, in order to arrive at certainty and the firm grounding in objective reality required by modern (which is to say Cartesian) philosophy and science. Quite to the contrary, the Nietzschean genealogy or redemption of the past requires our immersion in this movement of appearing itself, with the full confidence that what is to be thought and brought to light in our own creative taking up of that past is indeed presenting itself in that initial appearing. In this, Nietzsche's approach to history is, in a fundamental sense, phenomenological *avant la lettre*.

It must then be clear that the illumination and critical examination of the past's appearance to us does not then effect a mere negation or simple destruction of our historically generated concepts and values[11]. Rather, we must attempt to think it as Zarathustra indicates, as an *Erlösung*, which finds its root in the German "*los*" and thus entails a "redemption" only if this is understood as a setting "free" or setting "loose", a "releasing" of the past. Or more properly, it is a setting free or loose of the *origin* out of which our present concepts and values arose and of which these are then taken as the symptoms or the signs.

For example, Nietzsche traces the development of the moral value of selflessness or self-denial back to human society's utterly self-interested will to survival and advancement as requiring sacrifice on the part of its individual members[12]. Or, he finds the origin of our desire for and faith in scientific or scholarly "proof" *both* in the Protestant ethic's advocacy of "hard work" and the value it places on the blameless pursuit of a "finished job" *and* in the Jewish privileging of logic and "compelling agreement by force of reason" in order to supervene ethnic and religious prejudice and its threat of physical violence[13]. And in innumerable other examples, Nietzsche again and again traces our moral values and also our conceptualizations and intellectual certainties back to an origin that directly controverts them, exposing these as principles that disavow and then target the very urges and needs that gave rise to them.

When scholars attend to the genealogical project of Nietzsche, such as Michel Foucault in his brilliant and seminal essay "Nietzsche, Genealogy, History", they tend to focus on the overtly critical or destructive aspect, its destabilization and undermining of our current epistemological and moral prejudices. However, if we take seriously the "redemptive" character of the attitude towards the past for which Zarathustra explicitly calls, and if we understand this *Erlösung* as a "setting free" or "setting loose" of the past, then we must see the positive and productive moment in genealogy *as primary*. The tracing of our current attitudes and values back to their disavowed origin sets *this* origin free, as *our origin, our foundation*, such that we now can and must engage in what is then recognized as our own already ongoing creative activity as exposed to this origin.

This is nothing other than bringing the past, our still vital and determining past, into proximity to our future, the "nearness" which we heard Zarathustra above claim for his own soul. Indeed, the negative or destructive genealogical moment and the positive and creative moment are better viewed as one and the same. As Nietzsche writes in the section of *The Gay Science* entitled "Only as Creators",

> The reputation, name and appearance [*Anschein*], the value, the usual measure and weight of a thing – in its origin most of all an error and an arbitrariness [*im Ursprunge zuallermeist ein Irrthum und eine Willkürkichkeit*], thrown over things like a dress and wholly foreign to its essence and even to its skin [*seinem Wesen und selbst seiner Haut ganz fremd*] – through the belief in it and through its growth from generation to generation, it has slowly grown both on to and into the thing and it has even become its very body: the appearance from the outset almost always ultimately becomes the essence and functions as essence [*wird zuletzt fast immer zum Wesen und wirkt als Wesen*]! What fool would believe that it is enough to point to this origin and to this misty shroud of delusion [*auf diesen Ursprung und diese Nebelhülle des Wahnes hinzuweisen*] in order to destroy [*vernichten*] what counts essentially as world, so-called 'reality'! Only as creators can we destroy! (*GS* sec. 58, *KSA* 3:422)

And in "On Old and New Tablets", Zarathustra indicates precisely how there can be this creation at the very heart of genealogy's destruction. He says,

> Whoever has become wise concerning ancient origins [*alte Ursprünge*], you see, will in the end search for sources of the future [*Quellen der Zukunft*] and for new origins [*neuen Ursprüngen*]...
> The earthquake, that is – it buries many wells [*Brunnen*] and creates much languishing [*Verschmachten*]: it also brings inner strengths and secrets [*innre Kräfte und Heimlichkeiten*] to light.
> The earthquake makes new sources manifest [*macht neue Quellen offenbar*]. In the earthquake of ancient peoples new sources break out. (*TSZ* III, "On Old and New Tablets", sec. 25, *KSA* 4:265)

The uncovering of "ancient origins", the task of genealogy, becomes here nothing other than the search for "new origins". As an earthquake "of ancient peoples", that is, an earthquake *in our history*, in which the surface layer of initial appearance cracks and crumbles, revealing hidden depths, genealogy is not merely a violent annihilating upheaval, but also a revealing of "inner strengths and secrets", unnoticed "sources" for what is now recognized as our creative production of values and truths from out of what can be an energizing (but always dangerous) confrontation with these origins.

We must however ask what precisely these origins and sources are, which we uncover at work in our past and activate creatively. These are nothing other than the will to power itself. Zarathustra tells us that, "A tablet of goods hangs above every people [*über jedem Volke*]. Look, it is a tablet of the people's overcomings [*Überwindungen*]; look, it is the voice of its will to power [*die Stimme seines Willens zur Macht*]" (*TSZ* I, "Of the Thousand and One Goals", *KSA* 4:74). Tracing our values back through their histories, through their development by various peoples in various periods, we uncover the will to power that lay at the base of the creation of those values and that, even in our extreme phase of nihilism and with our pronounced weakness of the will, still functions at the base of our own blind, forgetful, but historically determined pursuit and elevation of those same values.

But this means that the origin that we find at the base of our own historically informed concepts and values is not a specifically determining and simple origin at all. It is not a source with a specific set of conditions and a fixed character, which would dictate a certain response and certain development. Rather, as will to power, it is an essentially multiple, dynamic, self-contradicting complex of forces, in contestation with one another, glimpsed *only* in the strange sparking up of effects that are then symptomatic not of this or that state of being, this or that subsisting reality, but only of their own violent and self-effacing emergence from out of a register of pure and innocent strife.

This excessive origin we confront at the base of our own historically determined condition. In the lightning flash and madness of the futural figure of the overman, we have the opportunity to take into ourselves this forceful and unpredictable historical emergence of values and concepts, of morals and truths, precisely *as arising from* the disavowed origin of the will to power. If we are healthy enough, we might leap into this "world of the madman", embracing the arbitrariness, the artiste's metaphysics and the illusionist's values. In doing so, in willing the arbitrary creation of value and truth, we do nothing other than redeem, or set free, the origin that lies secreted away in our own past. This, we see, is the meaning of Zarathustra's dramatic claim – "To redeem the ones who have gone before and to re-create [*umzuschaffen*] every 'It was' into a 'Thus I willed it!' – that I would first call redemption [*Erlösung*]!" (*TSZ* II, "Of Redemption", *KSA* 4:179).

Notes

[1] In the 1886 preface to the second edition of *The Gay Science*, Nietzsche writes the following of the passage that acts as both the last section (sec. 342) in the first edition of *The Gay Science*, entitled there "*Incipit tragoedia*", and as "Zarathustra's Prologue" in *Thus Spoke Zarathustra*: "'*Incipit tragoedia*' – reads the end of this dubious and non-dubious [*bedenklich-unbedenklichen*] book. Be on the lookout! Something utterly nasty and malicious is announcing itself: *incipit paroedia*, no doubt..." (*GS* Preface, sec. 1, *KSA* 3:346). All translations are mine unless otherwise indicated.

[2] The fact that the future Zarathustra has in mind here is not an ideal or a delimiting aim is indicated by what it is precisely that recommends this future to us. The future is to be allowed to act upon our present, not because this or that specific and to us admirable but not-yet present reality might come to be, but precisely because this future is open, indeterminate, unknown. Bemoaning the decay of the will in present-day human beings, Zarathustra exclaims, "This, yes this is bitterness for my bowels, that I can bear you neither naked nor clothed, you present ones [*Gegenwärtigen*]!/ Everything uncanny with the future [*Alles Unheimliche der Zukunft*], and whatever it is that makes flown birds shudder, that is truly more homey and more familiar than your 'reality' [*wahrlich heimlicher noch und traulicher als eure 'Wirklichkeit'*]!" (*TSZ* II, "Of the Land of Culture", *KSA* 4:154).

[3] In the section of *The Gay Science* entitled "*Prophetic Human Beings*", Nietzsche presents this sensitivity to "change in the weather" and an attunement to an "electricity in the air and clouds" as central to the prophetic mode. He writes on account of this sensitivity and attunement, "prophetic human beings are suffering human beings (*leidende Menschen*)", for whom, as animals when bad weather is approaching, "their strong pains are prophets for them" (*GS* sec. 316, *KSA* 3:549).

[4] From Athenaeus, *Scholars at Dinner*, 14.628a. See *Greek Lyric Poetry: From the Seventh to the Fifth Centuries BC*, *Loeb Classical Library* 259, ed. D.E. Gerber. Cambridge, MA: Harvard University Press, 1999, 160f. The verb *sunkeraunoun*, adds the prefix *sun*-, "together, with", to a verb related to *keraunos*, "thunderbolt".

[5] In *Ecce Homo*, Nietzsche describes a similar experience of the emergence of the figure of Zarathustra. He writes, "It was on these two walks that the whole first Zarathustra occurred to me [*fiel mir...ein*], and above all Zarathustra himself, as a

type – or better, he *assailed me* [*überfiel mich*]..." (*EH,* "Why I Write Such Good Books", "Thus Spoke Zarathustra", sec. 1, *KSA* 6:337).

[6] Although somewhat colored by the Schopenhauerian terminology he employs there, Nietzsche's discussion of an "artiste's metaphysics" in 1872's *The Birth of Tragedy* already indicates that Greek poetry's aesthetic "justification [*Rechfertigung*]" of the tragic groundlessness of human life does *not* amount to a mere Apollinian illusion, placed over a Dionysian reality. Rather, the creative response and the bringing forth of a beautiful appearance (*Schein*) is itself an expression of one's immersion in a dynamic, multiple, and conflicted reality and is, therefore, in a certain sense *true*, although not at all as an accurate representation of a present state of affairs.

[7] In the unpublished, but relatively polished and nearly complete text, *Philosophy in the Tragic Age of the Greeks*, Nietzsche challenges his readers to accomplish just such a "nearness" with respect to the Pre-Platonic thinkers. He begins the text, noting that, "With people who stand at a distance, it is enough for us to know their aims in order to approve or reject them as a whole. With those who stand nearer, we judge according to the means by which they advance their aims [*nach den Mitteln, mit denen sie ihre Ziele fördern*]: often we disapprove of their aims, but love them on account of the means and the mode of their willing [*wegen der Mittel und der Art ihres Wollens*]" (*PTAG* Preface, *KSA* 1:801). He then goes on to present not the abstract doctrines of these thinkers, but their *Persönlichkeiten* or "personalities", which must be understood not as their individual psychological characters but as the moment of their direct exposure to *phusis*, from within which they generate their philosophical systems. This entire text asks of the reader whether he or she is capable of *drawing near to*, and even of loving, such personalities revealed at the very foundations of the reader's own tradition.

[8] This claim seems to contradict directly Michel Foucault's claim in "Nietzsche, Genealogie, Histoire", that genealogy "opposes itself to the search for 'origins'" (146). However, Foucault is concerned here to indicate what differentiates Nietzschean genealogy from historical accounts that find a fluid and continuous development out of an identifiable and intelligible determining cause or set of causes. In this sense, as I indicate here, I am in complete agreement with Foucault and it is for this reason that I describe the "origin" that genealogy does uncover and activate as *excessive*. See Michel Foucault, "Nietzsche, Genealogie, Histoire", in *Hommage à Jean Hyppolite* (Paris: Presses Universitaires de France, 1971), 145-72. The more important difference is between the generative or positive focus of the presentation of genealogy here and Foucault's strong emphasis on its destructive function.

[9] We note here that, in the Preface to *On the Genealogy of Morals*, Nietzsche introduces the project he undertakes in these three essays, the examination of the *Herkunft* or "origin, descent" of our moral values, by saying that it is prefigured by the work done in *Human, All Too Human. A Book for Free Spirits*, which was written in the winter of 1876-77. He then even states, "The thoughts themselves are older" (*GM* Preface, sec. 2, *KSA* 5:248), indicating a fundamental continuity between the earlier radicalization of philology and the critique of historiography and the explicitly genealogical project he undertakes in this book.

[10] In 1873's second "Untimely Meditation", "On the Use and Disadvantage of History for Life", Nietzsche praises the "monumental" mode of history, which operates with approximations and somewhat misleading generalities in order to find compelling models of greatness in the past and which therefore has "no use for complete truthfulness" (II. UM sec. 2, 70, *KSA* 1:261). However, as he does with all three of the historical modes he outlines there (along with the monumental, he discusses the antiquarian and the critical), Nietzsche points as well to a danger this mode represents, whereby it can come to be harmful and inhibiting to life – the monumental mode can stray into "free poetic invention [*freie Erdichtung*]", producing not history but mere "mythical fiction [*mythische Fiktion*]", whereby "the past itself suffers *harm*, large parts of it being forgotten, despised, and flowing away" (II. UM sec. 2, 70, *KSA* 1:262). The proper or healthy mode of history must find its way between the extremes of complete truthfulness and pure invention.

[11] The tension here in play between a taking up of the past and a creation of new value and meaning is explicitly at stake in the mode Nietzsche recommends in "On the Use and Disadvantage of History for Life". Indeed, it requires a combination of all three of the historical modes that Nietzsche there discusses, the monumental, antiquarian, and critical, as well as the avoidance of each of their respective dangers. (See II. UM sec.s 2-4, *KSA* 1:258-78,).

[12] See especially, "To the Teachers of Selflessness", in *GS* sec. 21.

[13] See especially, "On the Origin of Scholars", in *GS* sec. 348.

"THE IMMEASURABLE FINENESS OF THINGS": NIETZSCHE AND THE QUIET MACHINERY OF THOUGHT

JILL MARSDEN

The psychologists' chief error: they take the indistinct idea to be a lower *species* of idea than the luminous one: but whatever moves away from our consciousness and thus *becomes obscure may* yet be perfectly clear in itself. *Becoming obscure is a matter of the perspective of consciousness.* 'Obscurity' is a consequence of the optics of consciousness, not *necessarily* something inherent to 'what is obscure'. (*KSA* 12:5 [55][1])

There is an elusive form of awareness which hovers at the shifting shoreline of consciousness, always just out of reach of the powers that would drive it into a precise mode of recognition. It may be that what is dimly sensed is too swift or too slight, too nebulous or too opaque to be organized into the world of the perceiver. Or it may be that this spectral sensitivity coexists with the life of an individual subject yet never coincides with it, flickering at the edges like a shadow. As such this twilight realm with its repertoire of obscure and orphan excitations goes unexplored and unaccounted until without warning its quiet machinery is fleetingly exposed. In these moments there is an intimation of something exterior, something unassimilable in the prevailing order of things. It haunts that interval on waking from a dream in which something from elsewhere is carried into the dawn, lingers only to evanesce and is inexorably swept back into the night.

To seek to capture the essence of this "experience" (if it can be called thus) is perhaps to risk losing its vital power. The desire to illuminate the shadowy margins of our knowledge, however modest in its scope, has a tendency to perpetuate a style of inquiry which is "overlit". Only when the searchlight of phenomenal consciousness has flooded the perceptual terrain with its beams is it possible to feel that one has been meticulous in one's endeavours: sharply focussed, exacting, incisive and acute. The delicate movements, the light agitations at the threshold of sense may tantalize the earnest inquirer but no amount of scrutiny will deliver them from the darkness. Mindful of these issues, in what follows I propose to explore Nietzsche's accounts of forms of awareness which elude empirical representation, understood here as the self-conscious expression of a relation to objects. To this end, the role which Nietzsche accords to non-conscious thinking in general and to subtle perceptions in particular will be examined in some detail, my guiding concern being to explore the methods which he employs to disclose their momentary revelation. In stating my aim thus it must be emphasized that to speak of that which is of necessity inchoate and indistinct will not entail clarifying the opaque or amplifying the muted. Try as we might to analyse the phenomenon *qua* phenomenon, to describe the constitutive characteristics of our representations, it is not a matter of looking harder but of looking away.

I.

In *The Gay Science*, Nietzsche suggests that the vast majority of our thinking, feeling and willing takes place without consciousness,

> The problem of consciousness (more precisely, of becoming self-conscious) first confronts us when we begin to grasp the extent to which we could dispense with it: we are brought to this initial realization by physiology and natural history (which have needed two centuries to catch up with the far-reaching suspicion of *Leibniz*). For we could think, feel, will, remember, we could also 'act' in every sense of the word, and yet none of all this would have 'to enter our consciousness' (as one says metaphorically). The whole of life would be possible without, so to speak, seeing itself in the mirror. (*GS* sec. 354, *KSA* 3:590)

In this passage and those adjacent to it, Nietzsche is wholly approving of Leibniz's "incomparable insight" that being conscious is only an accident of representation and not the constitutive ground of mental life as such (*GS* sec. 357, *KSA* 3:598). Indeed, in order to situate Nietzsche's interest in non-conscious perception in context, it is helpful to begin by examining Leibniz's idiosyncratic contribution to the debate. At first glance, Leibnizian rationalism might seem an unlikely precursor to Nietzsche's philosophy, not least because of Leibniz's adherence to the view that mind is by nature distinct from body, the "essence" of mind being always to think (*mens semper cogitat*). However, Leibniz's reasons for maintaining the latter position mark a profound divergence from the dominant Cartesian orthodoxy. Whereas for Descartes human being is to be regarded as *res cogitans* by virtue of its conscious representation of ideas to itself, for Leibniz the notion of an incessant "thinking'" fulfils another role, namely to take account of the existence of numerous minute perceptions which are too slight to be noticed at the level of consciousness. According to Leibniz we have countless perceptions of which we are unaware, so-called "*petites perceptions*",

> ...there are hundreds of indications leading us to conclude that at every moment there is in us an infinity of perceptions, unaccompanied by awareness or reflection. (*NE* Preface, 53²)

These perceptions are either too weak to be registered (because they lack intensive magnitude) or too fleeting (because they lack temporal extensive magnitude) or too unvarying (so that they are not sufficiently distinctive on their own) (*NE*, Preface, 54)³. However, when combined with other perceptions they do make themselves felt, albeit confusedly, within the whole. We may be unable to perceive the sound of each voice in the murmur of a crowd but our conscious perception of the overall buzz of conversation is *caused* by the minute, unconscious perceptions of which it is composed. Between the little perceptions which go unnoticed and the perceptions of which we are consciously aware there lies a difference of degree. Each conscious perception arises from a background of minor perceptions,

> ...noticeable perceptions arise by degrees from ones which are too minute to be noticed. To think otherwise is to be ignorant of the immeasurable fineness of things...[*l'immense subtilité des choses*]... (*NE* Preface, 57)

The extent to which the human animal is constitutively ignorant of this immeasurable fineness is in inverse ratio to its overestimation of the value of consciousness. Nietzsche contends that consciousness is the most unfinished and undeveloped outcrop of the organic yet it is popularly taken for what is "abiding, eternal, ultimate, and most originary" (*GS* sec. 11, *KSA* 3:382f.). Whilst Leibniz and Nietzsche have quite different philosophical agendas, it is possible to read Leibniz's model of human consciousness through a Nietzschean frame since "little perceptions" continually fade in and out of focus, approaching and receding from consciousness with a tidal ebb and flow. For both thinkers, it is those aspects of mental life which "move away from consciousness and thus become obscure" which appear to have a greater allure. According to Nietzsche,

> ..the human being, like every living creature, thinks continually but does

not know it; the aspect of thought that becomes *conscious* is only the smallest part, the most superficial and worst part... (*GS* sec. 354, *KSA* 3:592)

Of the countless influences acting in every moment (e.g. air, electricity) we sense almost nothing; there could well be forces that continually influence us although we never sense them. (*KSA* 10:24 [16], 654)

Scarcely sensed and seldom acknowledged, "the countless number of events that occur every moment" (*ibid.*) seem destined to do little more that mark the border separating our meagre life from the vast expanses that exceed it. The question, then, is what motivates Nietzsche's attempt to pursue these forces and how indeed is it possible to connect with them outside the optics of consciousness?

It is here that a return to Leibniz is instructive. For early modern philosophy "it is hard to conceive, that any thing should think and not be conscious of it" (*NE* 113). Since for Cartesian rationalism self-consciousness is a product of our awareness that we think, it would be simply incoherent to assert that there is thinking without an "I" that thinks. Leibniz grants that it is indeed perplexing to propose that thinking occurs in default of this self-reflexivity but he argues that our failure to realise that we think of many things all at once is due to our only paying heed to those things that stand out most distinctly. It is only when consciousness is relaxed that the myriad things which impress themselves on our senses vie for attention,

When we are in dreamless sleep, or when we are dazed by some blow or a fall or a symptom of an illness or other mishap, an infinity of small, confused sensations occur in us. (*NE* 113)

The role that Leibniz accords to the relative slumbering of consciousness is of special interest. When drowsy, dizzy, distracted by illness or even actually concussed, the world and its certainties start to sway and swim. Even in the relative serenity of dreamless sleep Leibniz identifies signs that undermine the Lockean position that the dormant state affords the soul necessary respite from the need to think. Rejecting the view that the absence of *known* thinking such as dreams entails the conclusion that all movement in the soul has ceased, he cites examples of the dim awareness that the sleeper may have of lights being extinguished, of having slept in a cold place or of hearing some noise or other[4]. This evidence recalls similar examples offered by the Stoic Hierocles who noted how the sleeper will draw a blanket up if it has fallen away in the cold, will avoid undue pressure on an injured body part and even will "wake at a set time" to keep an appointment[5]. Leibniz's position is that the constant yet imperceptible thinking of the soul is akin to the constant yet imperceptible movements of the body and to the sceptic his tireless response is to adduce examples of states in which the little perceptions might be inferred or even momentarily apprehended.

Whilst Leibniz's theory of unconscious perception does not seek to erase the "proper" conditions for perception it goes a long way towards unsettling the "given". In Leibniz's account there are a multitude of subtle senses which appear to operate at different frequencies to the normal perceptual array. The "little perceptions" remain unconscious and strictly speaking remain unperceived because they occur when consciousness is interrupted, suspended or disabled in some way. Nevertheless, they are encountered and it is the nature of this encounter that excites Nietzsche's interest. In his recasting of the Leibnizian challenge to self-consciousness, one of Nietzsche's aims is to redirect philosophical attention away from the perspective of consciousness and to dispute its role as representative of the *whole* of mental and affective life. Nietzsche asserts that it is entirely possible for life to think, feel, act and will without seeing itself externalized in reflective accounts of itself. In fact, the focus in Nietzsche's thinking is not so much on the conscious constitution of a world but on the quiet undoing of our meaningful involvements in things. Since for Nietzsche, "*consciousness overall has developed only under the pressure of the need for communication*" the movement away from consciousness must entail a progressive disinvestment in the *signs* of communication,

...with the best will in the world to *understand* oneself as individually as possible, to 'know oneself', each of us will only become conscious of what is not individual, what is 'average'. (*GS* sec. 354, *KSA* 3:592)

In moving away from consciousness and its available signs, life is brought into contact with something which exceeds its powers to represent it, an encounter which eclipses the habitual methods of securing knowledge. The sensory and conceptual coordinates for experience become hazy and imprecise as thinking is uncoupled from a kind of self-regarding. As part of his "method" for pursuing these trajectories, Nietzsche situates his investigation within the undetermined terrain of the "depths" or "inner world", as if the "bracketing out" of consciousness were the prerequisite for any truly exploratory philosophy. As he remarks in such contexts, it is necessary "to close the doors and windows of consciousness for a time" (*GM* II, sec. 1, *KSA* 5:291). In this way, in his various accounts of illness, recovery, contemplation and convalescence, Nietzsche appears to replicate the conditions of non-conscious experience to which Leibniz alludes.

This enterprise forms part of Nietzsche's abiding genealogical preoccupation with the relationship between illness, affliction and the material conditions of thinking. As is well known, this project seeks to determine the conditions for the production of bodies through a diagnosis of the values which shape them. This is most usefully illustrated in terms of Nietzsche's own symptomatology. As someone who was acutely sensitive to seemingly minor and "imperceptible" changes in atmospheric conditions Nietzsche regarded his pathological states as vital resources for his genealogical speculations. Convinced that minute changes in atmospheric pressure and electricity in the clouds had a deleterious effect on his physiology, Nietzsche made experimentation with different climatic conditions an essential aspect of his philosophical practice. In numerous places he alludes to this unusual sensibility, and his trial of different dwelling places, from the mountain heights to the coastal plains, is a constant refrain in both his published writings and his private correspondence. In the second section of "Why I am so Clever" in *Ecce Homo*, Nietzsche claims to be long practiced at using his body to read off climatic and meteorological effects as if from a "very subtle and reliable instrument" and declares that he is able to register "changes in the degrees of humidity" on himself physiologically (*EH*, "Why I am so Clever", sec. 2, 241, *KSA* 6:282f.). He likens himself to other primates that appear to be afflicted by impending climatic change,

> When a strong positive electrical charge, under the influence of an approaching, as yet far from visible cloud, suddenly changes into negative electricity and a change of weather is impending, these animals behave as if the enemy were drawing near and prepare for defence or escape; most often they creep away to hide. (*GS* sec. 316, *KSA* 3:549)

On the same theme he writes to Franz Overbeck,

> I should have been at the electricity exhibition in Paris, partly to learn the latest ideas, partly as an exhibit: for as one who can detect [*Witterer*] electrical changes and as a so-called weather prophet I am a match for the monkeys and am probably a 'speciality'. (Letter to Franz Overbeck, no. 167, 14th of November 1881, *KSB* 6:140)

Nietzsche's desire to both absorb the latest theories about electrical changes and to demonstrate his remarkable sensitivity to them indicates a fundamental interplay between ideas and their instantiation. Indeed, what these comments reinforce is that what is given as an exhibition of the "given" has always been determined in advance by prevailing ideas about what constitutes knowledge. In short, there is a reflux between bodies and their milieux such that ideas condition bodies (i.e., produce physiological experience or symptoms) and bodies thus cultivated present themselves as artefacts of these ideas. For example, whilst Nietzsche suggests that the weather actively conditions the sensitivity of which his affliction is a symptom, he also attributes his hyperaesthesia to an underlying nervous illness. In a letter to Franz Overbeck (no. 1056, 4th of July 1888) he complains that, "This extreme irritability in response to meteorological influences is *not* a good sign: it characterizes a certain general exhaustion, which is in fact my real illness" (*KSB* 8:347). The key point here is that this circuit of "stimulus and response" is not processed cognitively; rather, it describes a non-conscious assimilation of ideas into sensory experience in accordance with prevailing values, whether they be the "the latest ideas" or diagnostic categories. What a body is capable of perceiving is not simply a matter of what is "given" but of how its reality is achieved, whether through the consolidation of the commonplaces of experience or, more rarely, by their unsettling. Since all this takes place outwith the purview of consciousness it is to an examination of these processes that we now turn.

II.

In his assorted reflections on his powers of electro-reception and magneto-reception, Nietzsche undermines the humanist tendencies at work in the phenomenology of perception to commute sensitive and sensory experience to a narrow palette of capacities, ideally trimmed to the needs of consciousness and its already given world. Whilst echoing Leibniz's contention that the human animal is continually thinking without knowing it, Nietzsche goes much further than Leibniz by disputing whether thinking can be so easily distinguished from "willing" and "feeling" and questioning whether "what is designated by 'thinking' has yet been established" (*BGE* sec. 16, *KSA* 5:30). According to Nietzsche, for the human animal thinking has been compromised by its association with knowledge which is essentially the translation of the strange into the familiar, the alleviation of oppressive ideas by the attribution of meaning or cause to the general economy of "restraint, pressure, tension" and "explosion in the play and counter-play of our organs" (*TI*, "The Four Great Errors", sec. 4, *KSA* 6:92). These inner movements stimulate the "rhetorical drives" and only when they have become motivated or made meaningful – in short, when they have been explained away – are they delivered into consciousness. "Sound method" then dictates that the philosopher orientates his or her inquiries by starting from the "inner world" and the "facts of consciousness", because these are "*more familiar to us*" (*GS* sec. 355, *KSA* 3:594). In this way our habits of thought come to determine what we are able to see as thought, what we as a species "inherit" and incorporate (e.g., "that there are enduring things, that there are equal things, that there are things, substances, bodies...", *GS* sec. 110, *KSA* 3:469). As a result, "sense perception and every kind of sensation" works "with those basic errors which have been incorporated since time immemorial" (*ibid.*). However, as Nietzsche repeatedly insists, the fact that we need concepts such as "unity", "identity" and "causality" in order to translate the world of effects into a "visible world – a world for the eyes" (*WP* no. 634) is a product of our breeding as social animals and not the inevitable framework through which the world of "appearances" might be seen,

> 'Thingness' was first created by us. The question is whether there could not be many other ways of creating an *apparent* world. (*WP* no. 569)

If consciousness has only developed in concert with the need to make human experience communicable, the jettisoning of "herd signals" is the first necessary step away from transcendent gestures. To the extent that our sense perception is inhabited by metaphysical values, it prompts a form of perceiving based on believing (in "thinghood", for example). The pursuit of alternative ways in which to "recreate" phenomenal reality takes Nietzsche further into the depths of non-articulate becoming. As his own experience of rare and anomalous perception testifies, such paths will circumvent the familiar optics of knowing,

> There must have been thinking [*Es muß gedacht worden sein*] long before there were eyes; thus, 'lines and shapes' were not originally given; rather, for the longest time, thinking has been based on a sense of touch [*Tastgefühle*]. However, when this is *not* supported by the eyes, it only teaches degrees of the feeling of pressure, not yet shapes. Thus, before understanding of the world was practised as moving shapes there was a time when it was 'grasped' in terms of changing and differentially graded feelings of pressure. That thought can take place in images and in sounds there is no doubt but it can also take place in terms of feelings of pressure. Comparison in relation to strength and direction and sequence, memory, etc. (*KSA* 11:40 [28])

The "lines and shapes" which condition the temporal and spatial appearance of things are not simply constituted visually but depend upon a concord of the senses, most obviously the confirmation of sight by touch. It is clear from Nietzsche's emphasis on the "feeling" of pressure that what is being addressed here is to be distinguished from mechanistic conceptions of the world. In his assorted criticisms of the latter, the "mechanistic representation of pressure and impact" is dismissed as "only a hypothesis on the grounds of *visual evidence* [*Augenschein*] and the *sense of touch* [*Tastgefühls*]" (*KSA* 11:34 [247]). Mechanistic conceptions are translations of the world into the "*sign language of sight and touch*" (*WP* no. 625), a calculable world of measurable "things" (*WP* no. 635). It is here that Nietzsche, like Leibniz, contests the British empiricist model of perception as essentially the brutish impress of forces on matter and the (theological) presupposition that the "proper" medium of touch is the "surface". The intriguing question is what happens when touch is liberated from its dependency on sight. According to Nietzsche, if the prejudices of the eye and psyche are eliminated, nothing would remain but "dynamic quanta in a relation of tension to all other dynamic quanta" (*ibid.*). It is important to note that this tensional interplay does not unfold against the assumed givens of "lines and shapes". In other words, time and space as the *a priori* forms of intuition no longer provide a backdrop against which perceptual experience will be projected. Thinking in terms of feelings of pressure now emerges as something much more complex than the sense of touch. The "essence" of these dynamic quanta "lies in their relation to all other quanta, in their 'effect' upon the same" (*ibid.*). Each force exists only in relation to a multiplicity of forces, its difference from which is sensed or perceived as a difference in power. In this respect, thinking in terms of feelings of pressure presents an access route into Nietzsche's concept of *will to power* as micro-perceptive, "The will to power is not a being, not a becoming but a *pathos* – the most elemental fact from which a becoming and effecting first emerge" (*ibid.*). The will to power expresses itself as the differential sensibility of forces, sensitivity to what approaches and resists. In the most elementary way, thinking in terms of feelings of pressure concerns a relationship between forces capable of interacting with one another and like Leibniz once again, Nietzsche suggests that the most "pressing" forces may well be those which are imperceptible[6].

The verb "tasten" carries the sense of "to feel", especially in the sense of groping for something or touching with a light pressure as one would press a key on a keyboard. Nietzsche uses this word when describing his attempt to secure an ambient relationship with his environment,

It is *burdensome* [*Es ist schwer*] for my nature to find the right place with respect to heights and depths; at bottom it involves a *groping* [*Tasten*]. There are factors which cannot be strictly grasped (for example, the electricity in the drifting clouds and the effects of the wind: I am convinced that I have these influences to thank for eighty per cent of my torment). (Letter to Heinrich Köselitz, no. 119, 23rd of June 1881, *KSB* 6:95f.)

In his letter to Elisabeth Nietzsche (no. 121, 7th of July 1881) which lists the locations and resorts detrimental to his health, Nietzsche goes on to remark that the Engadine offers him some respite from the severity of his "attacks", "I experience continual calm and none of the pressure that I feel everywhere else" (*KSB* 6:98). Here, as in numerous other places in Nietzsche's writings, the word "pressure" has an odd valence. It often remains unclear within a given context how it is to be understood or indeed, how it is actually related to the subject matter in question. In the Preface to *The Gay Science* Nietzsche remarks that the title signifies the saturnalia of a spirit that has "patiently resisted a terrible long pressure" and although the text "seems to be written in the language of the wind that thaws", with hints of both April weather and the proximity of winter, it is not obvious that Nietzsche's allusion to pressure is a climatological one (*GS*, Preface, sec. 1, 32, *KSA* 3:345). Again, in *The Gay Science* section 354, in his criticism of language as the vehicle for maximal and mundane elevation of consciousness, the term "pressure" is listed somewhat curiously along with "look" and "gesture" as part of an alternative, tacit machinery of communication (*GS* sec. 354, 299, *KSA* 3:592).

Most significantly, perhaps, there is no "proper" organ for the sensation of pressure. The "groping" or "pressing" to which Nietzsche refers could be thought of as the primordial activity of the raw plasm of the body testing its environment and the establishment of boundaries between inside and outside. There are also copious resources for thinking about the changing and differentially graded feelings of pressure in terms of Nietzsche's sustained experimentation with heights and depths. However, as far as Nietzsche's own rare sensitivity to pressure is concerned, one may be permitted to address it in terms of a perception which one is unable to perceive – a little perception of sorts. This said, unlike Leibniz, Nietzsche's accounting of this anomaly does not rest on the conceptual appeal to parts and wholes or causes and effects but to *action at a distance*. He insists that "one cannot 'explain' pressure and stress themselves, one cannot get free of the actio in distans" (*WP* no. 618). To clarify, he goes on to add that one has lost the belief in being able to explain at all now that the dynamic interpretation of the world has supplanted the mechanistic, causal one. Since physicists are unable to eradicate action at a distance from their principles, one is obliged to understand all motion, all "appearances" and "laws" as "symptoms of an inner event" or "creative drive" (*WP* no. 619).

Provocatively, Nietzsche presents his account of action at a distance as a "pressing" which is not about proximity. Thinking in terms of "feelings of pressure" is not exclusively or fundamentally about contiguity. As Nietzsche remarks elsewhere in the context of his reflections on time, there is no obligation to plot movement as a relation between points (that is, as something proximate or spatial), "Time is...not at all a continuum; rather, there are only *totally different timepoints, no line*. Actio in distans." (*KSA* 7:26 [12], 579). The remote meteorological influences which Nietzsche reports need not be understood according to a model of distance as something spatially extended. "Distance" can also be addressed as something intensive and non-geometric. In fact, part of the problem of seeing time as either continuous or discontinuous is an artefact of our thinking of *things* as jointed or disjointed,

> An effect out of successive time moments is *impossible*: because two such timepoints would collapse into each other. Thus every effect is actio in distans, that is to say, through leaping [*Springen*]. (*KSA* 7:26 [12], 578)

It is one further proof of the monstrous tyranny of visually over-determined thinking that even when conceived dynamically, the notion of time *points* implies something quantitative and mathematically abstract. However, Nietzsche goes on to emphasize that it is only the habits of sensation and projection that reinforce the illusion of "thinghood". The key point about action at a distance is that one cannot picture it. "Leaping" is an intensive, wholly immanent process and not an interval between points. It is the vital upsurge of life, its subtle, imperceptible pulse.

Let us return to Nietzsche's claim that "at every moment" there are forces (such as air, electricity, etc.) which act on us without our knowledge. Arguably one of the most significant contexts in which Nietzsche explores this idea is in the Preface to *The Gay Science*, which also involves an unusual treatment of the notion of pressure. In a well-known section, Nietzsche presents the philosopher as a physician who diagnoses phenomena as if they were symptoms reflecting the interplay of forces within the tremendous multiplicity that is the body. Nietzsche notes that for a psychologist there are few questions that are as attractive as that concerning the relation of health and philosophy; in the event of the latter becoming ill himself, "he will bring all of his scientific curiosity into his illness" (*GS* Preface, sec. 2, 33, *KSA* 3:347). It is in this context that Nietzsche suggests that a person will express the kind of philosophical perspective that he or she deserves. Whereas some will employ philosophy as a means by which they express their superabundant gratitude for a charmed and exuberant life, for the most part, it is deprivations that philosophise. When it is distress that philosophises – which is the case with all sick thinkers – it is legitimate to ask, –"what will become of thought itself when it is subjected to the *pressure* of illness?" (*GS* Preface, sec. 2, 34, *KSA* 3:347). In formulating his question thus, Nietzsche alerts the reader to the material conditions of thought, to the needs which "unconsciously urge, push and lure the spirit" (*GS* Preface, sec. 2, 34, *KSA* 3:348). Thought is affected by the pressure of illness but illness (and its pressure) might equally be thought of as the well-spring of thought. If our sickness is an involuntary unravelling of the patterns associated with health, a falling away from good "constitution" in all its senses, it may be only when consciousness is disturbed that this pressure is apprehended,

> ...what will become of thought itself when it is subjected to the *pressure* of illness? This is the question which concerns the psychologist and here an experiment is possible. Just as a traveller determines to wake up at a certain hour before quietly abandoning himself to sleep, so we philosophers temporarily yield to sickness, body and soul (assuming that we are sick); we shut our eyes to ourselves, so to speak, and just as the traveller knows that something is *not* sleeping, that something counts the hours and will wake him up, so we also know that the decisive moment [*Augenblick*] will find us awake – that then something will leap forward [*hervorspringt*] and catch the spirit *in the act*; I mean, in its weakness, or backsliding, or surrender or hardening or darkening and whatever other names there are for the sick states of the spirit that on healthier days are opposed by the *pride* of the spirit... (*GS* Preface, sec. 2, *KSA* 3:347f.)

In this graceful declension of consciousness, to "yield" to sickness would imply a willing surrender to anomalous conditions. However, there is something very curious about this suggestion that in this process we might "catch the spirit *in the act*". As an image it is a peculiar one: either a successful piece of self-surveillance or self-entrapment, depending on how one reads the parties to the struggle. However, the situation is perhaps stranger than either of these two possibilities allow. This is a state which as yet fails to coincide with the element in which it is "discovered". Lacking both a determinate subject and a determinate object, this "act" stands apart from the temporal and causal continuum in which a narrative of human action might be interjected. It is a decisive moment which "finds us". It is in the moment that something "leaps forward" that the subject is "founded".

It is important to note that in this curious scenario, the reader is presented with an account of agency which is irreducible to any notion of decision, deliberation or purposivity. The sleeping traveller who is apparently able to rouse himself at the appropriate hour has not somehow stayed awake in order to do so. Beyond the simple opposition of waking and dormancy lies a far more subtly nuanced conception of the psyche in which different qualities of non-conscious awareness mark the peaks and troughs for all who travel in their sleep. Within this twilit realm there is no obvious causal relation between the spirit and the something that leaps forward. The issue might be better thought of as one of "catching a wave" or entering into a process rather than dividing up the current of thought into subject and object positions.

That which springs forward is as yet a vagrant vector of becoming, an acentred perception. It defines a moment when something springs forth in thought without any remotely discernible trajectory or telos. It is a kind of pure discovery but one which flares up against a darkness which it has caused to appear. It is not, then, a matter of making an idea luminous, rather it is a manifestation of its opacity, its utterly estranging power. Perhaps what thought apprehends when it approaches the relative idling of consciousness is a kind of economy of pressure, a sensitivity to nuances of strain, torpor, oppression, malaise. The "decisive moment" will "find us" in the precise sense of constituting a subject to reflect the "act" to itself, albeit darkly – in the blink of an eye (*Augenblick*). This moment of exposure to the silent machinery of thought is at the same time its closure – the arrival of a (self-)awareness which did not pre-exist its finding. If it is a question of vision at all, it is at best a matter of peripheral vision, that which can be glimpsed only by looking away from the light.

III.

To "look away" seems to be less a methodological gesture than an abdication of method. The identification of philosophy with effort (especially with "rigour") makes it difficult to discern the nature of a practice for which the *surrender* of struggle is a prerequisite. Of the numerous, elusive states of awareness which Nietzsche invokes – such as the passage from dreaming to a dreamlike wakefulness (*GS* sec. 54, *KSA* 3:416f.), the stirrings of memory, reverie and recollection (*WP* nos. 502,

809), the sudden and involuntary ecstasy of inspiration (*EH*, "Why I Write such Good Books", "Thus Spoke Zarathustra", sec. 3, *KSA* 6:339f.)[7] – the richest and most interesting are the states of self-"realization" in which one literally "comes to one's senses" after a period of "convalescence". In the new Prefaces of 1886, Nietzsche imagines the "free spirit" as a convalescent, drawing nearer to life again and again, puzzling over the question of its provenance ("where *had* he been?") and deducing that "he had been *outside* himself [*ausser sich*] – no doubt about that" (*HAH* Preface, sec. 5, *KSA* 2:19). The "herd signals" that Nietzsche associates with consciousness seem poorly equipped to convey the nature of this "experience". For anything to come to itself it must already find itself in an atmosphere which it does not yet identify. As "adventurer" and "circumnavigator" of that "inner world" called "human being", the "free spirit" is as yet nothing that accords with a subject of experience (*HAH* Preface, sec. 7, *KSA* 2:21). The accent, though, is not upon recollection of experience but on the experience of a kind of impossibility of experience. As Daniel Heller-Roazen intimates, the wide expanses traversed by a self prior to its fortuitous moment of self-realization can never be retrieved this side of appearance,

> If the process [of coming to one's senses] ever reaches an end, it is in the moment a self recovers itself: the instant in which I come, after sleep, shock, or stupor, to myself. Then it is difficult, if not impossible, to recall the wide expanses that must already have been traversed: all those regions in which a self comes to without yet coming to anything or anyone, let alone to that intimately felt but eminently forgettable being that is 'myself[8].

In section nine of "Why I am so Clever", Nietzsche offers his most sustained account of a kind of thinking constituted from within the mute obstinacy of the depths. In the context of exploring the question of "How one becomes what one is", the subtle senses are called upon to deliver an account of activity utterly opaque to the decisionistic modes of agency. We are told that, given the excessive nature of this task, there would be no greater danger than "catching sight of oneself *with* this task" (*EH* "Why I am so Clever", sec. 9, 254, *KSA* 6:293). It is a fundamental prerequisite of becoming what one is that "one does not have the remotest idea *what* one is" (*ibid.*). In this lengthy and highly cryptic passage, Nietzsche insists that the maxim *nosce te ipsum* ("know thyself") would be a liability. In fact, in this case blunders, wrong turnings, delays and self-misunderstandings attain a kind of reason of their own and Nietzsche even goes so far as to say that the position of moral selflessness – so much maligned elsewhere –

might even help to consolidate a more fundamental selfishness. The key point here is that the entire surface of consciousness has to be "kept clear of any of the great imperatives", even the "grand words" and "grand attitudes". These all constitute "a danger that the instinct 'will understand itself' too early" (*EH* "Why I am so Clever", sec. 9, 254, *KSA* 6:294). In line with Nietzsche's intuition that consciousness has only developed under the "pressure of the need for communication", an account of genesis is advanced which does not seek to "make sense" of anything in terms of the given habits of thought. On the contrary, this account makes of obscurity a virtue. Nietzsche suggests that if consciousness is unsolicited and held in abeyance, in the meantime the "organising 'idea' that is destined to rule" will continue to grow and grow "in the depths" (*ibid.*). Moreover, as it begins to command it "slowly leads *back* from sidepaths and wrong paths", it prepares individual qualities which will ultimately prove indispensable to the whole and constructs all "*subservient*" capacities one after the other before giving any hint of the "dominating task" or "goal" or "meaning" (*ibid.*).

What is so unusual about the "organising idea" is that it does not appear to direct activity in the conventional sense of the term. Any "advance" proceeds backwards – both in the sense of withdrawing from sidepaths and wrong paths and in the sense of constructing ancillary capacities prior to the primary idea. In fact, the organising idea appears to grow in "the depths" in the absence of any great imperative and in ignorance of its own *telos*. In the night-time of consciousness it would seemingly be a mistake to treat this "idea" as a guiding star. "Instinct" will push on instead in the dark, look for the darkest places, meander, wander for a while. Here pathways are created and retracted without reference to pre-established limits. Mechanistic laws are quite inadequate for describing this non-linear, discontinuous materialization. If there is a method to be discerned here, it is one of immersion in the elemental (the inner world, the depths), a surrender to the ebb and flow of things. Declaring abruptly and without any obvious justification that "regarded from this side" his life is "simply wonderful" Nietzsche continues as follows,

> For the task of a *revaluation of all values* more capacities may have been needed than have dwelt together in one individual, above all even contrary capacities which however are not allowed to disturb and destroy one another. Order of rank amongst capacities; distance; the art of separating without creating enmity; mixing up nothing; 'reconciling' nothing; a tremendous multiplicity which is nevertheless the opposite of chaos – this

was the precondition, the long secret labour and artistry of my instinct. Its *higher protection* manifested itself to such a high degree that I never had the remotest idea what was growing in me – that all my abilities one day *leapt forth* [*hervorsprangen*] suddenly ripe in their final perfection. (*EH* "Why I Am So Clever", sec. 9, 254f., *KSA* 6:294)

The apparent absence of logical connections between the clauses and the paratactic sequencing of sentences and ideas in this passage prompt the reader to question the "guidance" offered on the topic of "how one becomes what one is". As Nietzsche approaches the description of the "long and secret work and artistry" of his instinct, the sentences disintegrate into dissociative clauses, splintering further into lists of capacities and their relations. There is an inner distance signalled in these words which despite their precision dissolves the possibility of communicating anything. Unlike the account of a process in which successive states might be elucidated and cumulatively grouped, we are presented with an account in which differences enter into relations "amongst" one another whilst maintaining their "distance". The "art of separating without setting against one another" implies a thought of difference which is non-dialectical and non-extensive. Nothing is reconciled, sublated or equalized (mixed together). In spite of that, the tremendous multiplicity is not something that can be visualized as a set of juxtaposed entities discrete and divisible. The "leaping forth" of Nietzsche's "abilities" is the sudden fruit of a long and secret labour in which contrary capacities dwell together.

The "tremendous multiplicity" calls to mind the Leibnizian "immeasurable fineness of things", the minute differences which are formative and hence quite "the opposite of chaos". However, unlike Leibniz, Nietzsche presents the process of "coming to oneself" in terms of a difference in kind, not a difference in degree[9]. For example, in place of causal interpretations which rely on a notion of successive states [*ein Nacheinander*], Nietzsche's understanding of the activity of this multiplicity implies a process of interpenetration [*ein Ineinander*] (*WP* no. 631), a struggle between unequal elements in which a new series of differential relations is generated,

It is a question of struggle between two elements of unequal power: a new arrangement of forces is achieved according to the measure of power of each of them. The second condition is something fundamentally different from the first (not its effect): the essential thing is that different factions in struggle emerge with different quanta of power'. (*WP* no. 633)

The "essence" of the forces locked in combat with one another lies in their relation to all other quanta. This means that the next "moment" is now modified by the "outcome" of the struggle. Achieved "form" springs forward without warning and without obvious causal impetus. A threshold is attained at which something is registered but the memory of the former arrangement of forces is washed away in the surging wave of the next moment.

Thinking in terms of changing and differentially graded feelings of pressure is to be inhabited by the tensional interplay of forces and conditioned by them. It is to come to one's senses without yet coming to oneself. The something that springs forward in these remarkable moments is not yet thing-like. In the absence of any more suitable term Nietzsche calls it "instinct", a feeling unanchored to subject or object, a pulsion, a vector. This is why it is never really about how things "impact" on a subject but about coming to sense as such. Visual and spatial sense is so over-determined in terms of the co-ordinates by means of which understanding is possible. But one comes "to" one's senses from somewhere unspecified and this coming institutes the conditions according to which its arrival will be understood. The subtle senses are generative of "experience", they compose the perceiver in the decisive moment which "finds us". It is by means of the "changing and differentially graded feelings of pressure" that an "object" of perception is created *along with the spaces and times of its emergence*. This is why phenomena such as surprise, shock, daydreaming and "coming to one's senses" have such an extraordinary attraction for the thinker because it is here that everything is in the process of being "created". One becomes what one is as a momentary eruption in the thinkable. It is the view from outside, from the indeterminate element of formative forces.

Whereas for Leibniz it is true to say that the gentle flickering at the edge of vision might contract into an outline or the barely audible background melody might gain in volume, for Nietzsche our inchoate, subtle senses approach and move away from consciousness with a tidal ebb and flow yet retreat from every attempt to know them. Leibniz held that our distinct perceptions are composed of our myriad minute perceptions, proceeding by degrees to shape the whole. This is his general law of continuity, "Nothing takes place suddenly, and it is one of my great and best confirmed maxims that *nature never makes leaps*" (*NE* Preface, 56). In sharp contrast, Nietzsche presents us with an account of mental life which consists of surprising and unpredictable leaps. An incitement to explore ways of thinking beyond the familiar "reality" of our phenomenal world, Nietzsche's writing renders all that is "given" mysterious once again.

We cannot say how many twilights are yet possible. Nietzsche's philosophy conducts us through the dark labyrinths of the unknown to a mythic world wherein anything is possible at any moment. It would be futile to unite the inner tensions into intentionalities, to haul the inner pathos up on to the decks of daylight and consciousness, to make something egoic of the myriad signs of this indefinite life. All that remains is the background hum of the quiet machine, the eye pressed to the crack in the mirror, the last evaporating sentence of an unremembered dream.

Notes

[1] All translations from *KSA* and *KSB* volumes are my own.
[2] Gottfried Wilhelm Leibniz, *New Essays on Human Understanding*, trans. and ed. Peter Remnant and Jonathan Bennett. Cambridge: Cambridge University Press, 1981; hereafter NE. Page references according to the pagination of the Academie-Verlag edition of 1962.
[3] Leibniz remarks that although we might not be aware of background noise we do perceive it and it can be brought to our awareness, "This is how we become so accustomed to the motion of a mill or a waterfall, after living beside it for a while, that we pay no heed to it...Memory is needed for attention: when we are not alerted, so to speak, to pay heed to certain of our own present perceptions, we allow them to slip by unconsidered and even unnoticed. But if someone alerts us to them straight away, and makes us take note, for instance, of some noise which we have just heard, then we remember it and are aware of just having had some sense of it" (*NE*, Preface 53f.). This example suggests a mental landscape of differential zones of attentiveness with the capacity for the conscious retrieval of much that did not enter consciousness at the "time" of its occurrence.
[4] See Daniel Heller-Roazen, *The Inner Touch: Archaeology of a Sensation*. New York: Zone Books, 2007, 184.
[5] *Ibid.*, 121.
[6] It is perhaps worth mentioning in this context that chaos theorists explore the way in which matter becomes extremely sensitive to minor fluctuations in the environment, "perceiving" weak gravitational and magnetic fields and that this sensitivity is necessary for the emergence of self-organizing processes. See Manuel de Landa, "Nonorganic Life", in *Incorporations*, ed. Jonathan Crary and Sanford Kwinter. New York: Zone Books, 1992, 129-67, 131.
[7] Nietzsche's explorations of the experience of "rapture", especially in relation to artistic experience, are particularly interesting here (see *WP* nos. 799-811). If consciousness has only been "invented" to serve the needs of particular forms of life, it is possible to reconfigure the phenomenon from the perspective of the little

perceptions. In the context of his discussion of the inspiration surrounding *Thus Spoke Zarathustra* in *Ecce Homo*, Nietzsche describes a form of consciousness which is sparked into existence by the experience of revelation. In a passage of outstanding beauty and profundity, Nietzsche describes an ecstasy of terrific tension which discharges itself in involuntary paroxysms:...a complete being-outside-of self with the distinct consciousness of a host of subtle shivers and trickles down to the tips of one's toes. This consciousness, which is reconstituted from within the inscrutable "depths", is utterly distinct in itself but utterly opaque to intentional and decisionistic modes of agency. It is the distinct being of a multitude of subtle shudders, shivers and subtle sensations, incommensurate with any code.

[8] Daniel Heller-Roazen, *op. cit.* 211.

[9] In *Difference and Repetition*, Deleuze argues that Leibniz's thinking on the little perceptions is susceptible to a more radical view insofar as the latter can be read as both distinct and obscure: "distinct because they grasp differential relations and singularities; obscure because they are not yet 'distinguished', not yet differenciated" (213). The difference between the clear and the distinct is here no longer just of degree but in kind, "such that the clear would be in itself confused and the distinct in itself obscure" (*ibid.*). Gilles Deleuze, *Difference and Repetition*, trans. Paul Patton. London: Athlone, 1994.

NIETZSCHE, PANPSYCHISM AND PURE EXPERIENCE: AN EAST-ASIAN CONTEMPLATIVE PERSPECTIVE

GRAHAM PARKES

In one of his more incisive provocations Nietzsche ridicules the realists' naïve belief in the neutral purity of their experience,

> That mountain there! That cloud there! What is 'real' about those? Try taking away the phantasm and the entire human *contribution*, you sober [realists]! Yes, if only you could do *that!* If you could forget your heritage, your past, your training – your entire humanity and animality! For us there is no 'reality' – nor for you either, you sober ones. (*GS* sec. 57, *KSA* 3:421)[1]

In other words, it is impossible to extract from our current awareness the sedimentations, accumulated over millennia, of previous animal as well as cultural experience, impossible to escape the ways in which "some phantasy, some prejudice, some unreason, some ignorance, some fear and who knows what else" have woven their way into our "every feeling and sense-impression" (*ibid.*). And especially, it appears, when it comes to our experience of the natural world. However, one also finds passages in Nietzsche's works suggesting that it may after all be possible to check that ancient positing, perhaps through some kind of phenomenological *epochē*, and let natural phenomena like mountains and clouds simply show themselves, from themselves – perhaps even as they are in themselves? If this were possible, what would it be like? How would nature look?

Behind these questions is a practical concern. Insofar as things tend to go wrong when we lack clear awareness of the situation, any improvement of the currently dismal state of the world is probably going to come from a clarification of our experience. A particularly dismal situation is the ongoing devastation of the earth and its climate. One reason it is so difficult to persuade people in the developed countries to care about this crisis is that they have so little direct experience of natural phenomena, given the extent to which contemporary urban life enables us to insulate ourselves from them. It would surely be helpful if one could escape or subvert the "social construction" of the natural world that some theorists claim must always condition our experience, in order to get back "to the things [of nature] themselves". Nietzsche's talk of the possibility of our experiencing the natural world as "de-anthropomorphised", "de-divinised" or "newly redeemed" prompts the question of what exactly we would encounter under such circumstances[2]. The short answer is "will to power", which means that Nietzsche's monism of will to power can aptly be described as "panpsychist"[3].

Such a de-anthropomorphised engagement with the natural world could also be called "pure experience", since Nietzsche anticipates the use of this term by William James, and subsequently by the Japanese philosopher Kitarō Nishida, to describe a similar phenomenon[4]. Nishida came to the idea of pure experience from his Zen Buddhist practice, and it turns out to be illuminating, in outlining how Nietzsche effected such a transformation of his experience, to adduce some ideas and techniques from Daoist and Zen Buddhist philosophy. This shows that a way to begin to respond to Nietzsche's exhortation, through the person of Zarathustra, to "Stay true to the earth" is to cleanse the doors of our perception by removing all the egocentric clutter that we have pushed up against them, which gets in the way of seeing what the Buddhists call our "true nature" as well as the nature of the world around us[5]. This involves getting rid of consciousness, which is for Nietzsche "superficial" and ultimately "superfluous", and the language associated with and supportive of such consciousness. This undertaking does not preclude, but rather prompts, a change to a different kind of language, a more poetic discourse, which can conduce to more fulfilling lives – and perhaps even to saving the planet.

I.

As a way of showing the power of collective constructions of the natural world, Nietzsche emphasizes in his earlier work the vast difference between ancient and modern forms. He discusses the relations of the first humans to nature in connection with the origin of the religious cult, "The whole of nature is for those early religionists a sum of activities of conscious and volitional beings, an enormous complex of arbitrariness" (*HAH* I, sec. 111, *KSA* 2:112). This complex lacks any kind of natural causality, but is rather infused with unpredictable wills, magical forces, demons and gods, and inspirited things, all of which might be cajoled or compelled through affection or sorcery. A life in which "things (nature, tools, possessions of any kind) were animate and ensouled, capable of injuring and evading human purposes," gave rise to an extraordinary feeling of impotence on the part of human agents. Such a lack of power eventually engendered desire for the opposite, for a feeling of power, and this was later granted when Western science formulated laws of nature, which enabled people to exercise unprecedented power over the natural world – with a vengeance – by means of increasingly sophisticated technologies. Modern humans, for Nietzsche, tend to be impressed by the uniformity of the laws of nature, understood as utterly impersonal and devoid of irrational spirits. Nietzsche suggests that this uniformity derives from a change in the notion of the subject, which is now richer and more polyphonic than before, such that the uniformity comes to some extent from a projection of the human desire for order.

Although most early societies practised various kinds of ritual ceremonies and even magic in order to ensure success in the hunt or for agriculture, it was also clearly advantageous for our ancestors, especially when they were hunters and gatherers, to develop an accurate understanding of natural processes. But Nietzsche points out, on grounds that we would today call evolutionary-biological, that looseness in drawing certain kinds of conclusions also had considerable advantages.

> Whoever, for example, did not know how to find the 'similar' often enough, in the context of food or of dangerous animals, whoever subsumed too slowly or too carefully, would have a smaller probability of surviving than one who immediately assumed sameness in the case of similarities. (*GS* sec. 111, *KSA* 3:471)

These yellowish berries, for example, are not quite the same colour as those which my gathering companion so greedily devoured yesterday, just an hour before the stomach convulsions set in which killed him with gruesome rapidity. But they are similar enough in appearance for me to think twice about eating them. And that slight rustling sound is not quite the same as the sound I heard the day before, just seconds before the sabre-toothed tiger leapt upon my hunting companion and devoured him. But it sounds close enough, and sufficiently similar, for me to look for the nearest tree to climb, to a height beyond the range of a tiger's upward leap.

In order, then, for certain kinds of practical reasoning to take hold, it was necessary, Nietzsche goes on, for a long time not to see or feel what is changing about things; beings that did not see precisely had an advantage over those who saw everything 'in flux'. In and for itself every high level of carefulness in drawing conclusions, every tendency towards skepticism in this regard, posed a great danger for life. (*GS* sec. 111, *KSA* 3:472)

To get on more efficiently with the business of living, it is better not to pay too close attention to what is really going on. Nietzsche later draws an analogy with the process of reading. Just as a reader skims quickly over the individual words on a page,

so we scarcely see a tree exactly and completely, with regard to its leaves, branches, colour, shape; it is so much easier for us to phantasize an approximation of a tree. Even in the midst of the strangest experiences, we still do the same thing: we make up the greater part of the experience. (*BGE* sec. 192, *KSA* 5:113f.)

This passage suggests we might be able train ourselves to do what is less easy than phantasising the bulk of our experience, namely, to "see through" the persistent web of concepts and categories and linguistic labels to what is simply there. Given the survival value of the tendency to "phantasize approximations" of things, the strategy would be to suspend this aspect of what phenomenologists call "the natural attitude" – thereby effecting a switch from what one might call a "life perspective" to a "death perspective"

In an aphorism titled "Midday", Nietzsche writes of how "a strange longing for repose" can overwhelm the soul of one who has reached "the noontide of life",

Upon a meadow hidden among the woods he sees the great god Pan asleep; all the things of nature have fallen asleep with him, an expression of eternity on their faces – so it seems to him. He wants nothing, he frets about nothing, his heart stands still, only his eyes are alive – it is a death with open eyes. Then the man sees much that he has never seen before, and for as far as he can see everything is spun into a net of light and as it were buried in it. (*HAH* II, *WS*, sec. 308, *KSA* 2:690)

Nietzsche calls this condition a means of "procuring the advantages of one who is dead" – a condition not well appreciated, because of what he calls a "fundamentally false evaluation of the *dead* world on the part of the *sentient* world" (*KSA* 9:11 [35]).

The dead world! eternally in motion and without erring, force against force!...It is a *festival* to go from this world across into the dead world...Let us see through this comedy of sentient being and thereby enjoy it! Let us *not* think of the return to the inanimate as a regression! We become quite true, we perfect ourselves. *Death* has to be reinterpreted! We thereby *reconcile* ourselves with what is actual, with the dead world. (*KSA* 9:11 [70])

For Nietzsche this is also a way of getting beyond the human, all-too-human, "To think oneself away out of humanity, to unlearn desires of all kinds, and to employ the entire abundance of one's powers in *looking*" (*KSA* 9:11 [35]). And yet what often happens under such conditions (he is in the magical landscape of the Upper Engadine at the time) is that the ancient phantasms return, the immortals reappear, the mythic background comes to the fore,

Et in Arcadia ego. [Even here, perhaps especially here, I – *death* – am.] I looked down, over waves of hills, through fir-trees and spruces grave with age, towards a milky green lake: rocky crags of every kind around me, the ground bright with flowers and grasses...The beauty of it all made one shudder and reduced one to mute worship of the moment of its revelation; involuntarily, as if nothing were more natural, one projected into this pure, clear world of light (in which there was no longing, expecting, or looking forward and back) Greek heroes; this is how Poussin and his pupil must have felt: heroic and idyllic at the same time. (*HAH* II, *WS*, sec. 295, *KSA* 2:686f.)

A few years later (in 1881) Nietzsche elaborates these ideas in a series of passages in his notebooks. He praises "the will to know things as they are". For this, he writes, "What is needed is practice in seeing with other eyes: practice in seeing apart from human relations, and thus seeing objectively [*sachlich*]! To cure this enormous delusion of human beings!" (*KSA* 9:11 [10]). But then he presents a contrasting view,

The task: to *see* things *as they are*! The means: to be able to see with a hundred eyes, from many persons! It was a mistake to emphasize the impersonal and to characterize seeing with the eye of one's neighbor as moral. To see from the viewpoint of *many* neighbors and with purely personal eyes, that is the right thing. (*KSA* 9:11 [65])

But there need not be a contradiction here, as suggested by a similar move that one finds in the Chinese tradition.

Confucius, for example, advocates the cultivation of reciprocal perspectives – "putting oneself in the other person's position" or "seeing the situation from the other person's point of view" – as a way of reducing self-centredness and promoting social harmony. Not long after Confucius the classical Daoists thinkers (Zhuangzi in particular) recommend expanding the practice of experiential reciprocity beyond human beings to animals, birds, fishes, and even trees. Zhuangzi famously likens our normal, anthropocentric perspective to the situation of a frog at the bottom of a well who believes he commands a view of the whole world.

Some 1500 years later, in Japan, the Zen master Dōgen similarly encourages going beyond "looking through a bamboo tube at a corner of the sky" by entertaining the perspectives of an even broader range of beings, "dragons, hungry ghosts, celestial beings, mountains, and drops of water"[6]. In a similar vein, the Zen poet Bashō advises poets who wish to write about pine trees or bamboo – advice taken to heart also by many ink and wash (*sumi-e*) painters in Japan – to learn from the things themselves, "About the pine learn from the pine, about bamboo from the bamboo"[7]. A major tenet of East-Asian theories of creativity is that the artist needs to "enter into the spirit" or "resonate with the energies" of the subject of the work.

For Nietzsche this kind of understanding came easily in the Western tradition too, at least in the old days,

> During the great prehistoric age of humanity one presupposed spirit everywhere and never thought to honour it as a privilege of the human being…There was thus no shame attached to being descended from animals or trees…and one saw spirit as that which connected us to the natural world rather than as separating us from it. (*D* sec. 31, *KSA* 3:41)

Such a view is still possible in the modern age, at least for someone like Nietzsche, who writes in an aphorism with the title "Nature as Doppelgänger" that "the ultimate joy is found in being able to say of one's physical environment: 'This [nature] is intimate and familiar to me, related by blood, and even more than that'" (*HAH* II, *WS*, sec. 338, *KSA* 2:699)[8].

But what does it mean to say that the landscape of the Ober-Engadin is related to him "even more than by blood"? For one thing, from the "death perspective" mentioned earlier, from a standpoint beyond biocentrism, he appreciates the contribution to our lives that comes from the inorganic realm,

The inorganic conditions us through and through: water, air, earth, the shape of the ground...How distant and superior is our attitude towards what is dead, the anorganic, and all the while we are three-quarters water and have anorganic minerals in us that perhaps do more for our well- and ill-being than the whole of living society! (*KSA* 9:11 [210], [207])

Nietzsche was fascinated by what he knew, which was quite a lot, about the biology of his day – but he would have been truly delighted, had he been capable of registering it, by the discovery by Carl Benda in 1897 of *mitochondria*[9]. Mitochondria are organelles that reside within all cells in the human body and generate the energy necessary for the cells' activities and the body's life. There are some 10 million billion mitochondria in the body of the average adult, and they constitute almost half its "dry weight" (what remains after all the H_2O is extracted). The remarkable thing about mitochondria is that their DNA is quite different from the DNA of the body's own cells – and quite similar to the DNA of the mitochondria that power the cells of all multicellular organisms, whether animals or plants. One implication of this is that, if I attempt to assert my identity by pointing to my body and saying "This is me", most of what I am pointing to is water, and almost half the rest consists of mitochondria, which are very definitely *not* me. And it is this substantial "not-me" in the form of mitochondrial DNA – "even more than blood" – that relates this body physically to all other living bodies.

For Nietzsche, if one is going to understand the natural world properly, and aside from various human projections on to it, an appropriate research method is called for, "As a researcher into nature, one should get out of one's human corner" and thereby realise that "what *reigns* in nature is...abundance, extravagance...in accordance with the will to power, which is precisely the will to life" (*GS* sec. 349, *KSA* 3:585f.). One factor that allows us to get out of our human corner would be our intimate mitochondrial relationship to the natural world, on the basis of which we can entertain the perspectives of any other life-form. Nietzsche goes on to offer this advice to the natural scientists of his day,

Above all one should not want to divest existence of its *polysemic* [*vieldeutig*] character: that is what *good* taste demands, gentlemen, the taste of reverence in the face of everything that goes beyond your horizon! (*GS* sec. 373, *KSA* 3:625)

And in the next aphorism, "Our new 'Infinite'", he goes on to argue that the human intellect, being ineluctably perspectival in its view of itself and the world, is incapable of determining, how far the perspectival character of existence reaches or whether it even has any other character, whether an existence that lacks interpretation loses its 'sense' to the point of becoming 'nonsense', whether on the contrary all existence is not essentially existence that *interprets...* (*GS* sec. 374, *KSA* 3:626)

Leaving aside the question of whether something other than the intellect may be capable of determining such a thing, Nietzsche continues,

But I do think that today at least we are far from the laughable immodesty of decreeing from our own little corner that it is permissible to have perspectives *only* from this corner. Rather the world has become 'infinite' for us once again: insofar as we cannot dismiss the possibility that *it includes within itself an infinity of interpretations.* (*GS* sec. 374, *KSA* 3:627)

Not only multiple interpretations from each human being, but also from all other living and, ultimately, non-living beings.

II.

Another way of looking at this whole issue is in terms of what Nietzsche calls the drives (*die Triebe*). One of his most important statements about the drives makes the remarkable claim, generally ignored by the secondary literature, that the forces driving our psychical life do so with almost no awareness on our part,

However far we may drive our self-knowledge, nothing can be more incomplete than the picture we have of the totality of *drives* that constitute our being. We can scarcely even name the cruder ones: their number and strength, their ebb and flood, their play and counterplay, and above all the laws of their *nourishment* remain quite unknown to us. (*D* sec. 119, *KSA* 3:111)

Whether we are awake or dreaming, "our drives do nothing other than interpret nerve-impulses and posit 'causes' for them according to their own needs" (*KSA* 3:113). Since the patterns of stimulation received by the body during sleep are minimal, the drives have much more freedom of interpretation in their imagining – hence the phantastic nature of the dream. They are more constrained while we are awake and active, since the patterns of neural stimulation then are much denser, but Nietzsche emphasises that "there is no *essential* difference between waking and dreaming" insofar as the drives continue their interpretations during the day, dreaming and phantasising occasions for their fulfillment.

So, insofar as "all existence interprets", and the drives in particular interpret, and "will to power interprets", so that "interpretation itself [is] a form of will to power" (*KSA* 12:2 [148]), we end up with the picture Nietzsche proposes in *Beyond Good and Evil* section 36 of "the world as will to power and nothing besides". There, on the basis of the assumption that we cannot get to any reality other than the reality of our drives, Nietzsche asks,

> Is it not permitted to make the experiment and ask the question whether this given does not *suffice* for understanding on the basis of things like itself the so-called mechanistic (or 'material') world as well?…as a kind of drive-life, in which all organic functions…are still synthetically bound up with each other – as a *preform* of life? (*BGE* sec. 36, *KSA* 5:54f.)

It surely is permitted to make that experiment, and the results will be the realisation that as the drives interpretively project our (waking) world, what they encounter is will to power – as Nietzsche puts it, "'Will' can of course work only on 'will' – and not on 'matter' (not on 'nerves', for example)". Thus the drives encounter "will" in the form of *other interpreting drives* – not only the drives of our fellow human beings, but also those that animate animals, plants, and all other natural phenomena. In other words: panpsychism.

So what is ultimately going on, according to Nietzsche, if we manage to de-anthropomorphise the natural world, and "*naturalise* ourselves", as he puts it, "with pure, new-found, newly redeemed nature" (*GS* sec. 109, *KSA* 3:469)? He declines to elaborate, but it is helpful to consider here the traditional East-Asian practice of "emptying the heart-mind", referred to by the classical Daoist thinkers and followed to this day by Chan and Zen Buddhist practitioners, all of whom are engaged in a similar enterprise.

As one simply sits in the prescribed upright posture, following the inhalations and exhalations of the breathing, over time the internal dialogue – the incessant conversations and commentaries, thoughts and feelings, memories and phantasies, fears and anticipations that occupy our minds for so much of our waking lives – gradually quietens down. What supervenes is a calm openness and clarity. The Daoist and Buddhist thinkers account for this in terms of a falling away of the conceptual frameworks, ingrained thought-patterns, and emotional overlays and underpinnings that usually condition, and so preclude, our immediate experience of what is going on. Along with this comes a fading of the egocentric self that generates all this psychical clutter. Nietzsche describes this kind of self as,

> ...a phantom of ego, which for most people has been formed in the heads of those around them and communicated back to them, as a result of which they all live together in a fog of impersonal and semi-personal opinions and arbitrary, almost poetical valuations, each one in the head of the other, and this head in other heads again: a wondrous world of phantasms! This fog of opinions and habits grows and thrives more or less independently of the people it envelops. (*D* sec. 105, *KSA* 3:92f.)

This "general pale fiction" of the ego has internal as well as external origins, insofar as it also derives from the plurality of the drives. A contemporaneous note reads,

> The I is not the attitude of one being to several (drives, thoughts, etc.) but the ego is *a plurality of personlike forces*, of which now this one now that one stands in the foreground as ego and regards the others as a subject regards an influential and determining external world...As the drives are in conflict, the feeling of the I is always strongest precisely where the preponderance is. (*KSA* 9:6 [70], emphasis added)

Human reason "believes in the 'I', in the I as being and as substance, and *projects* its belief in the I-substance on to all things – thereby *creating* the concept of 'thing'" (*TI* "'Reason' in Philosophy", sec. 5, *KSA* 6:77). When this belief in the I is undermined, the concept of the "thing" is correspondingly weakened, and what comes to the fore as substance recedes is *relationships*. As we free ourselves from what Nietzsche calls "the error of the I", we come to recognise "the affinities and antagonisms among things, *multiplicities* therefore and their laws"[10]. This corresponds perfectly to the idea of "no-self" (*anatman*), which is central to Buddhism and, on the basis of a radically relational ontology, applies equally to the I and to things.

The practice of meditation has one simply sit, waiting for the words to subside and language to fade away altogether. Not something one can do when driven by the instinct for self-preservation, but rather in some temporary disengagement from the business of making a living in society. When this is working, a field opens up for the sitter that can persist through her rising from the cushion and returning to the opposite pole of dynamic activity.

With a diminishing of the thought-flow and a falling silent of language comes a dying down of consciousness, which is for Nietzsche a phenomenon that is "for the most part *superfluous*",

> The human being, like every living being, is thinking constantly, but without knowing it; the thinking that becomes *conscious* is only the smallest part, we say, the most superficial and worst part: – for it is only this conscious thinking that takes place in words, in signs that communicate, whereby the origin of consciousness itself is revealed. In short, the development of language and the development of consciousness …go hand in hand…Our thoughts are continuously generalised by the character of consciousness…and translated back into the perspective of the herd…An increase in consciousness is thus a danger; and whoever lives among the conscious Europeans knows that it is even an illness. (*GS* sec. 354, *KSA* 3:592f.)

A less sick way to live, then, would be to let the drives that give rise to our everyday consciousness and its thinking in words become quiescent, no longer interpreting the situation from their own perspectives, and to thereby allow what is going on beneath thinking to flow through the body in silence, without commentary. What is going on is basically drives – not exfoliating into consciousness or commenting on the text of experience, not the egocentric drives that sustain the illusion of the I – but now only the more ancient, deeper drives that through millennia of adaptation have kept the human body attuned to its physical environment. Paradoxically, it is by putting ourselves in a situation where we do not need to be concerned with preserving ourselves that we can get to a condition in which it is only those natural, environment-related and life-preserving drives that are operative. Under such conditions, one's responses to the world are naturally spontaneous, and one's actions stem not from the narrow confines of the small self, but from the forces of heaven and earth as they operate through the well-trained body. One thinks of Nietzsche's praise of Goethe in *Twilight of the Idols*,

> Goethe conceived of a strong, highly cultured human being, adept in a range of physical skills, self-controlled and with reverence for himself, who can dare to grant himself the full range and richness of naturalness, and who is strong enough for this freedom. (*TI*, "Expeditions of an Untimely Man", sec. 49, *KSA* 6:151)

And whatever thoughts may come when the chatter of consciousness has quietened down will then be genuinely results of Nietzsche's famous "*Es denkt*" (*BGE* sec. 17, *KSA* 5:31) rather than opinions of the egocentric self.

But, since Nietzsche did not engage in any formal meditation practice, how did he arrive at such Buddhistic ideas and experiences? By walking – or, as he often puts it, *marching* – six to eight hours a day. When he was in the Engadin, and hiking the paths around Sils-Maria, he kept to the well-trodden paths, avoiding dangerous terrain in which he would have to slow down and pay close attention to where he was putting his feet. (Several of his letters express gratitude for the successful efforts of the local authorities to keep the paths around the town smooth and even and clear of obstructions, so that he could march along them without fear of stumbling.) By keeping to ways that were safe and secure – whether around Sils-Maria, or among the lanes of Venice or the streets of Genoa – Nietzsche was able to practise a vigorous form of walking meditation (corresponding to the slower *kinhin* in the Zen tradition) that allowed him to hear the "inner voices" of his thoughts rather than the chatter of his I[11]. No wonder he reports that his creativity was always at its highest when the muscles were working at their most supple pitch, such that the body is experienced not as recalcitrant matter but as energetic flow (*EH*, "Why I Write such Good Books", "Thus Spoke Zarathustra", sec. 4, *KSA* 6:341).

To conclude with a return to the things of nature: how are things, then, when the body-flow is fully underway? Borrowing from the lyrical language of *Zarathustra*: Redeemed from their bondage under Purpose, the things of nature dance on the feet of Chance, and above each one: the Heaven Accident, the Heaven Innocence, the Heaven Contingency, the Heaven Exuberance. Zarathustra's gnarled tree at midday, wound around by the love of the vine. The world become perfect and we ourselves falling – Still! – into the well of eternity, up into the abyss of the heavens, from whence soul falls as dew, baptising all things in the vast transformative process of earthly becoming.

Notes

[1] From a concern to bring out certain nuances from the original, I have used my own translations throughout.
[2] For a discussion of these themes, see my essay "Nature and the Human Redivinized: Mahāyāna Buddhist Themes in *Thus Spoke Zarathustra*", in John Lippitt and James Urpeth (eds.), *Nietzsche and the Divine*. Manchester: Clinamen Press, 2000, 181-99.
[3] David Skrbina's all-too-brief presentation of Nietzsche as a panpsychist in his comprehensive study *Panpsychism in the West*. Cambridge, MA.: MIT Press, 2005, 137-39, aptly adduces the thesis of "the world as will to power and nothing besides" in *BGE* sec. 36, but he fails to mention the central role played by "life as

will to power" in *Thus Spoke Zarathustra*, for which see, especially, Part II, "On Self-Overcoming", and my remarks in the introduction to *TZ*, xx-xxii.

[4] See David Dilworth, "The Initial Formulations of 'Pure Experience' in Nishida Kitarō and William James", *Monumenta Nipponica* 24, 1969, 93-111, and Joel W. Krueger, "The Varieties of Pure Experience: William James and Kitarō Nishida on Consciousness and Embodiment", *William James Studies* 1/1, 2006. In his discussion of a new notion of the sublime in the fifth book of *Dawn of Morning*, Keith Ansell-Pearson characterises Nietzsche's task in that book as "liberating us from our human inheritance and looking at everything with searching eyes, new eyes", by way of pursuing "pure seeing" with a "pure, purifying eye", "On the Sublime in Nietzsche's *Dawn*", *Pli: The Warwick Journal of Philosophy* 20, 2009, 165-94, 187 and 191.

[5] "I beseech you, my brothers, stay true to the earth and do not believe those who talk of over-earthly hopes!...Once sacrilege against God was the greatest sacrilege, but God died, and thereby the sacrilegous died too. Sacrilege against the earth is now the most terrible thing...!" *TZ*, Prologue sec. 3. For an elaboration of this theme see my essay "Staying Loyal to the Earth: Nietzsche as an Ecological Thinker", in John Lippitt (ed.), *Nietzsche's Futures*. Basingstoke: Macmillan, 1998, 167-88.

[6] Dōgen, Shōbōgenzō, "Mountains and Waters as Sutras" sec. 4, in William Edelglass and Jay L. Garfield (eds.), *Buddhist Philosophy: Essential Readings*. Oxford and New York: Oxford University Press, 2009, 83-92.

[7] As recounted by a disciple of Bashō's, Hattori Dohō; cited in Toshihiko and Toyo Izutsu, *The Theory of Beauty in the Classical Aesthetics of Japan*. The Hague: Nijhoff, 1981, 162-63.

[8] See also *WS* , sec.s 14, 17, 51, 57, 115, 138, 176, 205, 295, 308, 332.

[9] See Nick Lane, *Power, Sex, Suicide: Mitochondria and the Meaning of Life*. Oxford and New York: Oxford University Press, 2005, 13. Lane notes that the importance of these tiny granules within the living cell as "the fundamental particles of life" was recognised by the German Richard Altmann in 1886, though he called them "bioblasts". The precise biological function of mitochondria was not determined until 1949, when they were proved to be the site of the living cell's respiratory enzymes.

[10] *KSA* 9:11 [21], 450. Compare the following notes, which make similar points:

The I contains a number of different beings. (*KSA* 10:4 [189], 165)

Within the human being reside spirits as numerous as the creatures of the sea: they fight with each other for the spirit 'I'. (*KSA* 10:4 [207], 169)

the cleverness of my whole organism, of which my conscious I is merely a tool. (*KSA* 11:34 [46], 433)

I regard the I itself as a thought-construct, like 'matter', 'thing', 'substance', 'individual', 'purpose', 'number': merely as a regulative fiction, then, with the help of which some kind of constancy [*Beständigkeit*], and therefore 'knowability', is made up and transposed into a world of becoming. (*KSA* 11:35 [35], 526)

[11] "I am in the Upper Engadine again, for the third time, and again I feel that here and nowhere else is my proper home and place of incubation. Ah, how much everything lies hidden in me still, and wants to become word and form! Only here is it quiet and high and lonely enough for me to be able to perceive my innermost voices!", Letter to Carl von Gersdorff, no. 427, end of June, 1883, *KSB* 6:386.

PART TWO:

NIETZSCHE AMONG THE PHILOSOPHERS

THE DESCENT OF PHILOSOPHY:
ON THE NIETZSCHEAN LEGACY
IN HEIDEGGER'S PHENOMENOLOGY

WILLIAM MCNEILL

The thinking to come [*Das künftige Denken*] is no longer philosophy, because it thinks more originally than metaphysics – a name that says the same thing as philosophy. However, the thinking to come can also no longer, as Hegel demanded, set aside the name 'love of wisdom' and become wisdom itself in the form of absolute knowing. Thinking is on the descent [*Abstieg*] into the poverty of its precursory [*vorläufigen*] essence[1].

Heidegger – Nietzsche. When one hears these two names intoned in the same breath, one cannot but think immediately of Heidegger's lectures and essays on Nietzsche dating from the mid-1930s to the mid-1940s, and published by Heidegger himself in 1961 in two volumes under the title *Heidegger: Nietzsche*. The seminal importance of the publication of these two volumes, and of their subsequent translation into French and English can scarcely be underestimated with regard to their impact on European philosophy, provoking a reassessment of the philosophical legacy of both Nietzsche and Heidegger, and spawning an extraordinarily creative range of responses to this monumental and ongoing *Auseinandersetzung*. In France, the translation by Pierre Klossowski that appeared a decade later gave rise to works by Derrida, Foucault, Deleuze, Sarah Kofman, Michel Haar, and Klossowski himself; on the American scene, one thinks at once of the work of David Krell, translator of Heidegger's *Nietzsche*, of Alphonso Lingis, Charles Scott, John Sallis, and David Allison, in each case to name but a few. With regard to the issue of descent that I wish to approach here, two of these thinkers merit special mention at the outset: David Krell, who has coined the term "descensional thinking" to characterize the movement and fate of thinking after Nietzsche (and this is a term that I shall adopt in my remarks here); and Michel Foucault, whose 1971 essay "Nietzsche, Genealogy, History" offers a sustained and incisive meditation on the meaning of descent with respect to Nietzschean genealogy.

What I propose to focus on here is the *other* Heidegger – Nietzsche: a much-neglected relationship that is found latent within Heidegger's early phenomenology, and specifically within his 1927 magnum opus, *Being and Time*. In pointing to the significance of Nietzsche in the project of *Being and Time*, I am not, of course, claiming that Nietzsche is the single most important influence behind Heidegger's phenomenology of Dasein: what would *Being and Time* be without the influences of Parmenides, of Plato and Aristotle, Descartes and Kant, Hegel and Husserl, St. Augustine and Dilthey, Jaspers and Kierkegaard, to name but a few? Part of what makes *Being and Time* a great work of philosophy is not just its radical, ground-breaking interpretation of the being of Dasein and of being itself in terms of originary time, but the fact that it is an ongoing dialogue, a critical encounter or *Auseinandersetzung*, with the entire history of philosophy and with the pivotal thinkers therein. As Heidegger would later remark, it is the privilege of great works to let themselves be influenced[2]. Yet, as he also repeatedly reminds us, it is precisely what remains unthought or unspoken, relatively hidden or concealed – the concealed sources within a thinker's work – that must be brought to light in their determinative force and influence. Such is the concrete work of hermeneutic interpretation, itself conceived as the ongoing, and ever to be repeated task of *Destruktion*: of a constructive dismantling or destructuring of the history of ontology.

Now in this perspective it is indisputable that there is also an influence and legacy of Nietzsche latent within *Being and Time*, a legacy that may be all the more significant precisely by virtue of its relatively hidden and unacknowledged character. David Farrell Krell, in his doctoral dissertation on descensional thinking in Nietzsche and Heidegger, has indeed argued – and convincingly so, in my view – that in *Being and Time* "Nietzsche lies concealed in a revealing way on every page"[3]. Jacques Taminiaux, in his perceptive essay "La présence de Nietzsche dans *Sein und Zeit*", has likewise suspected a profound, albeit largely unspoken complicity between Nietzsche's understanding of time and history and the project of *Being and Time*, asking whether, indeed, Heidegger's analysis of the ekstatic-horizonal temporality of Dasein does not in fact rest upon an "existential reappropriation" of the eternal return[4]. Certainly, if one asks concerning the Nietzschean thread within *Being and Time*, there are just three explicit references: 1. an allusion to *Thus Spoke Zarathustra* in the account of being-towards-death; 2. a mention of Nietzsche's account of conscience in a footnote to Heidegger's own analysis of conscience; and 3. an extended discussion of Nietzsche's second "Untimely Meditation" in the analysis of

Dasein's historicality. In these remarks, I shall focus on the first and third of these.

1. The first explicit reference to Nietzsche in *Being and Time* occurs in the pivotal section 53, a section that, in presenting what its title announces as the "Existential Projection of an Authentic Being-towards-death", prepares for the critical transition into the dimension of ekstatic temporality and the primacy of its futural ekstasis. Since Dasein is primarily possibility – since possibility, and not actuality constitutes the primary dimension of its very being – and indeed is the altogether indeterminate possibility of impossibility of being, the possibility that is itself possible at any moment (*Augenblick*); and since precisely this possibility is largely concealed and covered over by Dasein's everydayness, the uncovering and freeing of this possibility as such cannot mean its actualization (which would destroy its preservation precisely as possibility), but must mean a running ahead into (*Vorlaufen in...*) this possibility as such: a running ahead that first sets it free as possibility, that cultivates, understands, and sustains it as such (*SZ* 261f.)[5]. Yet freeing this possibility as such is thus nothing other than Dasein's freeing itself for itself, for its ownmost being, which is to say: for its ownmost possibility, for the possibility that only it can be and has to be in each case, the possibility that individuates its very being as Dasein. Freeing itself for itself as possibility, Dasein is, so to speak, deactualized: it ceases to understand itself as primarily something actual or as the actuality of the actual, the presence of what is present: it becomes futural – comes to be the being futural that it always already was: potentially was, that is, was precisely as a potentiality or possibility of being that had yet to be appropriated as such. Dasein's becoming free for its death, for its ownmost possibility as such, in running ahead, thus, as Heidegger puts it,

> discloses to existence, as its most extreme possibility, its relinquishing of itself [*die Selbstaufgabe*], and thereby shatters all petrification upon the existence that has been achieved in each case. In running ahead, Dasein guards itself against falling back behind itself and the potentiality for being that has been understood and 'of becoming too old for one's victories' (Nietzsche). (*SZ* 264).

Embracing its futuricity in running ahead, Dasein thus affirms the necessity of having to relinquish itself at any moment, of having to relinquish the particular possibility that it is and has been – and this is nothing other than the embracing of its ownmost freedom as such, as a freedom for death as its ownmost possibility. It ceases to understand itself as primarily something actual, or as the actuality of this or that possibility at this or that determinate moment, and does so in projecting itself upon – that is, understanding itself as – not this or that possibility, but the indeterminate possibility of impossibility, of death. This deactualizing of the actuality of its own being is nothing short of the shattering of itself as the one who is and has been, and the embrace of this deactualization or disappropriation as the primary moment of one's ownmost being is nothing other than an intensification of the vigilance (Dasein's "guarding itself") intrinsic to all existence as such, or, in other words, of the readiness of which Heidegger repeatedly writes. It is the projective character of Dasein's being, the fact that it exists primarily as possibility and thus has to be its "not yet" – or rather, more precisely, has to be a "not yet" that is never yet its own, that has always yet to be appropriated – that Dasein in each case faces the task of first becoming what it (potentially already) is. Heidegger had already noted this much earlier in *Being and Time*, when discussing Dasein as projection,

> And only because the being of the There is constituted by understanding and its projective character, because it *is* what it becomes or does not become, can it tell itself understandingly: 'Become what you are!' ['*Werde, was du bist!*']. (SZ 145)

The temporal analysis of Dasein's being is thus prefigured as nothing other than the explication of the temporality that enables and necessitates how one becomes what one is, Heidegger's words here more than likely alluding to the Nietzschean *ēthos* encapsulated in the subtitle of *Ecce Homo*.

Now, the explicit reference to Nietzsche in section 53 is taken from *Thus Spoke Zarathustra*, from the section "Of a Free Death", in which Zarathustra, insisting that we need to learn to "die at the right time" – at the appropriate Moment or *kairos* – laments, "All take dying seriously: yet death is not yet a festival". The work *Thus Spoke Zarathustra* as a whole, which begins with and is a continual celebration of and meditation on the necessity of *Untergang*, of descent as downgoing, is of course the preparation of this festival. Here, in this section, Zarathustra, in advocating the embrace of one's own death as a free death, as "the free death that comes to me, because *I* will it" – because, that is, my will now corresponds to, affirmatively gives itself over to, the intrinsically self-overcoming movement of the will to power (that can maintain itself only in and through its own self-overcoming) – insists that we must learn "to practice the difficult art of going [of departing] at the right time" (*die schwere*

Kunst üben, zur rechten Zeit zu – gehn); and this indeed, or something very similar, appears to be the art of authentic existence presented in *Being and Time*, or, as Heidegger simply called it in 1928, "the art of existing"[6]. The point here is not simply that Heidegger appears to take from Nietzsche the concept of *Freiheit zum Tode*, or freedom for death. It is, rather, that the very dimension of Nietzsche's thought, at least in *Zarathustra*, is undoubtedly what is being conceptually explicated in *Being and Time*: if Zarathustra is, as he himself insists, none other than the thinker of the eternal recurrence of the same, and if this thought is the thought that must be thought in and as the Moment *Augenblick* (as narrated in the section "On the Vision and the Riddle"), it is surely nothing other than the temporality of the Nietzschean Moment that we can already see latent within Heidegger's initial projection of an authentic being-towards-death. Is not this "deactualization" of myself (as Pierre Klossowski has called it[7]) as already having been, the deactualization that is the readiness for relinquishing oneself as one is and has been, and that is accomplished as the temporal ekstasis of running ahead, that is, of the authentic future – is not this deactualization the very experience of the thought of return, the necessary affirmation in response to Zarathustra's question in the gateway "Moment", "...and you [dwarf] and I in the gateway: must we not already have been there?" "Having been there", *Dagewesensein*, one might note, is the very same term used by Heidegger to designate the ekstasis of the "past": only insofar as Da-sein is *Da-gewesen-sein*, "has been there", can it be futural. In our affirmative response to the question "Must we not already have been there?" we are suddenly displaced from the present: the understanding of ourselves as purely present is disrupted, and we find ourselves displaced into the dimension of the future, of our not yet having been – and yet this "not yet" cannot be severed from our having been: it is the indeterminable "not yet" of our having been, whence the vortex of the eternal return into which we are sucked.

2. The second explicit reference to Nietzsche in *Being and Time*, which I shall note only briefly for now, occurs in the footnote that concludes section 55, on "The Existential-Ontological Foundations of Conscience". The note appears to be little more than a passing nod to Nietzsche, an acknowledgement of his analysis of conscience as one of several that should be heeded when undertaking a phenomenological analysis of conscience that seeks to understand it ontologically, and not as a faculty of the soul, the intellect, the will, feeling, or a combination of these. The allusion is presumably to Nietzsche's account of conscience in the *Genealogy of Morals*, but it is not entirely clear whether Heidegger

attributes any major phenomenological or ontological insight to Nietzsche; on the contrary, it appears that he simply lumps Nietzsche together with Kant, Hegel, and Schopenhauer as one more of the prevalent interpretations of conscience, one that, while noteworthy, remains phenomenologically and ontologically inadequate. The note simply reads, "In addition to the interpretations of conscience by Kant, Hegel, Schopenhauer, and Nietzsche, one should heed... ", and goes on to list Kähler, Ritschl, and Stoker (whose analysis ultimately rests on an adoption of Scheler's personalism). Of these, only Stoker's interpretation receives any explicit commentary. And yet, Heidegger's mere mention of Nietzsche here may conceal a greater significance of, and indebtedness to, Nietzsche's analysis of conscience than might appear to be the case.

3. I shall come back to this point shortly. But for now I would like to turn to the third and final explicit mention of Nietzsche in *Being and Time*. This third reference, by far the most extensive, extends over a page, and occurs towards the end of section 76, well into Part I, Division II of *Being and Time*. The section is entitled "The Existential Origin of Historiography in the Historicality of Dasein", and it purports to explicate the "ontological genesis" of historiography from the historicality of Dasein, in explicit preparation for an understanding of what is entailed in the task of a historiographical *Destruktion* of the history of ontology (392). Historiography is understood here as a "science", and science (*Wissenschaft*) is conceived in general as thematization, that is, as the explicit projection of the object of study in terms of, or upon the horizon of, its specific being. Every regional science thus presupposes a primary, guiding projection of the being of its thematic object, the opening of a horizon that at once delimits, and in turn first enables, a perspective upon the object in question. As Heidegger elucidates, "Every science constitutes itself primarily through thematization. What is familiar in a pre-scientific manner to Dasein as disclosed being-in-the-world is projected upon its specific being. With this projection the region of beings is delimited" (393). With regard to the "science" of historiography, the specific region of being in question is that of Dasein itself. Historiographical disclosure of the being of Dasein constitutes itself, that is to say: constructs itself, in and through the process of thematization, itself enabled by the primary projection of a horizon. The historiographical disclosure of Dasein's being is thereby shown to be possible only on the grounds of the ekstatic-horizonal temporality of Dasein, and in particular in the opening of the primary, futural horizon that delineates in advance how Dasein comes towards itself in coming back to its being as having been there. As Heidegger puts it, "Historiography,

therefore, [...] by no means takes its point of departure in the 'present' and from what is merely 'actual' in the present day, so as to grope its way back from there to something that is past. Rather, *historiographical* disclosure too temporalizes itself *from out of the future"* (395). Yet the point here is not that historiographical research is thus derivative with respect to the originary temporality (and by extension, historicality) of Dasein. Rather, in here broaching what was identified earlier, in the Introduction to *Being and Time*, as "the ontological task of a non-deductively constructive genealogy of different possible ways of being" (11) – and this is the sole occurrence of the term "genealogy" in *Being and Time* – Heidegger's focus is precisely on the meaning of construction, that is, on the formation of the primary horizons that delimit in advance particular ways of being. Phenomenological construction, elsewhere identified as intrinsic to the phenomenological method (together with reduction and destructuring (*Destruktion*))[8], if it is to understand itself in what and how it ultimately is, cannot proceed deductively, that is, starting from a given "present". Rather, insofar as the constructive formation of horizons, which enables historiographical thematization, is temporalized in and through the temporality of Dasein, it is also intrinsically historical, that is, bound to the historicality of Dasein itself. The futural formation of horizons is temporalized only in the retrieval or recovery (*Wiederholung*) of Dasein that has been there, and it is this future-oriented retrieval that not only constitutes the historicality of the present, but that also, by extension, first enables the possibility of an (authentic) historiographical disclosure of history (*Geschichte*) that would be what Heidegger explicitly calls a "history of the present" (393).

In what follows, I want to indicate how Heidegger's phenomenology of Dasein, accomplishing itself as a historiographical destructuring of the history of ontology, not only moves in the same dimension as Nietzschean genealogy in undertaking such a "history of the present", but also embraces and remains indebted to Nietzsche's tripartite conception of monumental, antiquarian, and above all critical historiography as outlined in the second of the *Untimely Meditations*. The discussion of Nietzsche in section 76 of *Being and Time*, I argue, is neither simply a passing reference to an important existing analysis of historiography, included for the sake of scholarly completeness; nor is it intended merely as a philosophical document that would justify Heidegger's own phenomenological analysis of Dasein by showing how Nietzsche's tripartite division is possible only on the basis of ekstatic-horizonal temporality and historicality of Dasein, and thus derivative with respect to this supposedly more original ground.

Both Heidegger's and Nietzsche's analyses of historical understanding must be understood in the context of the problem of historicism, to which Heidegger explicitly refers in this section. He writes,

> Thus the very prevalence of a differentiated historiographical interest that extends to the most remote and primitive cultures is in itself no proof of the authentic historicality of a 'time'. In the end, the emergence of a problem of 'historicism' is the clearest symptom of the fact that historiography tends to alienate Dasein from its authentic historicality. Such historicality does not necessarily require historiography. Eras without historiography are not as such unhistorical also. (396; cf. 21)

Historiography tends to alienate Dasein from its authentic historicality. Mere historical "interest" in the most diverse, differentiated, and foreign cultures and their histories is no proof of the authentic historicality of an age or time, if such historical interest occurs only from the horizonal vantage point of a distanced, theoretical gaze, supposedly impartial, scientific, and objective, and that remains fundamentally indifferent to and unaffected by the objects of its study, as in the case of historicism. Secure in its own present, such historical understanding is entirely alienated from the historicality of its own situatedness, the historicality that first forms and gives rise to its own horizon. By contrast with such inauthentic historiography, authentic historiography and the truth it discloses must, for Heidegger, be hermeneutic through and through, that is, critically attentive to the formation, transformation, and dissolution of horizons in the very process of thematization of its object, namely, the historical existence of Dasein. Heidegger writes,

> Historiographical thematization has its main component in the development of the hermeneutic situation which, with the open resolve of historically existing Dasein, opens itself to the disclosive retrieval of Dasein that has been there. The possibility and structure of *historiographical truth* is to be expounded from the *authentic disclosedness* ('truth') *of historical existence.* (397)

Yet what, more precisely, is to be the theme of authentic historiography? In authentic historiographical inquiry, the historical existence of Dasein is not to be objectified as something "past" and complete, something that now lies outside and beyond the present; yet nor is Dasein to be thematized simply in its present-day state of being. Rather, Heidegger insists, it is to be thematized in and from out of its primarily futural having-been, that is, in that temporality and historicality of its being from which possible horizons first emerge. The proper theme of authentic historiography, which can be undertaken only in and through the authentic existence and authentic historicality of Dasein, is nothing other than *the possible*, in its emergence and dissolution,

> If historiography is thus rooted in historicality, then we must also be able to determine from here what is 'authentically' the *object* of historiography. The delimitation of the originary theme of historiography will have to be undertaken in conformity with authentic historicality and the disclosure of what has been there belonging to it, that is, retrieval [*Wiederholung*]. Retrieval understands Dasein that has been there in the having-been of its authentic possibility. The 'birth' of historiography from authentic historicality then means: the primary thematization of the object of historiography projects Dasein that has been there upon its ownmost possibility of existence. Is historiography then to have the *possible* as its theme? (394)

Authentic historiography entails thematization of its proper object – Dasein – both from out of and with respect to Dasein's ownmost possibility of existence, a possibility that can be disclosed as such only in a distinctive movedness of Dasein, that of running ahead. ahead into the dimension of what is possible at any moment, and yet never calculable or determinable: the dimension of indeterminacy that permeates all existence as such. Running ahead into the dimension of possibility to come, Heidegger writes, holds the Moment (*Augenblick*) "at the ready": it brings about (temporalizes) a fundamental readiness for the possibility of a retrieval or recovery of our own having-been, of existence that has been there (343f.). Yet to the extent that our own having-been is never simply ours, but always also that of a historical world, a heritage, the enactment of this *ēthos* of readiness also bears within it the possibility of an explicit, that is, knowing appropriation of one's heritage – and this is the full sense of "retrieval" for Heidegger.

It is here, with respect to the issue of retrieval (*Wiederholung*) and its multiple temporal dimensions, that Heidegger explicitly embraces Nietzsche with regard to authentic historiography, appealing to the second "Untimely Meditation" and its distinctions of monumental, antiquarian, and critical history (or historiography). This threefold distinction, Heidegger remarks, is not accidental: it has its necessity and finds the grounds of its unity in Dasein's originary historicality and the ekstatic-horizonal temporality that it harbours. Authentic historiography, he notes, "must be the factically

112   The Descent of Philosophy

concrete unity of these three possibilities" (396). Existing futurally in running ahead, Dasein comes towards itself as coming back to a possibility that has been there, and in such retrieval is ekstatically open, in a horizonal manner, for the "monumental" possibilities of human existence – possibilities that can thereby become the thematic object of authentic historiography, guiding and grounding the future-oriented unfolding of historical Dasein. Such retrieval, as an appropriation of the possible, at the same time enables and calls for a recognition and preservation of the particular historical existence from which the possibility in question has been disclosed, giving rise to the "antiquarian" dimension of authentic historiography, oriented towards Dasein's having-been. Finally, Heidegger elucidates, the unity of futural having-been, as authentic, temporalizes the present day in the manner of the Moment or *Augenblick*, "...insofar as the present day [*das Heute*] is interpreted from out of the futural understanding, in retrieval, of a possibility of existence that has been seized upon", he writes, "authentic historiography becomes an unmaking of the present day [*zur Entgegenwärtigung des Heute*], that is, a suffering freeing of oneself from the falling publicness of the present day. Monumental-antiquarian historiography is, as authentic, necessarily a critique of the 'present' [*der 'Gegenwart'*]" (397).

Nietzsche's somewhat surprising appearance here in section 76 of *Being and Time* is a source of some mystery and of considerable speculation. For it is unclear when exactly Heidegger read the second "Untimely Meditation". The fact that one would search in vain for any mention of Nietzsche's meditation on history in any of Heidegger's work preceding *Being and Time* – although there are extensive discussions and mentions of other philosophers of history, including Dilthey, Spengler, Troeltsch (GA 60, 33), Simmel, Rickert, Windelband, Weber (GA 60, 39ff.; GA 58, 189ff.), Kant, Herder, Hegel, Niebuhr, Savigny, Ranke, Trendelenburg, Erdmann, Zeller, Fischer, Lotze (GA 56/57, 132ff.); not forgetting the infamous Count Yorck von Wartenburg (GA 64, 3ff.)[9], and many more, yet not a hint of Nietzsche – might lead us to suspect that Heidegger read Nietzsche's work only very late, when the writing of *Being and Time* was well underway, and decided to incorporate it at the last minute. Yet we know that this was not the case: Heidegger read Nietzsche – certainly the *Genealogy of Morals* and *Thus Spoke Zarathustra* – at least as early as 1909, and in 1912 indeed gave a public lecture on Nietzsche[10]. It is inconceivable that he would not have been familiar with such an important and ground-breaking text as the second "Untimely Meditation" from early on, despite the lack of any explicit reference to it that I have been able to unearth thus far in his early work[11]. Is it not rather the case, as I suggested earlier (and in this I concur with Taminiaux's suspicion), that Heidegger kept quiet about Nietzsche precisely because Nietzsche's meditation was a secret source and resource for his own account of historicality in *Being and Time*? Whatever the case, reactions to this appeal to Nietzsche are quite diverse. To mention just two: Hans Ruin, in his book on Heidegger and historicality, thinks that Heidegger "explicitly presents his own analysis as somehow providing a ground for Nietzsche's previous analysis"; but he finds Heidegger's argument "not very convincing" and his "grafting of Nietzsche's scheme onto his own account" "puzzling"[12]. Magda King, by contrast, finds it an "admirable example of a 'transforming' interpretation of an earlier thinker", remarking that "Even the most critical reader of Heidegger will hardly deny the brilliance of this exposition"[13].

So how are we, then, to assess Heidegger's appeal to Nietzsche in section 76? One of the most helpful assessments I have come across is that offered by Charles Bambach in his book, *Heidegger, Dilthey, and the Crisis of Historicism*. Bambach writes that "What Heidegger retrieved from Nietzsche, especially the early Nietzsche, was an understanding of historical time as horizonal" (254). He reminds us of Nietzsche's claim in the second "Untimely Meditation", "This is a universal law: every living being can be healthy, strong, and productive only within a horizon; if it is unable to draw a horizon around itself ... it will feebly waste away or hasten to a timely decline". And Bambach adds (allow me to quote at length here, because I think his suggestion is really quite enlightening),

The horizon offers a limit or threshold within which to situate one's own being, a boundary against which possibilities and resolutions can be projected, measured, and ultimately decided. What made Nietzsche's reading of horizonality unique, however, was that he moved beyond the traditional understanding of horizon as the static frame of the present and tried to express the unity of all three temporal modes in the dynamic possibilities of openness and interpretation. Heidegger pursued the hermeneutic implications of this reading for his own project, especially as it related to the problem of time. He found in Nietzsche's understanding of horizon an indication for a new beginning in thinking, a beginning marked by the openness of temporality against the closure of an eternal 'now'. The Nietzschean idea of horizon connoted for Heidegger a phenomenological opening or place within which beings show themselves. Horizon becomes, in this phenomenological sense, a place of disclosure – 'the open expanse' – rather than a limit, boundary, or container. Within this structure, time is grasped as the unity of horizons that mark the very being of Dasein. (254f.)

I think Bambach's remarks here are insightful, and I have tried to suggest how Heidegger, in *Being and Time*, can be seen to be explicating phenomenologically the ekstatic temporality that is implicit not only within the thought and experience of the eternal recurrence, but within the experience of historical repetition also, and doing so with a view to the formation and dissolution of temporal horizons that are the dimension within which genealogy moves.

In his essay "Nietzsche, Genealogy, History" that I mentioned at the outset – an essay that, in a finely nuanced manner, relates Nietzschean genealogy to the three modalities of history identified in the second "Untimely Meditation" – Michel Foucault argues that although the usage of the terms *Ursprung* (origin), *Herkunft* (descent), and *Entstehung* (emergence) is fluid in Nietzsche and never rigorously delimited, Nietzschean genealogy at its most incisive inevitably challenges the pursuit of origin, and casts its eye instead upon questions of descent and emergence[14]. "*Entstehung* and *Herkunft*", he remarks, "are more exact than *Ursprung* in recording the true objective of genealogy..." (145). Nietzsche challenges the pursuit of origin because it is indicative of a metaphysical desire to capture the essence of things, to posit an original identity or essential, immobile forms that "precede the external world of accident and succession" (142). Genealogy, by contrast, in studying descent and emergence, discovers that "What is found at the historical beginning of things is not the inviolable identity of their origin; it is the dissension of other things. It is disparity" (142). Genealogy cultivates "the details and accidents that accompany every beginning" (144); in following the complex course of descent, it seeks "to maintain passing events in their proper dispersion" (146), and precisely in this it rejoins the critical use of historiography which, in resisting the suprahistorical perspective of historicism, corresponds, as Foucault writes, "to the acuity of a glance [and one cannot but think here of the glance of an *Augenblick*] that distinguishes, separates, and disperses, that is capable of liberating divergence and marginal elements – the kind of dissociating view that is capable of decomposing itself, capable of shattering the unity of man's being through which it was thought that he could extend his sovereignty to the events of the past" (152f.).

In *Being and Time*, the question of the unity of man's being, of the being of Dasein, is, as a question of origin or *Ursprung*, from the outset displaced, initially into the tripartite structure of Care, whose moments are "equiprimordial", *gleichurspründglich*. The phenomenon of equiprimordiality,

Heidegger comments, "has often been disregarded in ontology as a consequence of a methodologically unrestrained tendency to derive the provenance [*Herkunft*] of everything and anything from a simple 'primal ground' ['*Urgrund*']" (131). This equiprimordiality of the structural moments of Care – Dasein's being ahead of itself, already in the world, as being in the presence of... – is subsequently unfolded as the three ekstases of temporality, ekstases which, although equiprimordial, nevertheless manifest a priority of the future, of the *possibility* of a retrieval of having been (329), at the same time as they manifest the derivative status of presence and of the present, which remains, as Heidegger puts it, "enclosed" within future and having-been (328). The analysis of the historicality of Dasein, however, which unfolds the horizonal structure implicit within the finite temporality of Dasein's being, increasingly brings to the fore the element of dispersion, of a primordial forgetting and irretrievability within historicality itself that first enables and necessitates the task of retrieval. It shows, for instance, that the very question of the unity of Dasein's being, of the unity of the self, is always *nachträglich*: it is always a retroactive attempt to think up or invent an encompassing unity, an attempt that presupposes and is indicative of an antecedent dispersion (*Zerstreuung*) (390). Here, in its emphasis on the finitude and closure within the ekstatic structure of temporality, Heidegger's phenomenological analysis approaches the themes of forgetting and of an active forgetfulness, themes that mark the beginning of the second "Untimely Meditation" and that of the analysis of conscience in the *Genealogy of Morals* respectively.

In sum, if Heidegger in *Being and Time* grants his explicit approval to the second "Untimely Meditation", asserting that Nietzsche there recognized and stated unequivocally and incisively "what is essential" concerning the "use and disadvantage of history for life"; and if he hints that the beginning of Nietzsche's "Meditation" lets us suspect that he, Nietzsche, "understood more than he made known", then it is this something "more", I would suggest, that Heidegger's own phenomenological analyses of ekstatic-horizonal temporality and historicality seek to unfold.

In closing, I should like to return to the theme of descent and in particular to the descent of philosophy in relation to Heidegger's appropriation of Nietzsche and to the issue of retrieval[15]. In the quotation from the "Letter on 'Humanism'" with which I began, Heidegger writes of a thinking that is on the descent and of a thinking to come. Yet this descent – a thoroughly Nietzschean legacy – was initiated, I have tried to suggest,

not in Heidegger's later work, but in a most radical and provocative
manner already in *Being and Time* (and, of course, in the lecture courses
that precede it, extending back at least to the *Hermeneutics of Facticity*).
In particular, it is Nietzsche's conception of critical history that Heidegger
appropriates here, understanding it as the critical moment of a
"destructuring" (*Destruktion*) of the history of ontology, and inscribing it
on the one hand within the ("monumental") priority of the future and of
the possible, and on the other within the ("antiquarian") necessity of
retrieval. Retrieval, writes Heidegger, in the sense of a knowing
appropriation of one's heritage, is neither a reactualizing of a Dasein that
has been, nor a return to the past, but is a response or reply – a
"reciprocative rejoinder" (*Erwiderung*) – to a possibility of existence that
has been there (386). As such, however, it is a "disavowal" or revocation
(*Widerruf*) of what is working itself out as the past in the present, in the
present day.

The task of retrieval, in other words, is understood by Heidegger as
essentially *critical* with regard to the present[16]. It is what, in explicitly
embracing Nietzsche's conception of critical history, he calls an unmaking
or undoing of the present (*eine Entgegenwärtigung des Heute*, 391, 397),
an undoing that understands history as the "return" of the possible, "*die
'Wiederkehr' des Möglichen*" – and here he invokes the Nietzschean term
for "return" (391). Such authentic historical inquiry, which is the task of
Destruktion, is a (suffering-undergoing) freeing oneself from today, a
critique of what appears to be the "present" (397). In other words,
Destruktion as critique retrieves, and in so doing transforms and rethinks,
reappropriates, the concealed forces at work in the present day, which is a
mere facade of history. It is in this sense that Heidegger invokes "the quiet
force of the possible" as that which is to be disclosed by authentic
historical inquiry (394): such inquiry has the task of disclosing history that
has been there "in such a way that the 'force' of the possible impacts
factical existence, that is, approaches that existence in its futural character"
(395). The essential past – i.e., having-been – is that dimension of
experience and/or of heritage that gets thrown forward, "metabolized", or
folded into the future[17]. The possible, the force of the possible, is that
which approaches us from out of what has been: it is what remains to be
appropriated in and through a thinking to come.

Destruktion as this critical confrontation with sedimented tradition,
that is, with the present, is thinking on the descent, a thinking that, in its
own descensional, regressive movement, traces the descent of the present.

For a tradition determined by philosophy, it is a critical confrontation with the history of philosophy itself. In his introductory remarks on the task of *Destruktion*, Heidegger insists that our vague and average understanding of being may be permeated by traditional theories and opinions concerning being. The tradition that comes to domination here, writes Heidegger, conceals the original "sources" of its own thinking. In fostering and instituting an understanding of being in general in terms of the "world" and of presence as mere presence-at-hand, this tradition (and this for us means the philosophical tradition) propagates and perpetuates a forgetting, as Heidegger describes it, of its own provenance, its own descent, its own *Herkunft* (21). Descensional thinking as critique is a critical response to such concealed forces of domination at work in the present. Its radicality consists in its excavating the roots of the present, the rootedness of the present in the essential past, thereby freeing the present for the possibilities of a thinking to come.

The descent from the theoretical and from the hegemony of the theoretical approach to history that gives rise to historicism is thus not to be enacted on a vertical plane: it is not to be enacted as a descent from the theoretical to the empirical or practical, for such a self-understanding would still leave this traditional, all-governing hierarchy in place[18]. If we may nonetheless speak in this context of "the descent of philosophy", then "descent" must here be understood in a threefold sense: 1) Descent as *Abstieg* names, not a descent from the theoretical to the practical, but the movement of philosophical thinking itself into the dimension opened up by Heidegger's phenomenological destructuring, the dimension of the historicality of its own provenance, its own emergence and disparition: in short, of its own experience. 2) This descent is thus that of an increased attentiveness on the part of thinking towards its own historical provenance, and this is the second sense of "descent": descent as *Herkunft*. 3) Yet descent is also the acknowledgement of thought's own finitude, and this is the third sense of "descent": of thought's descent as what, in *Being and Time*, is conceived as decline (*Verfall*) and dispersion (*Zerstreuung*), and will later be embraced as Nietzschean downgoing (*Untergang*), of its death as the condition of its birth – that is, of the possibility of a thinking to come: of a thinking to come that can be anticipated only in the temporality of *Vorlaufen*, of an explicit (taking up of and engagement with) running ahead into the indeterminacy of the "not yet" that grounds the possibility of experience. The determinacy of a world is itself always anchored and grounded in the happening of this "not yet", in the temporalizing of experience, and of the experience of thinking itself, in the dimension of this "not yet", as that of a thinking to come.

Notes

[1] Martin Heidegger, "Brief über den 'Humanismus'", in *Wegmarken*. Gesamtausgabe Bd. 9. Frankfurt a.m.: Klostermann, 1976, 364; "Letter on 'Humanism'", trans. Frank A. Capuzzi, in William McNeill (ed.), *Pathmarks*. Cambridge: Cambridge University Press, 1998, 276.

[2] Martin Heidegger, *Hölderlin's Hymne "Der Ister"*. Gesamtausgabe Bd. 53. Frankfurt a.m.: Klostermann, 1984, 62; *Hölderlin's Hymn "The Ister"*, trans. William McNeill and Julia Davis. Bloomington: Indiana University Press, 1996, 50.

[3] David Farrell Krell, *Nietzsche and the Task of Thinking: Martin Heidegger's Reading of Nietzsche*. Doctoral Dissertation: Duquesne University, 1971, 16. See also Krell's essay "Heidegger, Nietzsche, Hegel: An Essay in Descensional Reflection", *Nietzsche Studien* 5 (1976), 255-62; and his book *Intimations of Mortality: Time, Truth, and Finitude in Heidegger's Thinking of Being*. University Park: Pennsylvania State University Press, 1986, ch. 7.

[4] See Jacques Taminiaux, *Lectures de l'ontologie fondamentale*. Grenoble: Millon, 1989, 231-51.

[5] References are to Martin Heidegger, *Sein und Zeit*. 15. Auflage. Tübingen: Niemeyer, 1984; *Being and Time*, trans. John Macquarrie and Edward Robinson. Oxford: Blackwell, 1987, hereafter *SZ*.

[6] Martin Heidegger, *Metaphysische Anfangsgründe der Logik im Ausgang von Leibniz*. Gesamtausgabe Bd. 26. Frankfurt a.m.: Klostermann, 1978, 201; *The Metaphysical Foundations of Logic*, trans. Michael Heim. Bloomington: Indiana University Press, 1984, 158.

[7] Pierre Klossowski, *Nietzsche et le Cercle Vicieux*. Paris: Mercure de France, 1969, 94; *Nietzsche and the Vicious Circle*, trans. Daniel W. Smith. Chicago: The University of Chicago Press, 1997, 57.

[8] See *Die Grundprobleme der Phänomenologie*. Gesamtausgabe Bd. 24. Frankfurt a.M.: Klostermann, 1975, §5; *The Basic Problems of Phenomenology*, trans. Albert Hofstadter. Bloomington: Indiana University Press, 1982.

[9] All references are to the Gesamtausgabe of Heidegger's works, Frankfurt a.M.: Klostermann. Citations are by volume (GA) followed by page number.

[10] We do know that Heidegger read Nietzsche early on, although explicit references to Nietzsche in his early lecture courses are few and far between. In an early published article from 1909, which appeared in the *Heuberger Volksblatt*, Heidegger alludes to both the *Genealogy of Morals* and *Thus Spoke Zarathustra*. In 1912, he apparently gave a talk on Nietzsche to a Catholic social and youth group in Messkirch. *Zarathustra* is again mentioned by Heidegger in another article in the *Heuberger Volksblatt* from 1915, where, together with the New Testament and Goethe's *Faust*, Nietzsche's *Zarathustra* is reported to be one of the three essential texts that soldiers took with them when deploying. For these

references, see the *Heidegger Jahrbuch I: Heidegger und die Anfänge seines Denkens.* Freiburg/München: Verlag Karl Alber, 2004, 18-23, 463. Nietzsche is also mentioned in Heidegger's *Habilitationsschrift* from 1916. See *Martin Heidegger: Frühe Schriften.* Frankfurt a.m.: Klostermann, 1972, 138. Finally, the 1925 lecture course *Prolegomena zur Geschichte des Zeitbegriffs* explicitly identifies philosophy as phenomenological research with the atheism of what "one of the greats" called the "Gay Science". Gesamtausgabe Bd. 20. Frankfurt a.m.: Klostermann, 1979, 110; *History of the Concept of Time*, trans. Theodore Kisiel. Bloomington: Indiana University Press, 1985, 80, t.m.

[11] On the historical significance of the second "Untimely Meditation", see in particular Charles R. Bambach, *Heidegger, Dilthey, and the Crisis of Historicism.* Ithaca: Cornell University Press, 1995.

[12] Hans Ruin, *Enigmatic Origins: Tracing the Theme of Historicity through Heidegger's Works.* Stockholm: Almqvist & Wiksell International, 1994, 134f. To be fair, Ruin subsequently modifies the argument of founding, "Thus it seems more correct to say that instead of providing a foundation for Nietzsche, Heidegger thinks in the wake of his original claim, repeating it responsively for his own time", 135.

[13] Magda King, *A Guide to Heidegger's* Being and Time. Albany: SUNY Press, 2001, 324.

[14] See Michel Foucault, See Michel Foucault, "Nietzsche, Genealogy, History", in Donald Bouchard (ed.), *Language, Counter-Memory, Practice: Selected Essays and Interviews.* New York: Cornell University Press, 1988, 139-64.

[15] The following remarks borrow extensively from an already published essay, with greater emphasis on the Nietzschean aspects of Heidegger's conception of authentic historiography. See "The Hermeneutics of Everydayness: On the Legacy and Radicality of Heidegger's Phenomenology", in Jeff Malpas and Santiago Zabala (eds.), *Consequences of Hermeneutics: Fifty Years After Gadamer's* Truth and Method. Evanston, IL.: Northwestern University Press, 2010, 98-120.

[16] Cf. section 6 of *Being and Time*, where Heidegger remarks that *Destruktion* "does not relate negatively towards the past: its critique is directed towards the 'present day' [*das 'Heute*']... its negative function remains implicit and indirect". Its primarily positive aim is to stake out the "positive possibilities" – which also means, the limitations – of the ontological tradition, *SZ* 22f.

[17] This is indeed how Heidegger translates the Greek *metabolē*: it is *Umschlag*: a folding over and around, an enveloping: what *can* be is enveloped by what approaches us, approaches us as that which will have been.

[18] Cf. in this regard the beginning of the "Letter on 'Humanism'", which displaces the traditional ordering of theory and praxis, thought and action.

HEIDEGGER AND NIETZSCHE
ON HISTORY AND LIFE

ULLRICH HAASE

The less question-worthy 'life' becomes, the more irrevocable the alienation from Beyng[1].

In the following essay I will try to engage the question of the centrality of the notions of history and life in Heidegger's critical setting-apart from Nietzsche's thought. As such this theme is not particularly new. Early on it became evident to many commentators that Heidegger was not only the first philosopher who made us take Nietzsche seriously, but also that the thought of Nietzsche was critical with respect to developing his own philosophical thought. Scores of papers and books have been written on this topic and I will, therefore, not be able to do justice to the "state of play". I can promise that I have read much more of this work than I will quote in the following, which is also to say that I, while taking full responsibility for the following remarks, cannot take full credit for all of them.

The aim of this paper is to further the understanding of the *Auseinandersetzung* of Heidegger with and from Nietzsche. It will, therefore, not aim at a decision as to whether either Nietzsche or Heidegger is right about questions of history and life. While many critics originally tried to save Nietzsche from Heidegger's critique, the thesis developed in the following remarks is quite the obverse, namely that Nietzsche's thought, to a certain extent, demands the success of this very critique. The question thus is whether there is still something left of Nietzsche after Heidegger's critique or whether Heidegger has fulfilled Nietzsche's desire, as the latter expressed it in a letter to his friend Overbeck on the 2nd of July 1885, "My life now consists in the desire that all things may be *different* from how I understand them; and that someone will make my 'truths' unbelievable"[2].

In an essay published in the *Journal of the British Society for Phenomenology*[3], I attempted to outline what I see as the philosophical significance of Heidegger's *Auseinandersetzung* with, that is, his critical setting-apart from, Nietzsche. The question really is why Heidegger puts such emphasis on his interpretation of Nietzsche in the late thirties, that is, at the time that he dedicated to the Turning. There are many ready answers to such a question, ranging from the necessity to wrest Nietzsche's text away from its interpretation by Nazi Germany, to investigating a thinker who could give more to an understanding of the history of being than any other thinker, that is, maybe, apart from Hegel. Now, while the first point is not of a philosophical nature, it might just be true that the thinker for whom history has become the sole content of philosophy must be of special interest to Heidegger. And yet, Heidegger is here neither speaking about history nor about Nietzsche, which is to say that he is not interested in establishing correct judgements concerning either the true nature of history or the hermeneutics concerning Nietzsche's text.

In order to clarify the stakes of such an interpretation of Nietzsche in particular, let us remain for a while with the question why a philosopher like Heidegger would dedicate a considerable amount of time and energy to reading the work of another philosopher. Where is this work to lead him or her? What does she expect from the path on which she is walking? Indeed, Heidegger claims, any true philosophizing will have to address the "planetary mindlessness"[4] not only in terms of thinking about nihilism, but by means of philosophical method itself. In other words, we are not looking at Nietzsche merely because we can find "nihilism" as a "content" of his philosophizing, but we are looking methodically at Nietzsche's method of philosophizing. Thus "planetary mindlessness" is a word that Heidegger uses in *Besinnung*, first of all to characterize our very relation to philosophy, before looking at anything such philosophy would try to say or argue. Analysing these possible relations, Heidegger sums them up in five different forms,

> The 'historical' adoption of an earlier philosophy...and its approximation to variously perceived situations of the time...
> The 'historical' reckoning with philosophy as it is 'historically' handed down, without explicit, decisive and justified preference for a single thinker...
> A rejection of philosophy...
> An indifference vis-à-vis philosophy...
> All these...muddled up so that now the one, then the other 'posture' predominates arbitrarily, and remains ungraspable in its ground. (*BES* §15, 71-74/58-60)

Against such mindlessness Heidegger posits the exigencies of the *Auseinandersetzung* with history (*Geschichte*), in which alone, as he says, philosophy exists in its true meaning (*BES* §15, 74/60).

All the work that Heidegger did in the thirties and beyond belongs to this task of a critical setting-apart from the history of metaphysics, whether this concerns the *Beiträge*, *Besinnung*, or the lecture courses on Nietzsche, Hölderlin and others. Heidegger's lectures on the history of philosophy, on Leibniz, Kant, Schelling, Hegel and Nietzsche serve, then, the elucidation of this history of metaphysics, but not in the simple sense of repeating what they said and reckoning with their advantages and disadvantages. This is what Heidegger says in the *Beiträge zur Philosophie* about the aim of these historical lectures, thereby again clarifying the specific role taken up by Nietzsche's thought,

> To make visible the unfathomable breadth of Leibniz's way of questioning and yet to think Da-sein instead of the monas; to follow through Kant's major steps and still to overcome the 'transcendental' approach by way of the thought of Da-sein; to think through Schelling's questioning of freedom [*Freiheitsfrage*] and yet to move the question of 'modalities' on to another foundation; to bring Hegel's systematicity into an understanding view [*beherrschenden Blick*] and yet to think in an opposite direction; to dare the setting-apart [*Auseinandersetzung*] with Nietzsche as the one who is closest and yet to realize that he is furthest away from the question of being.

> These are some paths, in themselves independent while still belonging together, aiming at bringing *One and the Same Thing* [*das Eine Einzige*] to knowledge: that the essencing of Beyng depends on the founding of the *truth of Beyng* and that this founding has to happen as *Da-sein*. In this way all idealism, that is, traditional metaphysics and metaphysics as such have been overcome as a necessary unfolding of the first beginning, a beginning which only thus moves anew into obscurity, so as only to be comprehended as such first beginning from the perspective of another beginning[5].

It has often been said that Heidegger's interpretations serve his own purposes rather than making clear what the author in question really wanted to say, or at least what the text in question does actually argue. But such a difference does not really exist – or, rather, as Heidegger says, it exists only within the confines of the *Schulphilosophie* or a "history of ideas", themselves quite indifferent to philosophical thinking as such – and Nietzsche and Heidegger agree on the point that the necessity of thinking does not allow for the understanding of philosophy in the form of an *idios logos*, always bordering on voluntarism. When Nietzsche speaks of the

blood of the great philosophers flowing through his veins, he means to say
that a true philosophy has nothing subjective about it. When he uses the
image of Zarathustra being struck down by a thought, his point is that the
thinker does not make up a thought, does not "own" a thought, but is
owned by it. One might say as much in terms of reading *Being and Time*:
trying to understand the critique of truth as the property of positive,
affirmative judgements should lead to the realization that such critique
cannot itself be formed in terms of positive, affirmative judgement.

For the same reason it makes little sense radically to distinguish the
stance that Heidegger took at the time of *Being and Time* with that taken
here at the time of the Nietzsche lectures, though I might need to qualify
this claim. I am not saying that nothing happens between 1927 and 1936,
nor that one should underestimate the developments in Heidegger's
thought in the face of that which he himself called the *Turn*. But such
turning is often a quasi-dialectical movement which brings what was
unthought out into the open, which turns, as Hegel would say, the in-itself
existing truth into one that is known and therefore for-itself the truth. That
is why after the fact such a transformation often appears not at all as a
break with the former project, but rather as the realization of its truth.
Thus, for a reader of Nietzsche's work, it must appear surprising to read
about the emphatic description of his "sudden inspiration" in 1881
concerning the thought of eternal recurrence, while one can easily trace
this thought back to even his writings as a young school boy. It is therefore
not a contradiction that Heidegger himself does not seem to see this
development as "transforming his entire self-understanding", often
asserting, as late as the 1950s, that he never moved away from or beyond
Being and Time.

Instead of as a break, he comes to see this development as two phases
of his philosophical method. Every critical setting-apart, as Heidegger
says, is preceded by a destruction. While the latter had been effected by
Being and Time, as the destruction of ontology, this differentiation
between destruction and critical setting-apart already implies that the latter
is creative, rather than being merely destructive. It is with regard to this
difference between destruction and critical setting-apart as two parts of a
method, that I would deny the translation of *Destruktion* as deconstruction.
What first of all the critical setting-apart creates is the space that is opened
up between the historical necessity of metaphysics and this possibility of
another thinking. The difficulty here is the same that Nietzsche discusses
in the essay on "The Advantages and Disadvantages of History for Life",

namely the question as to which method should be capable of creating something new, rather than merely repeating the old, considering that anything new can only arise within the historical horizon of thought, within, that is, its necessity, rather than by means of taking up a theoretical stance of whatever novelty. The task of such a critical setting-apart is then not to find a new theoretical framework for thinking,

> The historical critical setting-apart [*Auseinandersetzung*]...moves us into those fundamental positions [*Grundstellungen*], in which and from out of which thinkers are no longer 'mutually intelligible' [*verständigt*], where 'agreement' is essentially declined, because no agreement of opinions within the same is able to bear whatever truth...For this reason an *Auseinandersetzung* never concerns a calculation of the correctness and incorrectness of doctrines or opinions; the ideas of a schoolmaster, thinking about the 'mistakes' which a thinker might have 'made' and which are to be eradicated, might have a place in the setting of a 'school', but not in the history of being and never in the conversation between thinkers. (*BES* §15, 69/56)

And every such *Auseinandersetzung* is always a setting apart from history, an attempt at becoming untimely, which is why the meditation (*Selbstbesinnung*) of philosophy "is only possible as *Auseinandersetzung* with *history*, in which *history* alone philosophy 'is'"[6].

Insofar as Heidegger comes to see the contemporary task of philosophy, this is bound essentially to an interpretation of Nietzsche's work. The question of metaphysics can be addressed only through the exhaustion of metaphysics in Nietzsche's thought. And the foremost question of our age, namely the question of technology, has to be addressed by means of a reflection on Nietzsche's critique of science. The question of the history of being can be opened up only on account of a differentiation from Nietzsche's thought on history. These points motivate the claim from the *Beiträge zur Philosophie*, where Heidegger says that "to understand Nietzsche as the end of metaphysics is the historical beginning [*geschichtlicher Ansatz*] of the future of Occidental thought" (*B* 89, 176). Rather than criticising Nietzsche in such a way that we would have to save him from such critique, Heidegger elevates Nietzsche to an incomparable rank, claiming that one cannot really philosophize at all today without thinking about the work of Nietzsche. In the following remarks I will therefore always bear in mind the question implied in the quotation above: if Nietzsche is at the same time the one nearest to Heidegger and yet the farthest away from the question of being, does that not cover precisely the distance that separates Heidegger himself from the question of being? And, if such a remark makes sense, then we should stop to speak about a "turn towards Nietzsche" in the 1930s, rather seeing Heidegger's work during these years as an attempt to move away from Nietzsche. This certainly makes sense in terms of the Nietzsche lectures, insofar as these explicitly attempt to distance us from Nietzsche. From this it follows that, insofar as *Being and Time* is the repetition of metaphysics with the intent of its destruction, while Nietzsche is interpreted as the "last metaphysician", the nearness to Nietzsche comes to express precisely the period of *Being and Time*, rather than the work of the late 1930s. And, indeed, *Being and Time* is a book whose problematic is, from the first to the last page, Nietzschean.

The critical setting-apart from Nietzsche is thus equally a critical setting-apart from *Being and Time*. As the latter is seen as the repetition of metaphysics with the intent of its destruction, it brings out the realization of metaphysics as the reality of our contemporary existence. Or, as Heidegger puts it,

> What has been explicated in *Being and Time* as 'destruction', does not signify a dismantling as a demolition, but *purification* in the direction of an exposition of the fundamental metaphysical positions. But all this is with respect to the accomplishment of *Anklang* and *Zuspiel* only a prelude[7].

In other words, *Being and Time* has found so much positive acclaim not on account of what this work intrinsically does, but on account of a misunderstanding. One forgot the *doing* of the work and thought that it merely described "what is the case" in a convincing fashion. If a Habermas consequently says that *Being and Time* is still fine, while the work consequent to it becomes quite meaningless, he therefore completely misses the point. One could happily say of *Being and Time* what Heidegger said of Nietzsche in the following quotation from *What is Called Thinking?*,

> In Nietzsche's thought that which now is comes to language, but to a language in which the tradition of occidental metaphysics of the last two millennia speaks, to a language that we all speak, that Europe speaks, just translated in manifold ways, but abraded, used up and without background. Plato and Aristotle still speak in our contemporary language. Parmenides and Heraclitus still think in our ways of representation[8].

✳

To repeat these points in all clarity: both Nietzsche and Heidegger attempt to understand philosophical thinking in historical terms. This does not mean that they simply follow the Hegelian idea of an identification of the philosophy of history and the history of philosophy, precisely insofar as such an idea depends on the possibility of taking a stance at the far end of history. Instead, we find in Nietzsche an understanding of the transient nature of thinking. The eternal return of the same, for example, is a thought which is in essential development, which is to say, in Nietzsche's words, that it is a teaching rather than a representation of reality, and, furthermore, it is a thought whose "success" is measured in its ability to disappear, that is, "to go under". While the thought of the last men, of the "philosophers" suffering from their Egyptianism, or of the "Masters of the Present", as Nietzsche variously calls them, depends on the ability to make their thought govern the future, the higher men are those who desire their own downfall. Pointing in the same direction we have already encountered Nietzsche's desire "that all things may be different from how I understand them; and that someone will make my 'truths' unbelievable"[9].

While Nietzsche tries to bring about the decision between overhuman and animal by means of the thought of the eternal return of the same, a thought that begins with the realization of "the infinite importance of our knowledge, our errors, of our habits and ways of life for all that is to come" (*KSA* 9:11 [141])[10], Heidegger thus staked the success of his thinking and the preparation of the turn towards another thinking on understanding why Nietzsche yet failed to bring about this crisis.

As Heidegger makes clear in his lectures on Nietzsche's "Second Untimely Meditation", "in truth there is no other form of a proper encounter with the thought of a thinker than the strife that puts this thought into question"[11], and as philosophical thought cannot be seen outside of such an encounter, both parties stand or fall in the differentiation of such *Auseinandersetzung*.

Three words of Heidegger, from the Schelling Lectures, the *Beiträge* and the text *What is Called Thinking?*, nicely sum up this thought. First, "whoever would truly understand the reason for this failure [of Schelling and Nietzsche], would have to become the founder of the new beginning of Occidental philosophy"[12]. Second, "the decisive question", as Heidegger says, is "whether Modernity can be understood as an end and a new beginning can become the object of our thinking, or whether we harden on a permanentization of the decline that has reigned since Plato" (*B* 134). And, thirdly, "Insofar as we are here speaking of a transition, Nietzsche's thought has completely to come to a standstill on this side of the transition...we can thus appropriate the whole of Occidental thought by means of Nietzsche's thought"[13].

In terms of the *Auseinandersetzung* of Nietzsche and Heidegger, we can see this in a double sense: to set them apart means to open the difference between the retrospective interpretation of Greek philosophy and the prospective possibility of another beginning. Nietzsche's return to the Greek notion of justice as it arises out of Greek *Beredlichkeit* will thus be measured with respect to Heidegger's return to the original notion of truth as *aletheia*. Whether we consider the question of the will to power as a liberation of the will from revenge; whether we investigate the decision made by the eternal return of the same between animal life and the overhuman; whether we think of knowledge as the highest affect; or whether we turn towards the schism inherent in the development of the sciences from their inception in Greece towards the modern "scientific world-view", all these conceptions lead us back to the questions of life and history and depend on the interpretation of truth as justice along the genealogical difference between *dike* and *iustitia*[14].

Life

> I realized at around the same time [1876] that my instinct wanted the opposite of Schopenhauer's: a justification of life, even in its most horrid aspects, in its ambiguities and its most dishonest moments: – to bring this about I had the formula 'Dionysian' in my hands. (*KSA* 12:9 [42])

One might write a short summary of Nietzsche's works from the perspective of life as follows: from the *Birth of Tragedy* and the early essays on "The Advantages and Disadvantages of History for Life" and "On Truth and Lie in an Extramoral Sense" onwards, it has been clear that Nietzsche's thought and philosophical endeavour turned around such a justification of life. His admiration for the Greeks is most powerfully expressed in the judgment that while we moderns are, without feeling, only capable of justifying the best of all possible worlds, the Greek could justify just about any world, even one from which the human intellect might feel alienated. His self-understanding as a reversal of Platonism takes as its fundamental revaluation the wresting of life from the clutches of death. In the essay on history, Nietzsche thus gave the first genealogical account of the alienation of life from itself and its consequent wilting in the historical malady. There is no philosophical recipe against such weakening of life; instead it is only life which can rejuvenate itself by means of what Nietzsche here calls a feeling of youth. And philosophy is rather a consequence of such feeling. It is life itself that drives Nietzsche to philosophize and to see such philosophizing under the sign of "great health". And once life has motivated philosophy, it takes it into its perspective. In other words, the grand problem of our age, the question of science, only becomes visible if approached from the perspective of art, while the phenomenon of art is not to be opened up via its objective nature, but, equally, from that which motivates it, that is, life.

Consequently, Nietzsche develops the idea of the philosopher as the physician of life and his first insight with respect to the history of philosophy is that "up to now" many of those who have called themselves philosophers have not been Greeks but Egyptians, that is, the antithesis to the Greek, and "nothing real has ever left their hands alive"[15]. The thought of the eternal return of the same is then the measurement of the strength of life. Its value seems not to be that of an "intellectual thesis" which one might evaluate as either right or wrong; rather, understanding it, life either affirms its rights or "*es geht zu Grunde*", i.e., "it goes to ruin". The thought of eternal recurrence is hence to effect a great crisis rather than a great insight. For those who suffer from life, life will become insufferable, while the life that is animated by a strength of feeling will find in that thought its "highest confirmation and seal"[16].

One is thus not to evaluate life itself. The problem of metaphysics is here precisely that it tries to take a stance outside of life in order to bring it into perspective, to evaluate and to judge it, while every value insofar as it is of any value is so only from the perspective of life. It is for this reason that we finally abolish the true world and, necessarily, the world is evaluated from this side of death, namely the world of appearances. The philosopher hence develops the means to look at this world, so to speak, from within. And the most sublime name for this looking at the world from within is the will to power. The will to power is thus Nietzsche's final conception. It does not replace any earlier thoughts, it does not stand against any of them, neither does it correct them. The will to power is that name for life which gives the whole of Nietzsche's thought its meaning. It is thus on account of the will to power that Nietzsche can say at this late stage of his work that all his work now "wants one thing". Accordingly, there is one last sentence of Nietzsche's work, written in June-July 1885, but rightly standing at the end of the concoction called *The Will to Power*,

> *This world is the will to power – and nothing besides!* And you yourselves are this will to power – and nothing besides[17].

✳

It is this, if here radically simplified, understanding of philosophy in Nietzsche which Heidegger calls the last metaphysics. As such, Heidegger does not see a new metaphysical system in Nietzsche's work. As he clarifies in the *Beiträge*, whatever comes after Hegel is only a decline into positivism, life-philosophy or doctrinal ontology (*B* 213). We can thus see Nietzsche's thought developing from the fundamental metaphysical positions of Kant and Hegel. On the one hand, Nietzsche explicates the truth of Kantian transcendental philosophy by grounding it on the notion of life. On the other hand, he fulfils the interpretation of being as becoming developed in Hegel's thought.

With respect to the first point we might clarify the problem with reference to the Nietzsche lectures by Georg Picht. Picht sets out the direction of his lectures as going through the Heideggerian critique and to make Nietzsche escape at the other end, by demonstrating how the properly understood notion of justice in Nietzsche makes him "explode the subjectivity of the subject"[18]. At the same time he happily describes Nietzsche's thought as transcendental philosophy and thus, if in a different sense, as inheritor of Kantian thought. But is it at all possible to speak of transcendental philosophy without subjectivity in the metaphysical sense? Heidegger certainly argues in the negative and adds to the overcoming of metaphysics the notion of dropping transcendental philosophy. And yet, is it meaningful to identify in such a way the form of subjectivity in Kant with the notion of life in Nietzsche? It certainly seems to be so, seeing that for Nietzsche everything that is of value and everything that is as such, is of such value and is what it is only from the perspective of life. This is, in the end, Nietzsche's point, that you are the will to power and nothing besides and that this world is the will to power and nothing besides. Following Leibniz, for Nietzsche the will to power makes the world as such appear as life. But if that is the case, Heidegger argues, then any further argument concerning the *ekstasis* of life, whether in pluralisation or in temporalisation, remains inconsequential insofar as it would here merely stand out into the same. Heidegger's conclusion from this is that such idea of life-philosophy is the furthest away from the question of being and that, equally, everything living is essentially without history (*BES* 182).

This dimension of Heidegger's argument is too often overlooked and, consequently, one all too often thinks one has escaped from Heidegger's criticism much too easily. We can see this point by giving the example of Dieter Thomä, who writes the following in an essay called "A Philosophy of Life Beyond Biologism and on this Side of the 'History of Metaphysics'",

> Heidegger's interpretation fails to do justice to Nietzsche's thought. In the course of his critique of subjectivity Nietzsche arrives at an internal pluralisation, at a 'societal structure'...which already on the level of the individual gives rise to multiplicity – and consequently also to an external pluralisation of the *will to power* on the social level. This pluralisation belongs essentially to the perspectivism championed by Nietzsche but dealt with by Heidegger only to the extend that he can centre it on the perceiving and willing subject or fasten it to the 'body' understood as central command...That is why Werner Stegmaier makes the difference between Nietzsche's 'thinking otherwise of the individual in relation to other individuals without relation to a common third' and Heidegger's 'thinking otherwise of being in relation to beings'[19].

I have quoted this at length because it can stand in for various strands of critique that think that the simple idea of multiplicity or pluralism is, as such, anti-metaphysical, and because it makes quite clear why this argument does not really work. The first part fails to address Heidegger's point precisely insofar as it does not seem to be aware that the notion of subjectivity is meant here not merely psychologically but metaphysically, that is, in the sense of the *hypokeimenon*, while the second part makes clear that it would have to claim that even Leibniz would have had to be pronounced as the one who first and finally overcame metaphysical thought. Furthermore, on a methodological level, such an argument would neither agree with Heidegger nor with Nietzsche, insofar as it implies that one would need, in order to overcome metaphysics, nothing but a clever thought.

When Nietzsche motivates his philosophy against Kant, and does so in an even more accentuated way with respect to the notion of justice, one might be able to see this motivation in line with Hegel's treatment of Kant. Kant, as Hegel has it, left the ground germane to philosophical thinking. Hegel expresses this by referring to Kant's barbaric terminology[20] and his barbaric exposition (*VGP* 343). This barbarity, and I cannot really go into the argument fully here, this non-Greekness, lies precisely in the abstraction of his notion of subjectivity. The "I" as apperception of self-consciousness supposed to accompany every apperception, this is what he calls a barbaric exposition, whereby the barbaric nature is clarified as a lack of unity,

> Thinking, the understanding remains something separate, sensibility something separate, both are united in an extrinsic, superficial fashion, like a piece of wood and a leg by means of a cord[21].

What Kant is thus lacking is what Hegel calls, in the *Science of Logic*, life as the immediate idea[22], whereby, at least for Hegel, the notion of a transcendental philosophy, which he likewise calls barbaric, is equally overcome. And what Hegel here calls barbaric, Nietzsche similarly calls the lack of a great style.

Herewith we come to that crux which Hegel, Nietzsche and *Being and Time* have in common. If in three different ways, we find these thoughts based on an explicit or implicit notion of life, even if, insofar as *Being and Time* is concerned, this is to clarify the fundamental metaphysical position of contemporary life. In Hegel this is given in the fundamental idea of desire, which gives rise to an understanding of the world as the product of human labour. When he distinguishes between logical life, natural life and spiritual life, the unity that desire gives to these is found in the absolute expression of absolute knowledge, whereby the individual recognizes itself in the world and identifies its objective existence with its subjective action. This foundation of life on the absolute concept is what Nietzsche turns around. Life is not the idea insofar as it is immediately given in order thus to overcome itself, but everything is what it is and insofar as it is from the perspective of life. The idea of the human being as *homo faber* here becomes absolute. The world is only interpretation, and, Nietzsche asks, who interprets? Answer: the will to power. And this interpretation, the labour of the will to power, concerns not only the reality of past and future, but the essence of this will to power itself. It is with this in mind that the essential task of the will to power is determined as *Zucht* and *Züchtung*, as discipline and breeding.

To see science from the perspective of art and art from the perspective of life means to see our existence on the ground of such an action that produces the human being as much as its world, which reduces everything that is to that which can be grasped with the hand. In Spring 1888 Nietzsche writes about the will to power as art,

The greatness of an artist is not measured by the 'beautiful feelings' that he excites...[b]ut by the extent to which he approaches the great style, to which he is capable of the great style. This style has in common with the great passion that it does not care to please, that it forgets to persuade; but that it commands; that it *wants*...To become master of the chaos that one is; to force one's chaos to become form; to become a formed necessity: logical, simple, unambiguous, to become mathematics; to become *law* -: that is here the great ambition. With this one becomes repulsive; nothing any longer stirs love for such 'men of violence' [*Gewaltmenschen*]. (*KSA* 13:14 [61])

In other words, all that was necessary to turn Hegel on his head was to base the notion of life not on the immediate idea, but on the body. Nietzsche, as Heidegger says in the lectures of the late 1930s, "[has] brought the metaphysically necessary subjectivism to completion...in that he determined the 'living body' to be the guiding thread for the interpretation of the world"[23].

Life as the ground of art, artwork and handicraft: it is not far from the "Second Untimely Meditation" to *Being and Time*. Even though Heidegger has difficulties using the words "life" and "living body", even though the question "who?" that can only be directed to Dasein and that is the only one that can be addressed to Dasein, is not the same as the will to power, it is still the case that the world is seen originally as that which is ready-to-hand and the work therefore shows at every step that "Nietzsche is the one closest to us"[24].

The following judgement on "biologism" in the widest sense of the word can thus equally be applied to Nietzsche as to a rather common interpretation of *Being and Time*,

Life as acting and doing is a going further and a going away, and it is, consequently, directed beyond itself towards 'meaning' and 'value', i.e., it is 'idealism'; and yet, one can immediately respond [to this claim of idealism], that one is not speaking of that life-form that represents and is 'conscious', but of lived-experience and interaction, *life and lived experience*; that sounds rather 'realistic' whilst still being able to afford, whenever necessary, its appearance as the highest idealism.
These ambiguities bestow an appearance of width and depth, while being the consequence of a complete groundlessness of this 'thinking', which in a quite superficial manner and intentionally blind towards its historical descent falsifies whatever can be grasped with the hand into the highest being. And it does so with the questionable advantage of immediately finding assent. (*B* 110, 221f.)

From here the notion of perspectivism and its essentially pluralistic quality finds its place in the doctrine of the will to power. While it understands cognition as the inner quarrel of the thinker, its affective qualities – which Nietzsche describes as making oneself many eyes, of seeing more and perceiving more – seem to be directed towards a more successful attempt at finding one's place in the world, at securing one's existence. In the best sense, as Heidegger says, such an idea of truth can lead to the victorious yes-saying to existence, but in this it only fulfils modern subject metaphysics and is not too dissimilar from Hegel's conception of absolute knowing. The pluralisation of perspectives is thus not at all an argument against Heidegger's interpretation of Nietzsche. Rather, as long as "to make oneself many eyes" is seen as an adaptive power of the will to power, as long as "to see more", "to hear more" belong to the subjectivity of life making its home in the world, truth as justice cannot be anything more than a reformulation of Greek *homoiosis* and, consequently, Nietzsche will not have found happiness, nor has he come to stand in the open after metaphysics. Instead, Nietzsche, at the height of his metaphysical thinking would himself have denied the Greek world in favour of the Roman world[25].

✱

Heidegger thus has to dare the critical setting-apart from Nietzsche precisely insofar as the latter is closest to him, and the distance that is opened up in this way is a distance within Heidegger's work itself, that is, the methodological step from the destruction of metaphysics to the critical setting-apart from metaphysics. We can rephrase this difference with respect to the development of the word Dasein within Heidegger's work. In *Being and Time*, Dasein appears to be a description of human reality, that is, of the being that we are in each case ourselves. It is not identical with that which we call the human being, but it is the disclosed foundation of that which since Plato we understand as the human being in terms of the *zoon politicon*, or the *zoon logon echon*, or the *animal rationale*, etc. In the 1930s, however, Dasein becomes more and more that which is "only" a possibility, the insertion (*Einsprung*) into which remains the possibility of an overcoming of the nihilism of the age of technology. In other words, our historical horizon is determined as this alternative between the technologically fixed animal and the insertion into Dasein. To understand the human being in terms of an essentially living being, a *Lebewesen*, is therefore essentially to miss the essence of the human being. Heidegger here appears to be following Descartes, if for entirely different motives:

the human being should not be understood at all as the symbolic animal *(animus or anima)* plus something. Rather, the human being is, to remain within Heidegger's praxis of tautology, human and not living, it is not *Lebewesen*, but *Menschenwesen*. In such *Wesen* it is what it is insofar as it indicates *(zeigt)* Being *(WhD* 95). The danger of nihilism can thus be described as the collapse of the human being into its animal nature. Insofar as it thus has to distinguish itself from this biologistic understanding, Heidegger has to distinguish himself from Nietzsche. And yet, the distinction between technologically fixed animal and insertion into Dasein is isomorphic to that crisis that, according to Nietzsche, is to be brought about by the thought of the eternal return of the same, namely that between animal and overhuman. Once again, thus, it is shown that Nietzsche is the closest to us, this time uncomfortably close. Here is to be found the reason for Heidegger's presumed exclamation that "Nietzsche has ruined me"[26].

Against such life-philosophy the human being – or at least a few apart – have to prepare for the historical *Zeit-Spiel-Raum* and to collect themselves for a nearness to being which has to remain alien to all those who are *lebensnah*, that is, too close to life (cf. *B* 116, 227). And yet, it is life itself which here escapes the "closeness to life",

> The 'living' will offer itself, as every objectifiable entity, to science as and in infinite possibility, and yet it will equally withdraw more and more from the sciences the more groundless these become[27].

We have thus not yet spoken the last word on Nietzsche's philosophy of life. And, indeed, at the beginning of the Nietzsche lectures, already cautious about "values", Heidegger says the following,

> According to Nietzsche, those who posit the highest values, the creative human beings, and, first of all, the philosophers, have to be experimenters and seducers [*Versuchende*]; they have to walk down ways and break up paths, knowing that they do not possess *the* truth. And yet, from this knowledge does not at all follow that they think of their concepts as chips in a game, so that they could exchange them at their will against any others; no, the consequence is quite the opposite: the absolute determination and obligation of thinking has to experience a foundation in the things themselves [*in den Sachen selbst*], a foundation as yet unknown by any prior philosophy. (*N* I 37)

This foundation is not to be seen anywhere else but in the notion of justice. And, insofar as this is a notion of justice or foundation "as yet unknown to any prior philosophy", it is a notion opposed to that which underlies the metaphysical tradition.

❋

It is true, in other words, that Kant, for example, could equally be seen as a thinker who conceives of the philosopher as a "judge" and "legislator", but it is always this Kantian idea of justice that Nietzsche does not want to be confused with. Indeed, as Nietzsche says, "we think differently about justice"[28] than Kant. The main contention in this objection to Kant lies in the construction of transcendental philosophy, which separates the human being from the world, so that it is human reason that, according to Kant, prescribes the law to nature. The hubris of this position lies for Nietzsche in the idea that justice could be reduced to subjectivity, to the judgement of a judge who can preside over nature precisely insofar as he can separate himself from nature,

> The whole pose of 'man *against* the world', of man as a 'world-negating' principle, of man as the measure of the value of things, as judge of the world [*Welten-Richter*] who in the end places existence itself upon his scales and finds it wanting – the monstrous insipidity of this pose has finally come home to us and we are sick of it. We laugh as soon as we encounter the juxtaposition of 'man *and* world', separated by the sublime presumption of the little word 'and'[29].

The danger of mistaking Nietzsche's philosopher for such a judge is not to be underestimated, especially since Heidegger is only a little less guilty of it than many other, less careful interpreters. And yet, it is only by way of this differentiation from the modern idea of justice and judgement that it becomes possible to look for another conception of justice. Nietzsche's claim is thus that we need a "new justice"[30], thought of as the basis of truth, a justice that requires us radically to rethink the identification of truth and knowledge.

True justice, for Nietzsche, takes the form of an affect, or what Heidegger calls a fundamental attunement. It is not spoken from the position of a *Weltenrichter*, but speaks to me, determines knowledge as the highest affect, "Justice confronted me: thus I destroyed my Idols and was ashamed. I repented and forced my eye to look where it did not want to look: and to carry love hither" (*KSA* 10:13 [1], 430). The critical setting-apart, which was to transport us into a fundamental attunement thus finds that it could not quite move us far enough, as it has failed to make Nietzsche "come to a standstill on this side of the transition"[31].

Following a description of how the world of the farmer arises from the emotion of value, the artist's from colour, the world of prehistoric man from anguish and ours from the desire for security – until we can see why Nietzsche says that finally there are only moral experiences – he asks whether justice has any meaning here and answers, "when we are on the way of justice, then the arbitrary, fantastic interpretations, with which we have hurt and violated things, die: because their *real* [*wirkliche*] qualities assert their right, and finally we have to value this more highly than ourselves" (*KSA* 9:6 [239]). This true notion of justice is, then, a step away from the humanistic identification of the world as a human world, a step in the direction of the "naturalisation" of "humanity in terms of a pure, newly discovered, newly redeemed nature" (*KSA* 3:469). This foundation of thought in the things themselves will finally lead to the denegration of the autonomy of reason, to the explosion of the subjectivity of the subject, that is, to the overcoming of metaphysics. But what are we talking about when speak of these *things themselves*? Nietzsche intimates an answer to this question in the following quotation, "we who are of a mixed nature, now heated up by fire, now cooled down by spirit, wish to fall to our knees before justice, as the only goddess we accept above us"[32].

We can, then, conclude again on the question why Nietzsche ruined Heidegger and why Heidegger brought to ruin Nietzsche's hope of finding in Heidegger someone who might have made his truths incredible, namely that Nietzsche is not only the one closest to us, but that he has also made some inroads into the question of being.

Notes

[1] Martin Heidegger, *Zur Auslegung von Nietzsche's II. Unzeitgemäßer Betrachtung*, Gesamtausgabe Bd. 46, Frankfurt a. M.: Klostermann, 2003, 54, hereafter *NUB*. A translation of this lecture course is forthcoming from Indiana University Press. All translations are mine unless otherwise indicated.
[2] Friedrich Nietzsche, Letter to Franz Overbeck, no. 609, 2nd of July 1885, in *KSB*, 7:63, "Mir besteht mein Leben jetzt in dem Wunsche, daß es mit allen Dingen *anders* stehn möge, als ich sie begreife; und daß mir Jemand meine 'Wahrheiten' unglaubwürdig mache...".
[3] Cf. Ullrich Haase, "Dike and Iustitia, or: Between Heidegger and Nietzsche", in: *Journal of the British Society for Phenomenology*, vol. 38, no. 1, January 2007, 18-36.

[4] Martin Heidegger, *Besinnung*, Gesamtausgabe Bd. 66. Frankfurt a. M.: Klostermann, 1997, §15, 74; hereafter *BES* followed by section and page number and, after the / by the reference to *Mindfulness*, trans. Parvis Emad and Thomas Kalary. London and New York: Continuum, 2006.

[5] Martin Heidegger, *Beiträge zur Philosophie*, Gesamtausgabe Bd. 65, Frankfurt a. M.: Klostermann, 1989, §88, 176; hereafter *B*, followed by section and page number.

[6] *BES* §15, 74, it is perhaps superfluous to point out that this statement is equivalent to the stance of Nietzsche's philosophy for which history has become the sole content of philosophy.

[7] "Was in 'Sein und Zeit' als 'Destruktion' entfaltet ist, meint nicht Abbau als Zerstörung, sondern *Reinigung* in der Richtung des Freilegens der metaphysischen Grundstellungen. Aber dies alles ist im Blick auf den Vollzug von Anklang und Zuspiel nur das Vorspiel" *B* 221.

[8] Martin Heidegger, *Was heißt Denken?* Tübingen: Niemeyer, 1954, hereafter *WhD*, 71,

> In Nietzsches Denken kommt zur Sprache, was jetzt ist, aber zu einer Sprache, in der die zweitausendjährige Überlieferung der abendländischen Metaphysik spricht, zu einer Sprache, die wir alle sprechen, die Europa spricht, nur mehrfach übersetzt, nur abgeschliffen, nur vernutzt und hintergrundlos. Platon und Aristoteles sprechen noch in unserer heutigen Sprache. Parmenides und Heraklit denken auch noch in unserem Vorstellen.

[9] Friedrich Nietzsche, Letter to Overbeck, 2nd of July 1885, quoted above.

[10] It is significant that this claim appears in the context of the first outline of the thought of the eternal return of the same.

[11] Martin Heidegger, *NUB*, 5f.

[12] Martin Heidegger, *Schellings Abhandlung Über das Wesen der menschlichen Freiheit*, Tübingen: Niemeyer, 1971, 4.

[13] Martin Heidegger, *WhD*, 21f.

[14] I have developed Nietzsche's thought on the genealogical difference of the term justice elsewhere and in more detail. While having to repeat some of the points made there, I would still like to refer to my "Nietzsche on Truth and Justice", *New Nietzsche Studies*, vol. 8, 1/2 Winter 2009 and Spring 2010, 79-97.

[15] *TIO* "'Reason' in Philosophy", sec. 1, *KSA* 6:74.

[16] *GS* sec. 341, *KSA* 3:570.

[17] *WM*, no. 1067. See also *KSA* 11:38 [12].

[18] See Georg Picht, "Nietzsche: Thought and the Truth of History", *Journal of the British Society for Phenomenology,* vol. 38, no. 1, January 2007, 8.

[19] Dieter Thomä, "Eine Philosophie des Lebens jenseits des Biologismus und diesseits der 'Geschichte der Metaphysik'", in *Heidegger und Nietzsche: Heidegger Jahrbuch 2*, Freiburg und München: Alber, 2005, 278.

[20] Georg Wilhelm Friedrich Hegel, *Vorlesungen über die Geschichte der Philosophie*, Werke Bd. 20. Frankfurt a. M.: Suhrkamp, 1970, hereafter *VGP* 337.

21 "Denken, Verstand bleibt ein Besonderes, Sinnlichkeit ein Besonderes, die auf äußerliche, oberflächliche Weise verbunden werden, wie ein Holz und Bein durch einen Strick", *VGP* 348.

22 Georg Wilhelm Friedrich Hegel, *Wissenschaft der Logik*, Werke Bd. 6, Frankfurt a. M.: Suhrkamp, 1970, 470.

23 Martin Heidegger, *Nietzsche*, 2 vols., Pfullingen: Neske, 1961, vol 1. 655; Nietzsche "[hat] den metaphysisch notwendigen Subjektivismus dadurch zur Vollendung gebracht…, daß er den 'Leib' zum Leitfaden der Weltauslegung bestimmte".

24 See note 5 above.

25 Cf. Martin Heidegger, *Hölderlin's Hymn 'The Ister'*, trans. William McNeill and Julia Davis. Bloomington and Indianapolis: Indiana University Press, 1996, 54.

26 According to a statement by Hans-Georg Gadamer. See Otto Pöggler, *Friedrich Nietzsche und Martin Heidegger*, Bonn: Bouvier Verlag, 2002, 16.

27 "Das 'Lebendige' wird wie alles Gegenstandsfähige dem Fortschritt der Wissenschaft endlose Möglichkeiten bieten und sich doch zugleich mehr und mehr entziehen, je grundloser zugleich die Wissenschaft wird." *B* 154, 276.

28 *KSA* 9:6 [403].

29 *GS*, sec. 346, *KSA* 3:580f.

30 *GS* sec. 289, *KSA* 3:530.

31 See note 13 above.

32 *HAH* I, sec. 637, *KSA* 2:362.

NIETZSCHE AND MERLEAU-PONTY: BODY, PHYSIOLOGY, FLESH

ANDREA REHBERG

This hatred of the human, even more of the animal, even more of the material...this desire to get out of all appearance, change, becoming, death, wishing, out of all desire itself – all this means...a *will to nothing*, a revulsion against life, an uprising against the most fundamental presuppositions of life, but it is and remains a *will*! (*GoM* III, sec. 28, *KSA* 5:412, t.m.[1])

Granted that 'the *soul*' was an attractive and mysterious thought, from which philosophers rightly only parted reluctantly – perhaps that with which they are now learning to replace it is even more attractive, even more mysterious. The human body, on which the entire most distant and nearest past of all organic becoming becomes alive and bodily again, through which, above and beyond which an immense inaudible stream seems to flow: the body is the more astonishing thought than the old 'soul'. (*WP* no. 659, t.m.[2])

What are the tasks left to philosophical thought in an epoch when metaphysics has become endlessly problematic, whether we think of the period in which "we" find ourselves as the end of metaphysics or the beginning of the self-overcoming of metaphysics, as the period which calls for the destruction of metaphysics, or, with Nietzsche, as the phase of impending nihilism, in which case the further question arises what kind of nihilism is meant, active or passive, complete or incomplete, affirmative or resentful[3]. However this malaise is precisely understood, framed or approached, the shared view is that traditional philosophy has – for complex, multiple reasons – run its course, and that something like a re-configuration of our philosophical modes has become necessary in order to take account of these tectonic shifts that appear to be underway. In the following these larger issues of historicity, periodicity, and the task of thinking will be bracketed in favour of attention to a more specific aspect of these complex questions.

I.

Nietzsche sees an all-pervasive contempt for the body and for the earth, a lack of attention paid to them, both in thought and in practice, as a sure indicator of the degeneracy he calls Platonism[4] and thus as a sign of incomplete nihilism. Therefore Nietzsche's works, from first to last, are permeated by different kinds of attempts at a rehabilitation of the body and of the earth[5]. In *Thus Spoke Zarathustra*, for instance, Zarathustra enjoins his disciples to "stay true to the earth", and asks that "your bestowing love and your insights serve the sense of the earth" (*TSZ* I, "On the Bestowing Virtue", sec. 2, *KSA* 4:99, t.m.). But what does this mean, rehabilitation of the body and of the earth? It is, I believe, the case that Nietzsche sees this as the comprehensive antidote to Platonic-Christian practices, and can therefore be seen as the other – "material" – side of the logic of "the overturning of Platonism"[6], as Heidegger calls it. It is all-pervasive in Nietzsche's writings, and therefore difficult to circumscribe briefly. For the time being, and in lieu of the extended discussion this side of Nietzsche's thought deserves, I will only attempt to sketch out the motivation for what will be thematised below in more detail as Nietzsche's physiological thinking.

If we were to participate in the fiction that it is possible to give a brief sketch of (Nietzsche's understanding of) Platonism, the following points would have to be made[7]. Platonism is above all characterised by a divisive thinking in terms of a two-world structure, in which value is exclusively accorded to the higher, "true", "real" world, whereas its "fallen" opposite, "this" world, the world of change and becoming, is considered ontologically deficient. But there is an even deeper, more obscure and sinister level to this. For it must equally be asked what the motivation is for this erection of a "higher" world, where there is eternal, unchanging and in fact unchangeable being, without having become and without passing away. The answer lies in the fact that it is supposed to be a realm immune from the very elements which characterise our earthly existence, namely material decomposition, disintegration and death. Because our manner of being, and of the world in which we are, is that matter comes to be and passes away, that our bodies are born in blood and slime, that they grow, age, die and decompose, and that whatever is in time must sooner or later pass away. This is *the* fundamental, ineluctable fact of our earthly, bodily being, but Platonism reacts to it by establishing an other-worldly, ideal realm free from all temporal materiality. And this is why all varieties of Platonism, including Christianity, all manner of idealisms, but also its mere inversions, such as positivism, scientism, and all kinds of (base) materialism, are finally motivated to participate in the same structure of thought, designed to save and preserve what is fundamentally beyond preservation, namely human being in the unstoppably temporal, self-overturning nature of matter. Thus it can be said that at bottom Platonism equals the fear and hatred of time and matter, becoming and the body (see, for example, *TI* "'Reason' in Philosophy", especially sec.s 1, 2, *KSA* 6:74f.).

But just as the oppositional stance that characterises Platonism cannot be overcome by opposing it, since any oppositional thinking merely duplicates its structure, so its fundamental, underlying anti-materialist orientation cannot be overcome through a simple contrary affirmation of matter. But it seems to me that Nietzsche's physiological thinking does neither. It neither denies the reality of Platonism and all aspects of this perspective, however nihilistic, nor does it attempt to oppose a simple valorisation of matter, the body and the senses to the Platonistic denigration of them. Instead, it shows – in a move as simple as it is elegant – that all oppositionality and all nihilism are always already immanent to the monism of life or will to power – which terms will be treated as virtually synonymous here, as two sides of the same coin, such that life indicates the monistic "field" within which everything occurs, while will to power emphasises the differential play of forces within this field. This monistic universe is neither unified nor adiaphoric, neither simple, nor single, nor morally invested. It consists of the strife of forces – will to power – in which different struggling perspectives seek to overcome each other, according to their respective powers of expenditure. Conversely, the failure of expenditure, the comparative weakness of this capacity, expresses itself as attempts at self-preservation, the blockage typical of metaphysico-moral constructions such as Platonism, Christianity, idealism, romanticism, etc. (see especially *GoM* I). But the important thing to remember is that all these struggles are immanent to life itself, which has no outside, no beginning or end (see, for example, *WP* nos. 1066 and 1067), and which is gloriously unconcerned about the petty scrabblings of humans and their metaphysico-moral systems. Thus Nietzsche says that, "When we speak of values we speak under the inspiration of life, from the perspective of life: life itself forces us to posit values, life itself evaluates through us *when* we posit values" (*TI* "Morality as Anti-Nature", sec. 5, *KSA* 6:86, t.m.[8]). So for Nietzsche, the only truly affirmative thinking is one that, starting from life, attempts to approximate this non-anthropocentric, anti-humanist, entirely impersonal and non-moral perspective and views all phenomena as expressions of it (*TI* "The Four

Great Errors", sec. 8, *KSA* 6:96). Such a thinking asks what a phenomenon's function might be in the overall economy of life, and it only finally judges as deficient those articulations of life which turn against it and judge life itself as deficient, as if there were a position to be taken up outside life from where it could be judged, and judged to be in any way lacking (see, for example, *TI* "The Problem of Socrates", sec. 1, *KSA* 6:67), when in fact life knows no lack, since it is the original, inexhaustible plenitude (see *WP* no. 1067).

But, and this is the crux of the matter, whilst it is surely the case that Nietzsche's thoroughgoing thinking in terms of life and will to power is not reducible to any of the known forms of materialism, neither is it the case that the original plenitude that is life is ever to be divorced from its essential materiality. Rather, whereas the former already operate within an oppositional framework, the latter mode of thought starts from an understanding of life as the self-articulation, and that means the self-overcoming, of matter. In other words, it sees all oppositionality, as well as all idealisms, as immanent, and even as in some sense and at certain times necessary, to this economy of life (see, for example, *GoM* I, sec. 6, *KSA* 5:264-6). And it is this intimacy between life and materiality, between an economy or play of unconscious forces and the material processes in which they play themselves out, that finally leads Nietzsche to thematise this new "world conception" (*WP* no. 1066) in terms of the body and specifically of physiology, a physiology not just of art, but of life. Thus birth and death, inspiration and expiration, ingestion, digestion and excretion, all manner of metabolic and catabolic exchanges and transformations, growth, decomposition, flows of matter and energy not only make up individual bodies, but all expressions of life. And so, by inhabiting this register of bodily becoming, Nietzsche's physiological thinking is balanced on the cusp between materiality and ideality, between sensuous and supersensuous, between individual and universal formations, such that it speaks of singularity and multiplicity at the same time and, furthermore, is thereby able to show how both only emerge from out of this ongoing physiological becoming. Nietzsche's thinking thereby constitutes a continuous practical revaluation (no longer deplorable but instead worthy of celebration) of the domain Platonism seeks to expunge, namely the fundament of our existence, physiology.

As has already been indicated, this physiological thinking, which attempts to view things from the perspective of life, has another important implication. In it the opposition between human consciousness, subjectivity or agency on the one side and, on the other side, the allegedly passive materiality of nature in its otherness, simply falls away if both are conceived as expressions of will to power, or if the former is seen as a specific articulation of the latter, and if attention is paid to physiology as the site of their perpetual exchanges and mutations. In the following note, for instance, Nietzsche understands "the entire conscious life" as working in the service of the enhancement of life (*Lebenssteigerung*), and he concludes that "what one used to call 'body' and 'flesh' is of such unspeakably greater importance: the rest is a small accessory" (*WP* no. 674). Thus Nietzschean thinking in terms of will to power importantly starts from a position beyond the compass of the merely or "all too" human. It views all human activity, including all culture, music, literature, art, philosophy, science, religion, etc., as so many processes internal to the overarching economy of life, as productions of its singular physiology. This thinking understands itself, like all thought, as an articulation of life and it is therefore from first to last thoroughly non-anthropocentric, arguably more so than that of any other thinker since before the inception of Western metaphysics by Socrates and Plato. That it simultaneously dissimulates its thoroughly impersonal character in a register of often vituperative rhetoric, seemingly traceable to the quirks and foibles of *Herr* Nietzsche, is part and parcel of its general strategy of concealing itself on "surfaces" of language, a strategy that has successfully befuddled generations of readers, and to which we will have to return below.

II.

Having thus briefly outlined both the motivation for Nietzsche's physiological thinking and – in general terms – its main features, it should come as no surprise that in the present paper the questions inherent in the title "Nietzsche and Phenomenology" are being pursued by way of tracing the outlines of Nietzsche's and Merleau-Ponty's respective thoughts of the body. Specifically, it is a question of how, if at all, Nietzsche's physiological thinking can be aligned with Merleau-Ponty's project of "an ontological rehabilitation of the sensible"[9]. But it can hardly be a matter of *comparing* a thought formed and honed over almost two decades (in the case of Nietzsche[10]) with the late flowering, roughly over two years, of a writer's output (as is the case with the later Merleau-Ponty's thoughts about the body[11]). So it can surely not be appropriate to carry out anything in the manner of a comparison, which would, at any rate, be in danger of simplifying their thoughts. Instead, perhaps it might be suggested that the encounter staged here between their thoughts is to be seen as something in the nature of a fortuitous, late, partial convergence, the temporary overlapping of two essentially very different trajectories, like the chance meeting of distant relatives *en route*, by different means, to far-off destinations on the same outlying continent.

Preliminarily, then, it suffices to say, in broad terms, that from his early *chef-d'œuvre, Phenomenology of Perception*[12], to the final working notes appended to *The Visible and the Invisible*, Merleau-Ponty sought to extend and deepen the scope of one of the cornerstones of Husserlian phenomenology, namely the concept of intentionality. For Husserl, this was still to be understood as a feature of consciousness, such that every act of consciousness is consciousness *of* something, is directed towards an object, and thus involved in the constitution of that object. By contrast, Merleau-Ponty strove to free the idea of intentionality from Husserl's understanding of it as essentially a feature of consciousness, such that, for example, he speaks rather disparagingly of Husserl's "senseless effort to submit everything to the properties of 'consciousness' (to the limpid play of its attitudes, intentions, and impositions of meaning)..." (PS in *S* 180). Instead, Merleau-Ponty sought to transpose intentionality into a broadly "material" – and thus fundamentally pre-subjective – register, specifically, to reinscribe it into the nexus of the human body as guarantor of the "always already" status of our embeddedness in material being. Thus, typically, in a statement that encapsulates Merleau-Ponty's late radical divergence from Husserl's project (insofar as this still accords central importance to consciousness) and his concomitant convergence with Nietzsche on the issue of the ontological importance of the body, Merleau-Ponty asserts, "It is the body *and it alone*...that can bring us to the things themselves" (*VI* 136, emphasis added)[13].

In one sense, then, to say that Nietzsche and Merleau-Ponty share an emphasis on the body as topic of their philosophical endeavours is to state an obvious truth, as it is to say that both do so as a response to metaphysical, Platonistic modes of thought in general, and to Cartesian, dualistic, intellectualist philosophies in particular. But in all this it remains a question whether the differences between their respective ways of approaching the problematic of the body do not outweigh any perceived shared concerns. This would, moreover, have certain implications for the project of situating Nietzsche vis-à-vis phenomenology. In the following I therefore simply aim to chisel out some of these differences, as well as of course the continuities between their respective projects, on the basis of which such questions become possible in the first place, and to draw out some of their implications. Rather than the full-fledged study that this fascinating topic deserves, this will be in the nature of a sketch, a mere outline of what I see as the central features of this issue.

It might be said that the differences between Nietzsche's and Merleau-Ponty's approaches to the body can simply be accounted for by the "fact" that Merleau-Ponty is categorisable as a phenomenologist, whereas Nietzsche is generally considered to be above all a genealogist, iconoclast and philosopher of life. This too has to be acknowledged as true, at least with certain reservations and qualifications[14], but of course both would agree that it is, to say the least, unhelpful to flee into labels when one tries to understand a phenomenon. So the bare "fact" of Merleau-Ponty's phenomenological, as opposed to Nietzsche's genealogico-physiological orientation does not explain anything, and in fact merely obscures the real issues. Similarly, the question might arise whether these differences can, at least up to a point, be accounted for by the very different routes by which they arrive at this stance: on the one hand, Nietzsche's project of quasi-Kantian critique (albeit radicalised to the point where it is barely recognisable as such), in tandem with Schopenhauer's influence on his thought; on the other hand, the provenance of Merleau-Ponty's project in that of Husserl and in a highly critical, if mostly subterranean, inexplicit, engagement with Heidegger. But, again, even this account, based on the very different trajectories of their thought, seems to me to be too broad-brush to begin with.

Perhaps, then, it might be more productive to open up this issue by looking at Nietzsche and Merleau-Ponty as concerns the issue of tone, the texture of their writing, because even the most casual reader of their respective texts must notice the gulf of difference between them as concerns tone. Thus one is struck by the highly nuanced hues of Merleau-Ponty's writing, which seeks to evade the tropes of metaphysics and instead weaves a *filigrane* web of deferrals and references, hints, suggestions and shades of meaning, especially so when compared to Nietzsche's seemingly "direct", confrontational, aggressively rhetorical, often bitterly sarcastic and frequently acerbic tone. But, I would suggest, without wishing to detract from the importance of the very different force of their tone, that in each case an element of dissimulation is involved, because it seems to me that, on one side, Merleau-Ponty for the most part – albeit extremely subtly – addresses quite traditional philosophical problems (above all those attendant on Cartesian dualisms). By contrast (as I was already trying to suggest in some of the opening paragraphs above), even the starting point of Nietzsche's reflections lies somewhere outside such traditional concerns (see for instance, *WP* Preface, no.3). They start from elsewhere, from a point or, more precisely, from a movement of thought beyond the circumference of traditional Western metaphysics, and only subsequently turn on it in order to expose what he calls "the idiosyncrasies of philosophers" (*TI* "'Reason' in Philosophy", sec. 1, *KSA* 6:74) or, more provocatively, "the brain ailments of sick cobweb spinners" (*TI* "'Reason' in Philosophy", sec. 4, *KSA* 6:76, t.m.). But this characterisation in terms of their respective positions in relation to the ground of metaphysics still lacks the requisite specificity, and so we must burrow deeper.

III.

How, then, can the truly important differences between Nietzsche's and Merleau-Ponty's philosophies of the body be delineated, given that both privilege it as the site of an attempted post-metaphysical manner of thinking? To my mind, as hinted earlier, the most far-reaching differences are generated by Nietzsche speaking from the outset in the mode of a vociferous advocate of life, of health, of the future and thus, finally, of self-overcoming. He never writes in a neutral mode, never even aims just to describe, just to let phenomena speak for themselves, because his genealogico-critical stance means that for him such simple description is simply not possible. Life is always biased, and pure, unbiased descriptions of phenomena are just not possible, from that perspective. Thus, because of the essentially agonistic and at the same time interpretative nature of life, the ideal of phenomenological description, stripped of all presuppositions, prejudices and assumptions is in practice unattainable for Nietzsche, if not even suspect, because of the will to power that can be read in it, namely a kind of will to purity. The doxa – whether as unthinking common sense, as reflexive-constructive philosophy, or as paradigmatic science – from which phenomenological description seeks to diverge (even if only temporarily, strategically, or by way of bracketting), for Nietzsche always catch up with thought because they (like error) are woven into it, and that means into the fabric of will to power. They are one of the means by which a specific will to power seeks ascendancy, namely in the attempt at equalisation (*Ausgleichung*) or eradication of differences. Ultimately, then, for Nietzsche, it is not doxa that is the problem, it is thinking itself, such as it is, namely wedded to the categorisations and simplifications of grammar (*TI* "'Reason' in Philosophy", sec. 5, *KSA* 6:78), suffused by the will to knowledge and the will to truth; thinking that equalises all difference in order to absorb, to incorporate, to make equal to what already belongs to an existing system or physiology. In other words, for Nietzsche it is our very modes and habits of thought that prevent us from ever encountering the things themselves (see, for instance, *TI* "'Reason' in Philosophy", sec. 5, *KSA* 6:77). And so for him every description is already deeply enmeshed in an interpretation, which in fact only makes it possible in the first place. According to Nietzsche, all phenomena, all perception, all descriptions of phenomena, and all reception of such descriptions are always already enmeshed in the struggle of forces which determines whether life is being advanced, enhanced, enriched and *risked*, or denuded, depleted, weakened and sapped in the attempt to *preserve* it. Nietzsche's is above all a philosophy of values, but the source of all values – even the most absurdly nihilistic ones, such as religious dogmatism – is life itself.

Thus, for instance, in the Preface to the second edition of *The Gay Science* (1886), Nietzsche reflects on the two most central elements of his physiological thinking, namely health and sickness. There he explores the entire nexus of illness, convalescence, health and, or as, (the history of) philosophy, to the point of asking whether philosophy as a whole has hitherto not been "an interpretation of the body and a *misunderstanding of the body*" (*GS* Preface, sec. 2, *KSA* 3:348), something in the nature of physiology concealing itself in abstractions and idealisations and only gradually coming to itself through the history of Western thought[15]. On the basis of this insight he states that there are essentially two types of philosophers, namely those predominantly life-affirming, thinking from the body and not seeking to deny or denigrate it, and those whose thinking remains slavish and nihilistic; those whose thoughts are born out of health, strength, gratitude and an excessive wealth of thought, and those who philosophise out of systemic disease, degeneration and weakness, and who use philosophy as a way of protecting themselves from themselves and from material becoming. The former practice philosophy as self-expenditure and enhancement, the latter as a means of self-preservation and curing themselves from life, from which they suffer (*GS* Preface, sec. 2, *KSA* 3:347f.[16]). For Nietzsche, it can thus never be a matter of describing the phenomena of the body, thereby to produce, perchance, a more accurately descriptive "rigorous science" of the body than do any scientifically-minded endeavours imbued with realist or, for that matter, idealist tendencies[17]. The project of phenomenological description in the (post-) Husserlian sense must therefore remain for Nietzsche something in the nature of a delusional phantasy, or the symptom of a declining life-form because it is no longer capable of speaking *for* life.

Making this point (about the values of health and sickness in Nietzsche's thought) does not, in my view, signify a relapse into dualistic modes of thought, as long as it is remembered that health and sickness mark the extremes on a scale on which every phenomenon's position oscillates, according to the forces which dominate it at one time or another, including the forces which dominate its interpretations. Also, parenthetically, it should be remarked that it would be a mistake unambiguously to equate health with the good and sickness with bad or evil evaluations. Sickness may be a good thing, it may in fact be the sign of a strong physiology regenerating itself and exposing itself to new possibilities by means of it. Everything hinges on the interpretations that constitute "health" and "sickness", in other words, what kind of will to power predominates (see, for instance, *WP* no. 643). And at any rate, for physiologically oriented philosophers all common sense and moral interpretations (where health equals good and sickness equals evil) are suspended. When they become ill they merely receive new, perhaps dangerous, but nonetheless stimulating impulses towards thinking (*GS* Preface, sec. 3, *KSA* 3:349f.).

In consequence of his advocacy of the all-encompassing, monistic, yet at the same time contradictory and tragic phenomenon *life*, Nietzsche must also be deeply suspicious of any valorisation of consciousness qua individual subjectivity above the myriad unconscious forces to which every consciousness is at the same time subjected. By these forces he does not predominantly mean the supra-individual, impersonal, "abstract", larger forces, such as those of history, society, politics, culture, etc. Rather, he pays attention to the concrete, material, local forces affecting a physiology, such as climate, diet, physical activity, sleep habits, etc., the "first things" (in order of importance), which have systematically been taken for the last things (to deserve philosophical attention, because of their allegedly low status as non-originary) throughout the history of philosophy (*HH* I, sec. 1, "Of First and Last Things", *KSA* 2:23-55; *TI* "'Reason' in Philosophy", sec. 4, *KSA* 6:76). In fact, he sees the revaluation of the "first things" in his writings as the most noble aspect of his entire philosophical endeavour (*WP* no. 1016). Attention to these "little things – nutrition, locale, climate, recreation" (*EH* "Why I am so Clever", sec. 10, *KSA* 6:295, t.m.), also, for example, "air, electricity", etc. (*WP* no. 676), is for Nietzsche not only a matter of individual health, it is a matter which indicates one's position within life and vis-à-vis metaphysics. He says of these "little things" that they are inconceivably more important than all abstract conceptuality ("über alle Begriffe hinaus", *EH* "Why I am so Clever", sec. 10, *KSA* 6:295), more important than everything considered important hitherto, namely those metaphysico-moral constructs that have tormented humanity, above all God, soul, virtue, sin, the beyond, truth, eternal life, etc. (*EH* "Why I am so Clever", sec. 10, *KSA* 6:296). Valorisation of these and contempt for the "little things" have tended to go hand in hand, but such a contempt is ultimately contempt for life itself, for the earth and for the body, and the resurrection of the "little things" – not least as topics of philosophical reflection – must be considered imperative for the project of the transvaluation of (Platonic-Christian) values. Nietzsche says, for example, that "the so-called 'good conscience'" is at bottom a physiological state, remarkably similar to the overall effects of a sound digestion, with which it is therefore easily confused (*TI* "The Four Great Errors", sec. 6, *KSA* 6:94, t.m.). In comparison to these profound forces, as Nietzsche says, "everything conscious remains on the surface" (*WP* no. 358) and "consciousness *is* a surface" (*EH* "Why I am so Clever", sec. 9, *KSA* 6:294). But still, when Nietzsche states that it is "the phase of the modesty of consciousness" (*WP* no. 676, t.m.), we should hear this not so much as the attestation of a fact than as a call to arms against any intellectual endeavour that takes consciousness to be an original source of meaning, when it is realised that meaning is always constructed out of interpretations.

In what I consider the *locus classicus* of his physiological thinking, namely the section called "Why I am so Clever" of *Ecce Homo*, Nietzsche examines his own life in terms of those concrete forces which have shaped it, and he examines those forces as to their effects on him and on humanity in general. The most serious lesson he conveys there is that "ignorance *in physiologicis*" – which ignorance he sums up as "that cursed 'idealism'" (*EH* "Why I am so Clever", sec. 2, *KSA* 6:283, t.m.) – has led to the most dangerous and far-reaching fatalities, errors and misunderstandings of his life, as of that of Western, Platonic-Christian humanity at large. The areas in which this ignorance tended to manifest itself in Nietzsche's life were those concerning the nutrition appropriate to the full exercise of his powers (*EH* "Why I am so Clever", sec. 1, *KSA* 6:279f.), the climate and locale most beneficial to the optimal working of his metabolism (*EH* "Why I am so Clever", sec. 2, *KSA* 6:281-3, t.m.), as well as the right kind of recreation (in his case literature and music) at the right time (*EH* "Why I am so Clever", sec.s 3-8, *KSA* 6:284-93). For Western humanity at large,

Nietzsche intimates, this ignorance led to the existential horrors of nihilism, that is, the most enigmatic and horrific spectacle of life turning against itself (*GoM* III, sec. 28, *KSA* 5:412).

Nietzsche thereby vividly demonstrates a number of points crucial to his overall philosophical stance. Firstly, for him there can be no substantial difference between reflecting on the importance of these physiological factors for human life in general and for his life in particular, since the errors of the former are also his errors, and vice versa. This is because – on the basis of his philosophy of life – every individual physiology, every life form, is merely the expression, continuation and instantiation of the entirety of forces, that is, life, because "one belongs to the whole, one *is* in and as the whole [*im Ganzen*],...there is nothing outside the whole" (*TI* "The Four Great Errors", sec. 8, *KSA* 6:96, t.m.). Secondly, the indivisibility of the thinker and the thought is thereby established, so that both are now seen as points on a continuum and the categories of subject and object become obsolete. Thirdly, the empirical person Friedrich Nietzsche ("Herr Nietzsche", as he calls it, *GS* Preface, sec. 2, *KSA* 3:347) and the thinker Nietzsche are inseparably embroiled in the same dynamic of forces, although the latter is of course not reducible to the former or simply identifiable with it. As he says in the Preface to *The Gay Science*, he is no "thinking frog, no objectifying and registering apparatus with neutralised viscera [*mit kaltgestellten Eingeweiden*]" (*GS* Preface, sec. 3, *KSA* 3:349, t.m.). Not for him the dispassionate distance, the stylistic remoteness of a disembodied voice which implicitly accepts the unspoken demand of a scientistic culture that the speaker keep himself (*sic!*) out of, apart and even aloof from the spoken, thereby unwittingly repeating the suppression of the physiological register from philosophical discourse that has characterised the Platonistic-Christian tradition. Insofar as the thinker is alive, *is* a human body, all philosophy is always already physiological, because produced by a thinking body. Physiological thinking is not just or even primarily a thinking *about*, but *by* the body. It stresses the always already open channel between a body and its thought, and it thereby reinstates and embodies the smooth transitions between phenomena that we habitually attribute to consciousness and those that we tend to attribute to our bodily being. Far from this indicating a thought mired in subjectivism, it is the most impersonal attitude imaginable, for according to it, when I think, life thinks through me. These are not "my" thoughts – in the sense of an organising, controlling agency to which they belong, such as in Kant's transcendental unity of apperception. They are instead thoughts expressive of particular concatenations of myriad forces agglomerating at this point in this way, and they are merely being articulated by this particular node in the "immense inaudible stream" of material becoming (*WP* no. 659, t.m.).

IV.

As has already been indicated, from his earliest explorations of phenomenology, Merleau-Ponty was concerned with deepening its investigations in such a way as to put its central concepts on a thoroughly material, corporeal footing, or, more precisely, on a basis which is prior to the ideal-material distinction. More concretely, towards the end of his life he reached for a term as similarly comprehensive as Nietzsche's understanding of life to denote a unitary material "field" in which the world articulates itself, namely his famous concept of "flesh" (*la chair*). This concept emerged in a number of late texts, such as "The Philosopher and His Shadow" (1959, arguably the most crucial of Merleau-Ponty's explicit *Auseinandersetzungen* with Husserl), as well as in "Eye and Mind" (1960), one of Merleau-Ponty's most important contributions to the philosophy of art. But the concept of flesh is most central to the discussion in the by now very well known chapter called "The Intertwining – The Chiasm"[18], chapter 4 of *The Visible and the Invisible*, the manuscript of which Merleau-Ponty was working on when death overtook him, in which, importantly, he distances himself from the orientation of *Phenomenology of Perception* in the following words, "The problems posed in *Ph.P.* are insoluble because I start there from the 'consciousness'-'object' distinction" (*VI* 200).

In the attempt to delineate the concept of flesh, Merleau-Ponty avers that it approximates most of all to the ancient sense of "element" – not to the dualities of matter, mind, spirit or substance (*VI* 139, see also *VI* 147), but to that which runs through every fragment of being as an "incarnate principle" (*ibid.*), such that it can be thought of as "an '''element' of Being" (*VI* 139). Flesh is therefore to be understood as something in the nature of a "formative medium of the object and the subject" (*VI* 147), in other words, something like a condition of possibility (*VI* 132f.[19]), constitutive of the things as of the one who sees them (*VI* 135), and, more importantly, constitutive of all relationality: to myself, to others, and to the beings in the world (*VI* 145). With the concept of flesh Merleau-Ponty seeks to reconnect the regions that have been separated in and by metaphysics, namely the regions of what he characterises as the touching and the touched, the viewing and the visible, the body and the world, the phenomenal body (*Leib*) and the objective body (*Körper*) and, at bottom, subject and object (see especially *VI* 137). Instead of the alleged divisions separating them, he finds between them a continuous movement of interlacing or intertwining (*l'entrelacs*). Merleau-Ponty's notion of flesh can, therefore, be seen as Husserl's understanding of consciousness – the universal condition of possibility for the appearing of the things themselves – radicalised and, as it were, made flesh. Furthermore, the reversibility between regions within this element, which reversibility Merleau-Ponty characterises as an ongoing process of intertwining, as a chiasmic figure, has the same explanatory function and force as does the concept of intentionality in Husserl's work.

Flesh is, for Merleau-Ponty, the guarantor of the possibility of my relation to myself, of reflexivity, although this too is now seen as embedded in a primordial materiality. Thus Merleau-Ponty at length discusses the chiasm that occurs when my left hand touches my right hand (*VI* 133, 136, 137, 141, 145; see also *Ideen* II, §37, the undoubted source of this discussion[20]). He calls flesh that "anonymity innate to Myself" (*VI* 139) for which traditional philosophy does not have a name (*ibid.* and *VI* 147). Because of it I am simultaneously fundamentally fused into the being of the world, and also profoundly alien to myself, yet without therefore being alienated *from* myself, in fact quite the reverse. Alienation from myself on the contrary only occurs as a result of the Cartesian intervention, which first of all splits the one material continuum of involvements into those aspects concerning alternatively subject or object. It is clear that flesh is one of the "first concepts" with which Merleau-Ponty aims to "avoid the classical impasses" (*VI* 137) of philosophy in general, and of Husserlian phenomenology in particular, in so far as it is still (namely in its privileging of consciousness) partly rooted in a certain adherence to the Cartesian paradigm. The first layer of Merleau-Ponty's thematisation of flesh as primordial condition of possibility of relationality is thus its enabling of my self-relatedness.

Secondly, being of elemental status, flesh also functions as the ontological basis of the possibility of every (e.g., linguistic) community, of communication, of the correspondence between your ideas and mine, and it is thus akin to what Husserl termed intersubjectivity. Merleau-Ponty hints at this provenance of this thought with the term "intercorporeity" (*VI* 141). In other words, what metaphysics has torn asunder into oppositional concepts is rejoined here, and it is shown how even this act of separation itself is first of all only made possible on the basis of the one "connective tissue" that is Merleau-Ponty's ontological concept of flesh (see, for instance, *VI* 142). Even every known thought belongs to a flesh, "toute pensée de nous connue advient à une chair" (*VI* 146, *VL* 189, t.m.). So the second layer of intertwining too, namely between the I and the other, is again a radicalisation of a Husserlian concept, this time from intersubjectivity to intercorporeity, just as earlier we saw the move from consciousness to incarnate being. A third layer of the titular intertwining is that interpenetration or "reciprocal insertion" (*VI* 138) in which "the body belongs to the order of things just as the world is universal flesh" (*VI* 137, t.m.). This is thematised in the text as the reciprocity between the touching and the touched (for example, *VI* 133), and between the tangible and the visible (for instance, *VI* 134). As indicated above, this is Merleau-Ponty's post-Husserlian explanation of how my relation to the things of the world is possible in the first place.

Beyond these three levels or layers of flesh as condition of all my relationality or involvements (with myself, others and world), Merleau-Ponty also sees in this primordial element indications of a self-relatedness of it with itself. Thus, what were previously still discussed as traditionally quasi-autonomous points (I, other, world), now emerge as "nodes" within this field, as conduits for its fundamental auto-affectivity. In this context Merleau-Ponty speaks of "the return of the visible upon itself" (*VI* 142), and of the flesh as "a texture that returns...and conforms to itself" (*VI* 146), and, most importantly, of "a relation of the visible with itself that traverses me" (*VI* 140). Also in this context, Merleau-Ponty advances an understanding of human being which entirely centres on the body and its essential belonging to a universal materiality, and which culminates in the statement "we are the world that thinks itself" (*VI* 136, n.2, "nous sommes le monde qui se pense", *VL* 177) This is to say that these nodes, including myself, are finally no more than expressions of an impersonal, pre-individual field, which constitutes them and which functions as guarantor of the relations between them. This is to say that with the notion of flesh, and especially through the way he understands its internal dynamic, Merleau-Ponty's thinking attains to an entirely non-anthropocentric perspective focused on a universal materiality, and it is therefore similar to the perspective we saw to be at work in Nietzsche's understanding of these issues, according to which all productions of consciousness are finally productions of the physiology from which it emerges, and which is in turn to be understood as an expression of life.

Furthermore, if we were to ask how exactly the relations between the whole of flesh and the nodes within in it are seen by Merleau-Ponty, the following comments would point the way. First of all, it should be stressed again that in Merleau-Ponty's understanding of it flesh is the source of the smooth continuity between the individual body and the entirety of the world, because "the world is made of the very stuff of the body" (EM 125) and "the world is at the heart of our flesh" (*VI* 136). But more specifically, in "The Intertwining – The Chiasm" Merleau-Ponty explores the idea that the body (as sensible mass) comes into being through an act of splitting off from and within the general mass of the sensible, "where it is born by segregation" (*VI* 136, "où il naît par ségrégation", *VL* 177, t.m.; see also *VI* 137, 143). Thereby too he indicates an in some senses similar understanding of the body as that found in Nietzsche's writings, namely as self-articulation of life. Here we recall the many points, discussed above, on Nietzsche's thought of the indivisibility of an "individual" physiology and all of life.

It must also be pointed out that there are signs which indicate that in his late thought Merleau-Ponty even appears to approach Nietzsche's aim (briefly mentioned near the beginning of this essay) of a return to the earth in thought[21]. Towards the end of "The Philosopher and His Shadow" Merleau-Ponty finds that what the later Husserl's analyses of constitution finally reveal is that on the far side of things we discover a region "that we have not constituted", specifically beings "beneath our idealisations and objectifications which secretly nourish them", foremost among them "the Earth...the 'soil'/'ground' or 'stem'/'stock' of our thought as of our life" (*S* 180, "la Terre,...'sol' ou 'souche' de notre pensée comme de notre vie", *Ss* 293, t.m.).

Finally, in a somewhat programmatic statement, Merleau-Ponty summarises his understanding of post-Husserlian phenomenology in the following terms,

> In the last analysis, phenomenology is neither a materialism nor a philosophy of mind. Its proper work is to unveil the pre-theoretical layer on which both of these idealisations find their relative justification and are gone beyond. (*S* 165)

It is arguably the case that Merleau-Ponty's concept of flesh – or what we understand of it from his late elaborations of this concept – satisfies the demands of just such a pre-theoretical layer. It may also be suggested that in this respect there is a direct continuity between the structural properties of the notion of flesh and Nietzsche's understanding of physiology, as elaborated above.

V.

Having chiselled out in a little more detail the continuities between Nietzsche on the topic of life, the body and physiology on the one hand and late Merleau-Ponty's understanding of flesh and body on the other, it remains for us to address one final question. On the basis of the understanding of Platonism as not only a formally dualistic ontology but – as has been argued and emphasised here – a thoroughgoing denigration of the body and of the earth, it behoves us to ask which one of our two thinkers accomplishes a more radical overcoming of the nihilistic, idealising metaphysics that characterises the entire Western tradition and thereby achieves a more radical rehabilitation of the body. But this is clearly a huge question, and here a possible response to it can only be sketched out, and it would be two-pronged. Firstly, it has to be recalled that Platonism, even though it sets out from the Platonic articulation of it, undergoes a host of transformations throughout the history of Western metaphysics, and shows, as it were, a series of different faces. Thus, in the modern period it shows itself in the form of Cartesianism, specifically in the double Cartesian dualism of subject and object, and mind and body. Put simply, then, the degree to which a thinking in the modern period manages to divorce itself from this paradigm at the same time indicates its distance or otherwise from the Platonistic vilification of the body. Secondly, and related to it, the core aspect of Cartesianism, namely the subject-centred perspective taken up by it, can only finally be overcome by a thinking which inhabits a thoroughly non- or pre-subjective, completely non-anthropocentric, wholly impersonal plateau, on which the uninterrupted continuity between different points within a single material-constitutive field is the starting-point of thinking, and on which differentiations between these points are accounted for by an economy of self-differentiations within that field. Such a thinking, it seems to me, represents the only true "twisting free" of metaphysics.

Merleau-Ponty begins to attain to this in the final years of writing, but even then, in the gloriously exuberant explorations of flesh and the reciprocities within it, his thinking seems periodically to be being pulled back into the very framework which it so audaciously seeks to leave behind. Innumerable instances of this (in all the texts of his under discussion here) could be cited. Here it must suffice to give one or two exemplary indications of this tendency. For instance, even though Merleau-Ponty's investigations of flesh are initially meant to lead him away from an individual consciousness posited as originary, and its alleged opposition to a world of objectivity, and instead towards intercorporeity and other forms of the interlacing, at one point they culminate in the statement "one sole body [encompassing all 'individual' bodies] before one sole world,...a Sentient in general before a Sensible in general" (*VI* 142). Although this might on the one hand be read as an advance on the Cartesian insistence on individuated consciousness, it can, on the other hand, be seen as a relapse into the dualism of subject and object from which it sought to escape – albeit now inscribed in a less idealist register and, as it were, sublated on to a higher level of generality.

Similarly, Merleau-Ponty's language indicates a certain degree of being beholden to the most traditional schemas when he says of the body that it "offers to him who *inhabits* it [*qui l'habite*] and senses it the wherewithal to sense everything that resembles himself on the *outside* [*au-dehors*]" (*VI* 135, *VL* 176, emphases added). Here the bizarre designation of my body as "the sack in which I am enclosed" (*VI* 134, "le sac où je suis enclos", *VL* 174) could also be mentioned. Both of these instances point to a certain implicit conception of an I that initially precedes its bodily being, and only subsequently finds itself "in" a body. This duplicates, almost exactly, one of the most egregious of Plato's statements of this "relationship", when he writes of the body as the "walking sepulchre" in which an otherwise pure "unpolluted" soul is entombed (*Phaedrus* 250b, c[22]). In fact, to my ears even the register of *in*carnation and *em*bodiment retains such an accusative sense which indicates that something previously (essentially?) not of this "location" has subsequently been "enclosed" in the body. But what then is this pre-physiological I, how did it come to be "in" the body, and how should its relations to, and differences from this physicality be understood? In other words, this kind of register precisely leads back to the questions which Descartes himself was unable to resolve satisfactorily, and which, I would claim, remain unresolvable as long as one sets out from anything like the substance dualism that fuels Cartesian thinking. As the saying has it, "you can't get there from here".

It must then be admitted that Merleau-Ponty oscillates between two very different orientations, in one sense pointing "outward" towards the impersonal "tissue" of the flesh, that "lines,...sustains,...nourishes" (*VI* 132) all things, and in the other sense periodically relapsing into the Cartesian paradigm from which Husserl's thought had attempted to liberate modern philosophy. But, I would claim, the very attempt to overcome this dualism remains marooned in it as long as it is not, from the outset, motivated by an understanding of the whole of beings as issuing from a prior monistic field[23]. Another way of grasping these oscillations within Merleau-Ponty's thinking might be to say that it is moving between, on the one hand, a conception that starts from an originary relationality, and from out of it accounts both for the existence of the relata themselves and for their actual relations; and, on the other hand, a conception that presupposes these relata as quasi-substantial entities and only subsequently asks about how their relation might be possible.

Finally, then, if we might speculate about the reasons for these oscillations which often strangely occur cheek by jowl in Merleau-Ponty's texts, three elements could be pointed to. Firstly, Merleau-Ponty's philosophy, whether early or late, is not underpinned by a thought of will to power, so it has no sense of (the strife of) forces, and therefore no sense of the need for a genealogical reading of them. Thus it is constantly in danger of a certain indifferentism, a general acknowledging of the primacy of – in the case of the later texts – flesh, but without a sense of the *agon* of forces permeating it, and hence it is prone to a somewhat overly benign, as well as unspecific, sense of *how* precisely matter articulates itself. Secondly, the movement of his thought, although outward bound, away from a foundational consciousness and subjectivity and their alleged interiority, therefore also retains, however remotely, a distant affinity to this point of departure, so that it is never completely able to leave behind this original mooring. Thirdly, there is its indebtedness to a phenomenological problematic, a debt, it seems, of which it can never fully divest itself, because to do so would also mean to give up that which motivates it to pursue its course in the first place. Thus, to sum up, Merleau-Ponty's late thought tends towards a close approximation of the radical stance sustained throughout Nietzsche's writings, but in the end it retains a certain hidebound element by dint of the Cartesian framework which is still partially, distantly operative in it, as it is in the thought that it seeks to work through, namely Husserlian phenomenology.

Notes

¹ "[D]ieser Hass gegen das Menschliche, mehr noch gegen das Thierische, mehr noch gegen das Stoffliche,...dieses Verlangen hinweg aus allem Schein, Wechsel, Werden, Tod, Wunsch, Verlangen selbst – das Alles bedeutet...einen Willen zum Nichts, einen Widerwillen gegen das Leben, eine Auflehnung gegen die grundsätzlichsten Voraussetzungen des Lebens, aber es ist und bleibt ein *Wille!*" *(KSA* 5:412).

² "Gesetzt, daß 'die *Seele*' ein anziehender und geheimnisvoller Gedanke war, von dem sich die Philosophen mit Recht nur widerstrebend getrennt haben – vielleicht ist das, was sie nunmehr dagegen einzutauschen lernen, noch anziehender, noch geheimnisvoller. Der menschliche Leib, an dem die ganze fernste und nächste Vergangenheit alles organischen Werdens wieder lebendig und leibhaft wird, durch den hindurch, über den hinweg und hinaus ein ungeheurer unhörbarer Strom zu fließen scheint: der Leib ist der erstaunlichere Gedanke als die alte 'Seele'" *(WM* no. 659).

³ Here the following key instances of this come to mind: Hegel and the trope of the end of history; Heidegger's project of the "Destruktion" and investigation of the history of Western metaphysics to discover its unthought, his conceptions of the age of technology; Derrida's project of "deconstruction"; Irigaray's venture to trace the unthought feminine at the foundation of the texts of philosophy; Lyotard's attestations of post-modernity, etc., to name but a few of the most salient. What all these share, despite the differences between their projects, is a sense that there are tremendous, profound historical changes afoot, and that these call for a response in thought.

⁴ It is important to distinguish the term "Platonism" from the understanding of Plato's thought that emerges from a careful reading and examination of his works. By "Platonism" a certain schema of thought is meant that has been highly influential throughout the history of Western philosophy, and has been so not least because it has eschewed such a careful reading. "Platonism" is therefore something like a title for a tendency within philosophy or other attempts at thought, rather than to be strictly associated with the *texts* of Plato.

⁵ From *Birth of Tragedy* to *Ecce Homo*, whether in the more "incantatory" *Thus Spoke Zarathustra* or in the more quasi-systematically argued *Genealogy of Morals*. See also Gilles Deleuze, *Nietzsche and Philosophy*, trans. Hugh Tomlinson. London: Athlone Press, 1983, 87; as well as Michel Haar, *Nietzsche and Metaphysics*, trans. Michael Gendre. Albany: SUNY Press, 1996, 50, where Haar speaks of "the rehabilitation of the sensuous and of the living body".

⁶ The German phrase is "Umdrehung des Platonismus". Martin Heidegger, *Nietzsche*, 2 vols., 4th ed. Pfullingen: Neske, 1961; trans. David Farrell Krell. San Francisco: Harper & Row, 1991. See especially *Nietzsche* I, 151-61, 200-10.

⁷ The *locus classicus* for the nexus of issues to be outlined here is *Twilight of the Idols*, especially sections 1-7.

⁸ Hollingdale, in his translation, unaccountably omits the phrase translated here as "life itself forces us to posit values", which in German runs "das Leben selbst zwingt uns Werthe anzusetzen".

[9] This is how Merleau-Ponty generously characterises the Husserl of *Ideas* II and III, but I believe it more accurately describes Merleau-Ponty's own extension and intensification of Husserl's phenomenological project in the direction of a materially grounded phenomenology. Maurice Merleau-Ponty, "Le philosophe et son ombre" in *Signes*. Paris: Gallimard, 1960. Hereafter *Ss*. "The Philosopher and His Shadow", hereafter PS, in *Signs*, trans. Richard McCleary. Evanston, IL: Northwestern University Press, 1964. Hereafter *S*; 167.

[10] Roughly between 1870 and 1888, the last full year of lucidity for Nietzsche, given his breakdown on the 3rd of January 1889.

[11] It is thought that he was working on his late texts, especially "The Intertwining – The Chiasm" and "Eye and Mind", between 1959 and 1961, when he suddenly and prematurely died. Maurice Merleau-Ponty, *L'Œil et l'Esprit*. Paris: Gallimard, 1964. "Eye and Mind", hereafter EM, in *The Merleau-Ponty Aesthetics Reader – Philosophy and Painting*, ed. Galen Johnson. Evanston, IL.: Northwestern University Press, 1993. "L'entrelacs – le chiasme", hereafter EC, in *Le visible et l'invisible*, ed. C. Lefort. Paris: Gallimard, 1964. Hereafter *VL*. "The Intertwining – The Chiasm", hereafter IC, in *The Visible and the Invisible*., trans. Alphonso Lingis. Evanston, IL: Northwestern University Press, 1968. Hereafter *VI*.

[12] Maurice Merleau-Ponty, *Phenomenology of Perception*, trans. Colin Smith. London: Routledge, 1962.

[13] Although it falls outside the scope of the present enquiry to go further into this issue, we might speculate whether there is not a constant correlation between the extent to which Merleau-Ponty diverges from Husserl and the extent to which he approaches Nietzschean concerns.

[14] But then a more in-depth investigation of the shades of Merleau-Ponty's version of phenomenology, for instance as concerns the differences between its earlier and later articulations, would be required, but this falls outside the scope of the present paper.

[15] This should not be mistaken for a quasi-Hegelian thought of Spirit's progress towards self-realization, because in Nietzsche's account no overarching, controlling intelligence or agency is posited and there is no thought of (historical) progress, telos, or of a transcendent truth to be reached.

[16] See also *TI* 'The Problem of Socrates', sec.s 1 and 2, where Nietzsche identifies Socrates and Plato as such sick or, as he puts it there, "declining types" (*Niedergangstypen*) (*KSA* 6:67), and he diagnoses them as similarly physiologically degenerate because of their disparaging attitude to life (*KSA* 6:68f.).

[17] Here one is reminded of the psychologies, physiologies, and philosophies which are the object of Merleau-Ponty's critique in *Phenomenology of Perception*.

[18] This chapter, and specifically its central concept of "flesh", is considered so important that an entire volume of essays has been devoted to it. Fred Evans and Leonard Lawlor (eds.), *Chiasms – Merleau-Ponty's Notion of Flesh*. Albany: SUNY Press, 2000.

[19] See also PS in *S* 173, where he states that "The body is nothing less but nothing more than the condition of possibility of the thing" (*Ss* 282, t.m.). What is remarkable here is the use of the restrictive "but", with which Merleau-Ponty subtly indicates the as yet rather reserved stance of Husserl's thinking about the

body, even though he simultaneously unfolded it for phenomenological research –
this, incidentally, also being the point, as I see it, of PS.
[20] Edmund Husserl, *Ideen zu einer reinen Phänomenologie und phänomenologischen
Philosophie*. Zweites Buch. Den Haag: Martinus Nijhoff, 1952.
[21] One might speculate whether this approach is somewhat mediated by
Heidegger's reflections on (world and) the earth, most notably in "The Origin of
the Work of Art". As the opening paragraphs of PS also seem to suggest, perhaps
the later Merleau-Ponty's thought as a whole rather stands under the influence of
Heidegger, whilst at the same time pushing his project too, like that of Husserl, in a
more materially grounded direction.
[22] Plato, *Phaedrus*, trans. Walter Hamilton. Harmondsworth: Penguin, 1973. The
quotation as a whole runs as follows,

> Whole were we who celebrated that festival, unspotted by all the evils
> which awaited us in time to come, and whole and unspotted and changeless
> and serene were the objects revealed to us in the light of that mystic vision.
> Pure was the light and pure were we from the pollution of the walking
> sepulchre which we call a body, to which we are bound like an oyster to its
> shell.

[23] Arguably, Heidegger's sense of being formally achieves this, but it is hampered
by a certain nervousness (to put it mildly) it displays about the body and about
materiality. See, for instance, Martin Heidegger, *Seminare*. Gesamtausgabe Bd. 15,
2nd ed. Frankfurt a.M.: Klostermann, 2005, 236, Heidegger famously states, "Das
Leibphänomen ist das schwierigste Problem" ("The phenomenon of the body is the
most difficult problem").

NIETZSCHE IN DERRIDA'S
POLITICS OF FRIENDSHIP

DAVID FARRELL KRELL

Wo aber sind die Freunde?
—Friedrich Hölderlin, *Andenken*

"Nietzsche and phenomenology"? A sense of abashment and even chagrin accompanies the topic every time it is broached, and it is often broached. If phenomenology is the project of securing apodictic if not adequate *evidence* from acts of consciousness through eidetic and transcendental reductions, the reasons for this are clear enough, if not evident. There *is* a place for Nietzsche in Husserlian phenomenology, but that place is in the margins of, say, the time-consciousness lectures or the analyses of passive synthesis, where Husserl is wont to comment on his own work with phrases like this: *The problem with this description is that there is no such thing – it never happens this way.* One only has to read "On Truth and Lie in an Ultra-Moral Sense" (1873) and then the "Logos" article (1913), back-to-back, as a professor of mine back in college, Manfred Frings, forced us to do, in order to despair of thinking Nietzsche and Husserl together. (We never dreamt that Husserl could have neglected to *read* Nietzsche, just as in later years we could not believe that he had failed to confront Fichte and Schelling, to say nothing of Leibniz and Plato.) If Nietzsche's complaint with respect to philosophers is this lack of a sense of history, we know how matters stand with "Nietzsche and Husserl", even and especially the Husserl of the *Crisis* and the "Origins of Geometry".

Phenomenology is considerably larger than Husserl, however. Heidegger's existential-hermeneutical phenomenology brings Nietzsche out of the margins to centre page, particularly when it is a page on knowing as a founded mode of being in the world, on falling, on the anxiety that frustrates every effort to evade it, on our being as a temporalizing unfolding from one end, birth, to the equally ineluctable end, death – and in fact on every page where Heidegger labors over the fundamental methodological problem of access (*Zugang*) to the phenomena in question. If in later years Heidegger reportedly complains to Gadamer, "*Nietzsche hat mich kaputt gemacht!*" that is only because from time to time Heidegger confused himself with Hegel. Indeed, when we read the essays of the *second* volume of Heidegger's *Nietzsche* and his unpublished notes on Nietzsche from the late 1930s, which express the regret that Nietzsche is insufficiently *German,* we may upbraid our good European for not having made Heidegger *kaputt* enough. Even so, Pöggeler is right to say that a Sils-Maria wind blows through the *Beiträge* (1936-38); one may even venture to say that those wonderful mythopoeic essays of the 1950s ("Das Ding", "Bauen Wohnen Denken", "...Dichterisch wohnet der Mensch") are periodically cleansed of the piety that threatens to suffocate them precisely by that bracing wind.

And of Nietzsche and Merleau-Ponty what will we say? How little Merleau-Ponty writes of Nietzsche, how few the signs! The thinker of the body as alive and of the body's senses as more knowledgeable than our knowledge of them will ever be, the critic of high-altitude philosophy and of the retrospective illusion, the one who calls "eternity" a hypocritical sentiment – it is impossible to say whether we are describing Merleau-Ponty or Nietzsche here. In fact we are describing both. How lucky we are to have Merleau-Ponty's lectures on Schelling, yet how long do we have to wait before some young scholar discovers and excavates the lectures on Nietzsche, which surely are buried somewhere in the Bibliothèque Nationale?

If Husserl, Heidegger, and Merleau-Ponty belong to phenomenology, however, then it seems to me that we may also include under that rubric the author of *Voice and Phenomenon, Of Spirit,* and *Memoirs of the Blind*, who also happens to be the author of excellent books on Nietzsche. And so I will speak of Nietzsche in Derrida's *Politiques de l'amitié* (1994)[1].

Nietzsche figures large in Derrida's course of 1988-89, "Politics of Friendship", as in the resulting book. Although the sources of the seminar are many, from Plato, Aristotle, and Cicero to Jean-Luc Nancy and Maurice Blanchot, Nietzsche's reflections on friendship hold a special place in the seminar – the place, if it *is* a place, of interruption, inversion, and revolution. From the second to the tenth and final hours of the seminar Nietzsche is powerfully present, to the extent that one may say that *Politiques de l'amitié* is, among other things, the last of Derrida's

Nietzsche books, following upon *Éperons* (1978) and *Otobiographies* (1984).

As Derrida himself explains in the Preface to *Politics of Friendship,* the seminar and the resulting book are the culmination of many years' work, presented in seminars from 1983 to 1988, all under the rubric of "Philosophical Nationality and Nationalisms". Following this seminar on the politics of friendship are those from 1989 to 1993 devoted to the themes of "the secret" and "testimony". The Preface also tells us that Derrida opened each of the *séances* of 1988-89 with an apostrophe attributed by Diogenes Laertius to Aristotle but nowhere recorded in the latter's works, an exclamation repeated by countless philosophers through the ages, among them Montaigne and Nietzsche, in these words: *O mes amis, il n'y a nul amy!* "O my friends, there is no friend!". Almost all the authors treated in Derrida's seminar uttered or penned those remarkable words at one time or another, with one sort of inflection or another. The Preface also relates in the most cryptic and concentrated form the thesis of the book as a whole, which reportedly records no more than the opening *séance* of the seminar. (It must have gone on for quite a few hours.) The thesis is that friendship in Western philosophy is regularly defined in terms of the figure of the *brother,* producing a politics that is at once familial, fraternalist, and androcentric. Derrida suspects that political violence and political crime cannot be unrelated to this fraternity.

Without being able to do justice to the analyses of this text, which is some 340 book pages in length, let me try merely to state for each of its ten chapters the principal sources and the thesis – as though there were but one thesis per section, whereas we know that Derrida, an adroit juggler, always tosses multiple theses into the air all at once, so that the reader can hardly believe that they will be gotten in hand again. They always do return to his hands, to both of them, except when the juggler wants them to fly off and form a constellation on their own.

In chapter 1 the main sources are Montaigne's famous *Essai* "De l'amitié", Cicero's *Laelius de amicitia,* Aristotle's *Eudemian Ethics,* and Plato's *Lysis.* The thesis: an unavoidable mourning accompanies both friendship and politics, a regret or grief expressed in the exclamation *O mes amis, il n'y a nul amy!* For friends must stand the test of time, and there is not time enough for many such tried and true friends; to most of the "others" in our lives we will not give the time of day, much less the time for friendship. Even in a successful democratic society, if there is one, we therefore confront a double-bind,

> No democracy without respect for singularity or irreducible alterity, but no democracy without a 'community of friends' (*koina ta philon*), without the calculation of majorities based on stabilizable, representable, identifiable subjects who are equal among themselves. These two laws are irreducible to one another. They are tragically irreconcilable and they always lacerate. The wound itself gapes with the initial necessity of one's having to *count* one's friends, count the others, in an economy of what is ours, there where every other is altogether other. (*PA* 40, *PF* 22)

Chapter 2 has among its main sources Maurice Blanchot's *L'amitié* (1971) and *La communauté inavouable* (1988), along with Jean-Luc Nancy's *La communauté désœuvrée* (1982), and, before all of these, "the event that is signed 'Nietzsche'" (*PA* 56, n. 1, *PF* 47, n. 15), specifically, section 376 of Nietzsche's *Human, All Too Human* I, and sections one and two of *Beyond Good and Evil*, "On the Prejudices of Philosophers" and "The Free Spirit". The thesis: All those who today are avidly seeking genuine sociality and a new form of community will have to become, in Nietzsche's words, "jealous friends of *solitude* [*Einsamkeit*]" (*BGE* sec. 44, *KSA* 5:63, *PA* 54, *PF* 35).

Chapter 3 focuses once again on section 376 of *Human, All Too Human* I, "On Friends", which contains that famous apostrophe attributed to Aristotle, "O friends...", and which Nietzsche knows via the *Fables* of Jean-Pierre Claris de Florian (1755-1794)[2]. The thesis of Derrida's chapter, if it has one, has to be excavated from this remarkable text, which closes the section on "The Human Being in Traffic", or "The Human Being in Social Intercourse", *HAH* I, "*Der Mensch im Verkehr*", and which reads as follows,

> Consider merely your own case at some point or other: how different are the sensibilities, how disparate are the opinions even among the closest companions; just so, the identical opinions in the minds of your friends have an altogether different status or intensity [*Stellung oder Stärke*] than in yours; how hundredfold is the occasion to misunderstand, to flee one another on the most invidious terms. After all that you will say to yourself: how uncertain is the ground on which all our confederations and friendships rest, how close are chilly rain showers and bad storms, how lonely is each human being! [*...wie unsicher ist der Boden, auf dem all unsere Bündnisse und Freundschaften ruhen, wie nahe sind kalte Regengüsse oder böse Wetter, wie vereinsamt ist jeder Mensch!*]. If one

has this insight, and also understands that all opinions in their type and intensity among one's fellow human beings are every bit as necessary and unaccountable as their actions, then one gains an eye for the inner necessity of opinions as emanating from the ineluctable intertwining of character, occupation, talent, surroundings – and in this way he may perhaps rid himself or herself of the bitterness and acrimony in the sensibility of that wise man who cried, 'Friends, there are no friends!' ['*Freunde, es giebt keine Freunde!*']. He or she will far rather concede that, yes, there are friends, but it was their error and their being deceived about you that led them to you; and they must have learned silence [*Schweigen*] in order to remain your friend; for almost always these human relationships are based on the happenstance that one or other thing is never said, indeed, never touched on; if that pebble were to start to roll, the friendship would be dragged along in its wake and would shatter. Are there human beings who would not be mortally wounded were they to discover what their most trusted friends at bottom know about them? – To the extent that we know ourselves and view our very essence as an ever-transforming sphere of opinions and dispositions, so that we learn to take a dim view of it all, we bring ourselves into equilibrium with the others. It is true that we have good reasons to take a dim view of all our acquaintances, even the greatest of them; but just as valid reasons to turn this sensibility against ourselves. – And so we will want to hold out with one another, since, of course, we hold out with ourselves; and perhaps that more joyous hour will befall every one of us, when we can say:?

'Friends, there are no friends!' cried the moribund sage;
'Enemies, there is no enemy! – is what I cry, I, the living fool.'

[– *Und so wollen wir es mit einander aushalten, da wir es ja mit uns aushalten; und vielleicht kommt Jedem auch einmal die freudigere Stunde, wo er sagt:*

'*Freunde, es giebt keine Freunde!*' *so rief der sterbende Weise;*
'*Feinde, es giebt keinen Feind! – ruf' ich, der lebende Thor.*']
(*HAH* I, sec. 376, *KSA* 2:262f.)

This is the text that perhaps more than any other yields so much fruit for Derrida's reflections throughout *Politics of Friendship*.

The main sources of chapter 4 are Plato's *Menexenus,* Carl Schmitt's *Der Begriff des Politischen* (1932), and Nicole Loraux's essays and books on democracy and the status of women in ancient Athens. The thesis: Up to the present moment, every politics of friendship has been based on a belonging-together (*appartenance*) that invariably brings exclusions with it; according to Schmitt, every concept of the friend rests on an experience of the enemy – and not the other way around.

Chapter 5, "Of Absolute Enmity [*De l'hostilité absolue*]", has, again, Carl Schmitt as its main source, with references, however, to Walter Benjamin's "Kritik der Gewalt" and Martin Heidegger's *Sein und Zeit*. The thesis: Deconstruction must go to work on Carl Schmitt's principal concept, which Schmitt calls "a possibility in reality", *eine reale Möglichkeit,* and which he takes to be "the concrete", *das Konkrete;* the work of deconstruction must confront Schmitt's two principles, first, that the distinction between friend and foe has as its basis "the real possibility of physical liquidation [*die reale Möglichkeit der physischen Tötung*]" (*PA* 147, *PF* 124), and second, that war, if not the goal of politics, is nonetheless "the ever-present and really possible *presupposition* [of politics] [*die als reale Möglichkeit immer vorhandene* Voraussetzung [*der Politik*]]" (*PA* 149, *PF* 126).

Chapter 6 deals with Carl Schmitt's later writings, including his prison memoir, with reference back to Plato's *Lysis*. The thesis: Appurtenance, or *appartenance,* the German *Zugehörigkeit* or *Zusammengehörigkeit,* which since antiquity functions as the ground of the possibility of friendship, is perennially identified as brotherhood. Meant is not the brotherhood of male siblings within any given family, but what Schmitt calls a *Schwurbrüderschaft,* a sworn brotherhood. *Philia* is fraternization. Yet, to repeat, brotherhood is a matter of oath-taking, whereby the metaphor of fraternity as consanguinity seems to be in the blood, flowing from the pen as naturally as blood from the vein. Derrida wonders about the "naturalness" of the metaphor: why is it – supposedly a mere metaphor – omnipresent in Western philosophical discussions of friendship? A mini-thesis with regard to Schmitt's writings accompanies this chapter: You will look in vain in Schmitt's writings for a single reference to womankind, in vain for "*…une figure de femme, une silhouette féminine, et la moindre allusion à la différence sexuelle*" (*PA* 179, *PF* 156).

Chapter 7 has as its main sources, again, Cicero and Montaigne, though this time Montaigne in the company of his soul-brother Étienne de La Boétie, and Book IV of Augustine's *Confessions*. The thesis: Since antiquity, and through the Enlightenment in both France and Germany, the one who accompanies me as a friend (*celui qui m'accompagne*) is a male. Woman, and especially the wife, need to be and are excluded. Women, we and they are told, are *not yet ready* for friendship.

Chapter 8 has only one source, and it is Diogenes Laertius, whose attribution to Aristotle might in fact mean something quite different from what the tradition – from Cicero to Blanchot – has taken it to mean. It may be, some classicists argue, that the omega that opens the phrase *O my friends* does not at all indicate an apostrophe; rather, it is a dative-case personal pronoun, an omega with a rough breathing and an iota-subscript, not ὦ but ᾧ. The sense of Diogenes' attribution would then have to do with the specific problem of the number of one's friends, the fact that such a number must be very small, as small as one. Not *O my friends,* but, "*For him who has* multiple friends, there is no friend"[3]. Against the backdrop of this restriction and constriction, Derrida offers this thesis: To think about friendship is properly to think about what is other (*de l'autre*), and this is to think mortality as a mortal (*la pensée du mortel*). Perhaps in recollection of Lacan's parody of the Cartesian cogito in "L'instance de la lettre", Derrida writes, "...je pense, donc je pense l'autre: je pense, donc j'ai besoin de l'autre (pour penser): je pense, donc la possibilité de l'amitié se loge dans le mouvement de ma pensée en tant qu'il requiert, appelle, désire l'autre, la nécessité de l'autre, la cause de l'autre au cœur du *cogito*" (*PA* 252, *PF* 234).

Chapter 9 has as its main sources the historical literature surrounding the French Revolution (Edgar Quinet, Jules Michelet, and others), Heidegger's *Was ist das – die Philosophie?*, and Kant's *Metaphysik der Sitten*. The thesis: Liberty and equality are subsumed under fraternity, as sworn brotherhood. Kant too stresses the fact that friendship needs distance, not intimacy or tenderness (not *la tendresse, la douceur, die Zärtlichkeit*), which can only be a disturbance or an interruption to friendship (*Störung, Unterbrechung*).

Finally, chapter 10 has as its main sources texts of Kant, Ferenczi, Blanchot, and Michel Deguy – but above all Nietzsche's *Die fröhliche Wissenschaft* and *Also sprach Zarathustra*. The thesis: One must try in our time, for the sake of a democracy to come, to think and to practice a friendship without *phratrocentrisme,* which is the military equivalent of fraternity. The question remains, "...is it possible to think and to put to work a democracy that would preserve the old name 'democracy' while at the same time uprooting everything that all the figures of friendship (whether philosophical or religious) prescribe for it in terms of fraternity, which is to say, in terms of the family or of the androcentric *ethnos*?" (*PA* 339, *PF* 306).

What this list of sources and theses lacks, of course, is the alpha and omega of Derrida's book, namely, the nuanced reading and the infinite patience of his questioning. He objects to his own book that it is nothing more than a series of quotations – should one not, precisely in a text on friendship, make a sort of declaration, take a stand, speak out as an author? Naturally, when it comes to friendship one has to act, one has to move oneself and accept all the risks. Yet at the moment one wants to take a position and to formulate something about that move and its risks, the massive impact of a tradition is felt. One hopes with Foucault that there are moments of resistance at every stage of the history of the concept and the institution of friendship – little gaps that enable resistance and a certain freedom of expression. Derrida is clearly skeptical: he pleads for a long and detailed deconstruction of the leading concepts of friendship and politics alike. What a mere listing of his sources and theses fails to show is the thoroughness of Derrida's research, the seriousness of his deconstructive task, the modesty of his claims, and the brilliant intellect and the subtle humor that we encounter on every page of *Politiques de l'amitié*. Perhaps some of this injustice can be remedied if we take a closer look at Nietzsche's role or roles in Derrida's book, focusing on chapters 2, 3, and 10.

It is not surprising that Derrida's desire to think of *l'a-venir,* the to-come, should lead him to Nietzsche's "Philosophy of the Future", *Jenseits von Gut und Böse.* What is perhaps surprising is how much of Nietzsche's harshest rhetoric and how many of his hardest ideas – hard and heavy, we might say, thinking of Heidegger, that is, of those political ideas that still strike us as fraught with danger – Derrida is able to affirm and to think through. It is not difficult for Derrida to acknowledge and to embrace Nietzsche's insistence on the word *perhaps,* inasmuch as both the event and the to-come in general are imprevisible and, as Bloom under the heaventree of stars hung with humid nightblue fruit would add, *impredictable.* "Someone is sighing, a sage is dying perhaps", writes Derrida in his very first reference to section 367 of *Menschliches* (*PA* 44, *PF* 26). He then repeats that last word as a second, independent sentence, "Peut-être". (Derrida is clearly proud of these two verbs, *pouvoir* and *être,* these verbs of power and being, that come together and enact in French what the rest of us mutter adverbially in our *per-haps* or *viel-leicht,* although he does not go so far as to say that when speakers of German or English have to *think* they perforce lapse into French.) Derrida's messianicity-without-messianism is in fact contained in this *per-haps*: what arrives, what is haply to-come through the smallest portal, is itself the undecidability of everything we wish were already decided so that we might have, happily, nothing to decide. Derrida even wonders whether in some sense the *perhaps* precedes the "yes" or the *Zusage* that itself precedes all questioning. Or, if it is obtuse to speak of precedence, then, to realize that yes-saying always already affirms the *alea,* the chance of a *perhaps,* without which there is no future to affirm (*PA* 46, *PF* 28f.). More on this in a moment.

Nietzsche reverses the performative contradiction of "O my friends, there is no friend!" by invoking the enemy, and he is the first to do so in the tradition. As though in parody of the Christian commandment to love your enemies – love 'em to death, one might say – Nietzsche, as the vital fool, the fool of life that he is, cries, "O my enemies, there is no enemy!" Derrida says of this parody that it constitutes a "seismic revolution in the political concept of friendship that we have inherited" (*PA* 44, *PF* 27); one remembers Carl Schmitt's insistence that only if one has enemies to kill can one have friends to love. If there were no enemy, the Christian would have no Crusade and Schmitt no political relevance for the Age of Bush – which, they say, is now drawing to a close. A seismic revolution, to be sure, for those who rotate on the axis of evil. Nietzsche is in fact interrupting a long tradition of the politics of friendship, even if he continues to exclude women from friendship and politics, that is, as he admits, even if he has trouble with sisters, grandmothers, aunts, moms, and Lou – and, finally, even if all of these are Ariadne and thus, in a word, life. Nietzsche interrupts and inverts the tradition with his insistence that the fundamental belief of all metaphysicians, namely, that values are oppositional and exclusionary, self-identical and immune to their opposite, has crumbled (*BGE* I, sec. 2, *KSA* 5:16f). *Perhaps* philosophers in the past have forsworn their duty to doubt all; *perhaps* their value-estimations are "foreground estimates" from a "frog perspective"; *perhaps* the very opposite of every positively esteemed value "is in a fatal way related to, knotted together with, knitted into, and perhaps even essentially identical with" its opposite – "Perhaps!" (*BGE* I, sec. 2, *KSA* 5:17). And Nietzsche concludes,

Yet who is willing to bother with such hazardous perhapses! For this one must wait upon the arrival of a new species of philosopher, one that has some other, some inverted taste and proclivity [*umgekehrten Geschmack und Hang*] compared to the earlier ones – philosophers of the hazardous Perhaps in every conceivable way. – And to put it with all seriousness: I see such new philosophers on the rise. (*BGE* I, sec. 2, *KSA* 5:17)

Such philosophers, to repeat, are friends of solitude above all. By insisting on this, Derrida seems to be remonstrating ever so slightly with his friends who are writing constantly about community, if not about ethics and politics. The nostalgia for community and the precipitation with which one wants to institute community by talking about it are things that Nietzsche spent most of his time and ink warning us against. Yet Derrida remonstrates ever so slightly because he does not want to join in the ridicule that emanates from a familiar, well-protected corner – the ridicule of those "who believe they can hold out forever in the shadow of the Enlightenment" (*PA* 63, *PF* 42). He does not mention Habermas by name. Instead, he reflects on *why* community nowadays must be of those who have nothing in common, *why* community is *inavouable* and, like a pope, out of work. Nietzsche is the key figure in this reflection. On Nietzsche's idea of a community of new philosophers, the philosophers of the hazardous "perhaps", Derrida comments,

> Thus a community of anchorites announces itself, designed for those who love to keep their distance. The invitation comes to you from those who *love to split off and remain afar.* That isn't all they love, but they love the magnetism of love [*l'aimance*], they love to love, whether in love or in friendship, only on the condition of this retreat…They invite you to enter into this community of social disconnection [*déliaison sociale*], which is not necessarily a secret society, a conjuration, an occult participation in some esoteric or crypto-poetic knowledge.
> …But how, now?…Is this possible?
> Perhaps it is impossible. Precisely. Perhaps impossible, it is the only possible chance for something new to happen, for some new philosophy of innovation [*de quelque philosophie nouvelle de la nouveauté*]. Perhaps, perhaps in truth the *perhaps* still names this chance. Perhaps friendship, if there is such, ought to do right by what appears here to be impossible. (*PA* 54, *PF* 35f.)

Derrida pushes the sense of the *perhaps* quite far, rejoining the conversation he had with Françoise Dastur some years earlier. That discussion was about whether for Heidegger the question, *die Frage*, is pre-eminent for thinking. Dastur insisted, and Derrida had to concede, that for the later Heidegger a kind of affirmation must precede all questioning, in that one must say *yes* to the question – a *Zusage* or consent opens the way to questioning. Yet here in *Politics of Friendship,* to repeat, Derrida wonders whether the *perhaps* precedes all consent and affirmation (*PA* 58, *PF* 38). Why? Because even an originary affirmation, even a double-affirmation, "yes, yes", dare not be blind to its chances, which can always prove to be, as Derrida likes to say, *méchantes*. Every affirmation has to tack on to its most fervent wish the phrase *s'il y en a,* "if there is such a thing" (*PA* 59, *PF* 39). It is this hyperawareness of the *perhaps* that instigates those hard words that Nietzsche has in sections 43-44 of *Beyond Good and Evil* for the democracy and the "modern ideas" of his time. The new free spirits will have to be freer and hardier than ever before: *Härte, Gewaltsamkeit, Sklaverei, Gefahr auf der Gasse und im Herzen, Verborgenheit, Stoicismus, Versucherkunst und Teufelei jeder Art* – those are the requirements (*BGE* II, sec. 44, *KSA* 5:61). Nightowls and scarecrows alike, proud of their genealogical research and all its new categories, yet ready at a moment's notice to turn such research against itself. For all their hardness, therefore, the new philosophers have a delicate sensibility and an eminent vulnerability. In section 43 Nietzsche affirms that one can entertain great expectations only of those who heed their own abysses as they plumb the depths of things, only of those who possess certain tendernesses or vulnerabilities, *Zartheiten,* only of those who in the face of rare and fine things experience a *frisson* [*Schauder*] (*KSA* 5:60). Nietzsche believes he sees such new philosophers on the rise, but they scarcely form a pack or a flock or a majority, for all are "sworn and jealous friends of *solitude,* our own deepest solitude at darkest midnight and brightest noontide" (*BGE* II, sec. 44, *KSA* 5:63).

Yet Nietzsche's opening blow for the *perhaps* – that is, the conviction that there cannot be the to-come without ineluctable chance – is perhaps the strongest, and Derrida reverts to section 376 of *Human, All-Too-Human, I.* He focuses on the silence that friends must keep if they are to remain friends – Derrida is a great friend of the secret, even if there aren't any. His first remark is, "Friendship does not preserve silence; it is preserved by silence" (*PA* 71, *PF* 53). It is not that one practices deception with one's friends; it is that one grants and receives the vital silence so gladly. Derrida comments,

> The protection granted by this safeguard assures the truth of a friendship, its ambiguous truth, by which friends protect themselves from the error or the illusion that founds the friendship – more precisely, founds it on the foundation without foundation on which friendship is founded in order to resist its own abyss. To resist the vertigo or the revolution which causes it to turn on itself. Friendship is founded in truth to protect itself from the abyssal foundation or the without-foundation. (*PA* 71f., *PF* 53)

Nietzsche, the classicist, dignifies by its Latin name the silence that safeguards. Section 252 of *Human, All Too Human* II reads, "*Silentium.* – One dare not talk about one's friends: otherwise one blabs the feeling of friendship into oblivion" (*KSA* 2:489). Once again, it is not a matter of taciturnity vis-à-vis one's friends. Silence, remarks Derrida, "is nothing other than a certain manner of speaking: secret, discreet, discontinuous, aphoristic, elliptical, a stretch of time sufficient to avow the truth that one must hide, hiding it in order to save a life because it is mortal" (*PA* 72, *PF* 54).

And yet we are not free of the *perhaps* even here. For who can say whether we preserve silence in order to retain the comfort and avoid the fuss? How many stage-plays have been written about such noncommunication and cowardice! Yet there is no safety in confrontation, either: those who like to confront, who take their pleasure in their conception of self as one of candor, frankness, honesty, and courage, those who honor friendship only in the breach and never in the observance – perhaps they are never happier than when, like a god, they strike their disarmed friend in the back, playing Apollo to every Patroclus. Impossible to know in some general way. Derrida here remembers Husserl, who meets his *alter ego* with the not very confident modicum called "analogical appresentation" (*PA* 73, *PF* 54). Hard to be friends like that. Hard to be friends by pretending one can do more than that. "There is no solidarity between these two", comments Derrida; "they are solitary, but they ally themselves in silence upon the necessity of keeping quiet together, each one on his or her own side nonetheless" (*PA* 73, *PF* 54f). Such shared silence, *das miteinander Schweigen,* according to Derrida takes precedence over every form of *Zusammengehörigkeit.* The section that precedes the one we just heard says, "It is not how one soul approaches another, but rather how it takes distance from the other [*wie sie sich von ihr entfernt*], that enables us to acknowledge their affinity and their belonging together" (*HAH* II, sec. 251, *KSA* 2:489). Finally, silence often follows or initiates laughter, which is a way of saying what is not said. Derrida, "Silence among friends does not do without laughter, and laughter bares the teeth, as death does. And the worse it is the better it gets" (*PA* 74, *PF* 55).

And that, as we might suspect, brings Derrida back to one of the most persistent questions of his seminar and his book, namely, *qu'est-ce qu'une amie?* What does it mean to have "a woman friend", as our maiden aunts used to say? A number of the variants of section 2 of *Jenseits* show Nietzsche toying with the idea that is expressed in the Preface to his book, "Presupposing that truth is a woman…" (*BGE* 13, *KSA* 5:12). These texts on the one who gives herself out as…, but who is not as she seems, reminiscent not only of Schopenhauer but also of Kant's pragmatic *Anthropology*, preoccupied Derrida decades earlier in his *Spurs*. In *Politics of Friendship* the issue becomes even more intense. If the entire tradition, from Plato's *Lysis* to Nietzsche's *Zarathustra,* understands friendship as fraternization, what does it mean to fraternize, or to fraternize *with,* a woman? Molly Bloom is not the first – though she may be the last – who asks, "Why can't we remain friends over it?" By contrast, what does it mean when one turns the sister into a brother? Who *is* that famous woman who, according to a brotherhood she does not disquiet, can really be a pal, *just* a pal? What does it mean – to name a more serious case – when Heidegger suggests that by becoming a brother to Trakl's elusive stranger one thereby becomes a brother to the still more elusive sister, a brother to her of the lunar voice? One wishes that Derrida had gone to meet Irigaray, and Cixous as well, in *Politiques de l'amitié,* and especially that he had taken up Irigaray's notion of *la seule tendresse* (in *L'oubli de l'air chez Martin Heidegger).* For both Irigaray and Derrida, the future of friendship, if there is one, surely involves this crossing of friendship and all the sexes and genders, choices and inclinations, there can be. We pride ourselves on being there already, but perhaps we are nowhere yet. At all events, here is a final word, from Derrida, on the qualities of silence, "Not all silences are consonant. Each time the quality, the modality, the tonality of 'keeping quiet together' removes itself from the common measure" (*PA* 76, *PF* 57).

The lack of common measure affects the friends themselves, inasmuch as friendship is – *pace* Aristotle – forever asymmetrical and nonreciprocal, even if the friend reciprocates in every way (*PA* 82, *PF* 63). The logic of the gift applies above all to friends, and it is a logic of disproportion. Never one soul in two bodies, never fusion, never another self. All these trademarks of fraternal friendship go by the boards for that friendship to-come that is Derrida's fascination. We need, as Nietzsche says, "a new concept of *justice*" to understand the friendship of nonreciprocity in the age of the *perhaps* (*GS* IV, sec. 289, *KSA* 3:530; *PA* 83, *PF* 64). Why justice? If only because the usual concept of what one calls *amor* and *amicitia,* which reputedly make justice superfluous, often have to do with appropriation and possession. The final pages of chapter 3 are devoted to a close reading of section 14 of *The Gay Science, "All those things we call by the name* love". Herewith a few extracts, those on which Derrida focuses,

> *Avarice* and *love:* how differently we feel about these two words! – and yet it could be the same drive named twice, first condemned from the standpoint of those who already possess, in whom the drive has grown

more calm and who now fear for what they 'have'; then from the standpoint of the unsatisfied, the parched, and therefore hailed as 'good'. Our love of neighbor – is it not the compulsion for additional *property?* And equally so our love of knowledge, of truth, and every compulsion for novelty in general?...When we see someone suffering, we gladly take advantage of the opportunity to take possession of him...Love of the sexes betrays this compulsion for property most clearly, however: the lover wants to be the unconditional sole possessor of the person he yearns for; he wants to enjoy unconditional power over the soul as well as the body, he wants to be the sole beloved, wants to dwell alone in that other soul as supreme, as the most desirable, and he wants to rule in that soul...Here, obviously, the nonpossessors, the desirous ones, have determined the way we use language – there always were so many of them. Those who in this area were favored with magnificent possession and satisfaction often, it is true, dropped a word here and there about the 'raging daemon', as did that most lovable and best beloved of Athenians, Sophocles; but Eros always laughed at these blasphemers – they were always his greatest darlings anyway. – There is, to be sure, here and there on the earth a kind of extension of love by which that avaricious demand of two persons for one another vanishes in the face of a new craving and avarice, a *shared* and higher thirst for an ideal that stands over them: but who knows this love? Who has experienced it? Its right name is *friendship.* (*KSA* 3:386f.)

Cupid here appears under the guise of cupidity, and Derrida is driven to wonder whether everything that has gone under the name of love – or even friendship – has not involved the desire to appropriate, with all the envy, jealousy, and vengeance (instead of *Gerechtsein, Gerächtsein*) that accompanies such desire (*PA* 83, *PF* 64). One thinks of Sophocles' warnings concerning Eros (those lines of Dianeira's and of the chorus in *Trachiniai* and above all the fourth choral ode, or third stasimon, of *Antigone*), although Derrida does not offer a detailed analysis here. With every hope for something new, for something new *to come* with regard to friendship, the unsettling question-and-answer haunts us, "Yet another ruse? Yet another desire for appropriation?/ Yes. Yes, perhaps" (*PA* 84, *PF* 65). No event, no *a-venir,* without the absolutely undeterminable *perhaps* (*PA* 86, *PF* 67); no *decision,* which can be a decision only after it leaves all motives and rationalizations in its wake, without the aleatory *perhaps* (*PA* 87, *PF* 68). Given such a condition, where even the names of friend and foe are confounded by wisdom and foolishness, one can understand the desperate cry of William Blake to his former friend and current nemesis, Hayley, "Thy friendship oft has made my heart to ake/Do be my Enemy for Friendships sake" (*PA* 91, *PF* 72).

Chapter 10 begins with a reference to how short life is – something Derrida and I alike ought to be aware of by this time – and the effect such brevity has on our most stellar friendships. The chapter begins with Kant, Kant on woman, who through her *pudeur,* which is but a feigned virtue, can make men more virtuous than they might be, even though their virtue too is feigned, but maybe someday their shared counterfeit virtue will be traded in at the Bank of Righteousness for hard moral currency – legal tender, as it were. (Even those who account themselves no friend of Derrida have to be grateful for one thing: he has shown how terrifically funny Kant can be, whether writing of picture frames or the moral law, whether making reflective aesthetic judgments or demonstrating just how kinky the analogue of those starry heavens above us can be.) But the chapter soon turns to Nietzsche's *Zarathustra* and its passage "On the Friend", which opens as follows,

> 'There is always one too many around me' – that is what the hermit thinks. 'Always one times one – eventually that makes two'.
> I and Me are always too avidly in conversation: how could they hold out if it were not for a friend?
>
> For the hermit, the friend is always a third: the third is the bob that prevents the conversation of the two from sinking into the depths. (*KSA* 4:71)

This doubling of the isolated individual, such that the friend is always a third, enables Derrida to speculate that narcissism is always a dual relation, and therefore always jealous. Nietzsche's text "On the Friend" wants to interrupt "the jealous narcissism of the dual relation, which always remains enclosed between 'me' and 'me', 'I' and 'me', doing all it can to prevent the plunge into the abyss of a specular jealousy" (*PA* 307, *PF* 276). By addressing his "brothers", Zarathustra seems to continue the tradition of *phratrocentrisme* (*PA* 309, *PF* 278), yet it is his interruptive text, if one may put it this way, that will incite Derrida's recurrent question concerning "the interpretation and the experience of friendship in our culture". Derrida asks about "the *double exclusion* that one sees at work in all the grand ethico-politico-philosophical discourses on friendship, that is, on the one hand, the exclusion of friendship between women, and, on the other, the exclusion of friendship between a man and a woman" (*PA* 310, *PF* 278f.). To be sure, in the notorious passage "On the Friend" Zarathustra will deny three times that woman is "ready" for friendship. Always a *noch nicht,* whether in the Revolutionary discourse of Michelet or the sermons of *Zarathustra,* when it comes to women and friendship.

Perhaps the key is Zarathustra's insistence that brothers need to be prepared to be enemies, respected enemies, whereas woman can only be unjust and blind towards what she does not love. We know of course where Zarathustra's sermon is headed – namely, towards cats and birds and cows – and we are ready to cringe. Derrida does not shy from the passage, yet he notes the lines immediately following, which assert that *men too* are not yet capable of friendship: in this respect men and women are equal, equal in their capacity for avarice (*Geiz*), and equal in their incapacity to give and receive friendship. Zarathustra's sermon, in short, is a prayer to the future, a hope for the to-come of a friendship that would be new. This becomes clear in Zarathustra's commentary on "love of neighbor". Not *Nächsten-Liebe*, love of the near or close by, the *Nachbahr, Nah-gibur,* but love of the farthest-removed, *die Fernsten-Liebe,* is Zarathustra's object. If Nietzsche is here parodying Matthew 5:43-8, which enjoins love of one's enemies, Derrida is grateful for the parody, for it seems to forestall in some way Carl Schmitt's disastrous (and yet perhaps historically accurate) reading of the gospel: Schmitt distinguishes between *inimicus* and *hostis, ekhthrós* and *polémios,* the former a private or personal enemy, the second a public or national foe (*PA* 108-9, 317, *PF* 89, 285). Whereas Christianity requires us to love the former, Christendom has never hesitated to urge us to kill the latter, and Schmitt sees this as its saving grace, so to speak. The respect in which Zarathustra wants us to hold our enemies, however, is not murderous – that is the sense of Nietzsche's apostrophe of the living fool who says, "Enemies, there is no enemy". To love those who are at the greatest distance from us implies that there is no expected return, no reward for love. Friendship, for Zarathustra, is "a gift without return and without a salary", a gift given on the basis of "terrestrial finitude" (*PA* 318, *PF* 286). It is the gift of a world, but "a finite world" (*PA* 319, *PF* 287). The respect in which one embraces friend and enemy alike is itself spectral, not as a ghost of the past but as the future that Zarathustra calls the overman. Derrida cites these remarkable words from "On Love of Neighbor", "Higher than love of neighbor is love of the farthest and of what is to come [*die Liebe zum Fernsten und Künftigen*]; higher still than love of human being is love of things and love of specters [*die Liebe zu Sachen und Gespenstern*]" (*KSA* 4:77). Zarathustra adds, emphasizing the futurity of this ghost, "This specter that is running ahead of you, my brother, is more beautiful than you are; why not give him your flesh and your bones? But you are afraid, and you run to your neighbor" (*ibid.*). Perhaps the Nietzschean ideal of friendship is closest to that of the ancient Greeks: whereas autonomy and autarchy are highly esteemed Greek virtues, the commitments involved in profound friendship, even if they should imply a kind of surrender to the other, are still more highly esteemed. Indeed, for the ancient Greeks friendship is of inestimable value (*GS* sec. 61, *KSA* 3:425).

It would be another task altogether to show how the Nietzschean heritage marks the friendship – and the texts *on* friendship – of Bataille, Blanchot, and Lévinas. Yet these pages of *Politics of Friendship,* which are devoted to the task of "thinking and living the soft rigor of friendship" (*PA* 322-39, *PF* 290-305), are perhaps the most affirmative of the entire book. They emphasize the *who?* of friendship, as opposed to the *what?* They invoke the *interval* of friendship, which speaks *to* the friend but not *about* her or him. They evoke the mourning that accompanies friendship and the disastrous dissymmetry to which mortal friendship is heir, the nonreciprocity that caused Derrida to say many times, both at conferences and in private conversations, "Try to say this: 'We will see one another die'. Try to say it; it is the impossible sentence". A friendship without appropriation or appurtenance, without community – this is the challenge of the politics of friendship to come. Blanchot perhaps more than any other notes the impossible difficulty of such friendship, and I will close my account of chapter 10 with this attempt by Blanchot – almost entirely in the negative – to respond to the death of a friend,

...not the deepening of the separation, but its effacement; not the enlargement of the caesura, but its leveling, and the dissipation of this emptiness between us that used to allow for the unfolding candor of a relation without history. To the effect that what made us close not only ceases to approach us in the present but is lost to the truth of extreme remoteness...We can, in a word, remember. But our thinking knows that you don't remember: without memory, without thought, our thinking struggles already in the invisible, where everything collapses in indifference. There is its profound pain. Our thinking must accompany friendship into oblivion. (Blanchot, *L'Amitié,* 329; *PA* 328, *PF* 295)

Some scattered thoughts, by way of conclusion, about Nietzsche in Derrida's *Politiques de l'amitié*:
1. If Derrida loves above all those philosophers who are close to tears (Augustine, Rousseau, Nietzsche), those tears perhaps prove to be tears of condolence; among all the philosophers I can think of, Derrida and Nietzsche are the two whose condolences to friends are utterly remarkable. The collection of funeral orations edited by Michael Naas and Pascale-Anne Brault, *The Work of Mourning,* called in French *Chaque fois unique – la fin du monde,* "Unique Each Time – The End of the World", is

perhaps the best introduction we have to Jacques Derrida. Likewise, Nietzsche's letters to his grieving friends are extraordinarily tender as well as relentlessly intelligent. And there are entire correspondences – that with Erwin Rohde is perhaps the prime example – that are acts of mourning, namely, the mourning of an astral friendship that could not survive on Earth. Derrida selects Nietzsche's section on "astral friendship" for the exergue of his tenth and final chapter of *Politiques de l'amitié,*

> *Sternen-Freundschaft.* – We were friends and we became estranged. But that was right, and we don't want to hide it or obfuscate it as though we had to be ashamed of it. We are two ships, each with its own goal and its own route; our paths can cross and we can celebrate a feast together, as the two of us did – at that time our good ships lay at anchor so peacefully in the same harbor and under the same sun that it seemed they had reached their goal and their goal was one and the same. But then the all-powerful dominion of our tasks drove us apart again to different seas and different streaks of sunlight – perhaps we will see one another again, but we won't recognize one another: the different seas and suns will have changed us! That we had to be estranged from one another is the law that rules over us: on account of it we ought to become more estimable to ourselves! On account of it the thought of our former friendship ought to become more holy! Probably there is a vast, invisible curve and astral orbit that encompasses our so very different avenues and goals as though they were tiny stretches of the way – let us elevate ourselves to this thought! Yet our life is too short and our vision too weak to allow us to have been more, to have been friends in the sense defined by that sublime possibility. – And so we will want to believe in our astral friendship, even if on earth we had to be enemies to one another. (*GS* sec. 279, *KSA* 3:523f., *PA* 301, *PF* 271)

Friends were immensely important to Derrida, and though they seem to have been legion and devoted, there was an aura of loneliness about the philosopher, as though the outskirts of Paris were equivalent to "mountain heights" or even "astral" courses. As for Nietzsche's solitude, surely it is incomparable. When Overbeck sends him a birthday greeting in 1885, here is Nietzsche's reply,

> It was the only birthday greeting that anyone put to paper for me this year; – I thought about this fact of a forty-first birthday long and hard. It is also a kind of *result,* perhaps not in every respect a sad one, at least if one may grant oneself the right to say that the meaning of one's life has been staked on knowledge. To that pertains estrangement, isolation, and perhaps freezing. You will have had many occasions to observe that the scale of 'frosty feelings' is practically a specialty of mine by now: that comes of having lived so long 'in the heights', 'on mountaintops', or also, like the

outlaw, as free as a bird 'in the air'. One becomes sensitized to the smallest
sensation of warmth, increasingly so as time goes by – and oh, one is so
grateful for friendship, my dear old friend! (no. 636, *KSB* 7:101)

2. Such friendships were perhaps even more important to these two
thinkers than their most beloved ideas were. Recall Nietzsche's expressed
willingness to abandon every idea of his the moment he feels it might do
someone harm or cause grief. This was, often at least, not mere coyness or
disingenuousness on his part; it was because people were more important
to him. Even dead people. His letters to Cosima Wagner and Paul Deussen
in 1876-77 about the importance of Schopenhauer to him – a man he did
not know – show that such friendship extended even to specters of the
past. To Cosima he writes, "...even while I was writing about him I
noticed that I was already beyond all questions of dogma. For me, what
was important was the *human being*" (no. 581, *KSB* 5:210). Heidegger
chides Nietzsche for this tendency when it comes to the Presocratics:
whereas Nietzsche achieves a relation to the *personalities* of the ancient
Greeks, his translations of the fragments and his remarks on their *thinking,*
Heidegger says, are banal[4]. Heidegger surely took great pride in not
having or showing any interest in the people behind the ideas, since
philosophers merely live, work, and die – and it is the work alone that
survives. Derrida, for his part, was intrigued by the *and* of the universal
phrase, "life and work of x". Nietzsche always wanted to know why even
the most assiduous excavators at some crucial point and for very hidden
reasons, very personal reasons, put his or her spade aside and refuse to
inquire any farther. As for Derrida, it is impossible to conceive of the
seminar and the book in question without the background of his
friendships with Blanchot and Lévinas, Jean-Luc Nancy and Michel
Deguy, to name but a few.

3. In *Politiques de l'amitié* it is Nietzsche whom Derrida follows and
pursues – in the sense that he reads text after text by Nietzsche in order to
discover his own thoughts concerning friendship and the future. The
critical or deconstructive distance that Derrida shows when reading Plato's
Lysis or Aristotle's *Eudemian Ethics,* to say nothing of Carl Schmitt's *The
Concept of the Political,* is with Nietzsche radically reduced. If
deconstruction is an event that is always already occurring in the text
under examination, we may say that in Nietzsche's texts – particularly
those on friendship, which are many and varied – that deconstruction is
already well under way. One senses that Derrida joins forces with
Nietzsche with less reserve than he evinces elsewhere, even if the
fraternity of *Thus Spoke Zarathustra* still smacks of the tradition that

Derrida wants to overcome. Even to his brothers, Nietzsche is always good for surprises, and Derrida is always good for the reception of surprises.

4. To revert for a moment to those thinkers who are close to tears. There is to be sure a "hard" Nietzsche and a "hard" Derrida. There is the relentless genealogical critic and the equally relentless deconstructionist of genealogy. There is the Nietzsche who frightens students, who affirm, not knowing whom they are quoting, "This is dangerous, this is dynamite!" And there is what one frightened critic in a letter to me once called *la machine derridienne,* a machine, he felt, designed for the penal colony. And yet there is a very soft Derrida, and a soft Nietzsche. Yet when we remember what Nietzsche's best friends showed him (Overbeck both before and throughout the years of Nietzsche's deepening darkness) and what his best friends wrote of him (the incomparable testimonies of Meta von Salis and Resa von Schirnhofer) we need not be apologetic about Nietzsche's extraordinary humanity. Richard Ellman once said of James Joyce that if the author of *Ulysses* had known how very humane and humanistic his book was he would have been frightfully embarrassed, and one could say the same of Nietzsche. And what about Derrida? If you want to know what he was to his friends, read the book by Michael Naas called *Derrida From Now On*[5]. Or ask those who in spite of all the memorial journal issues and colloquia to which they were invited were unable to write or say a word. Perhaps that is one of those qualities or tonalities of silence that friends share. Derrida himself was fond of a line by Paul Celan that itself seems to have been written in response to Freud's "Mourning and Melancholia",

> *Die Welt ist fort, ich muss dich tragen.*
> The world's gone, I'll have to carry you.

Although Derrida does not mention it, that is Zarathustra's response, his response in deed to his very first friend, the fallen, shattered tightrope-walker, whom Zarathustra comforts then carries on his back until he finds a hospitable living sepulchre. Friend Derrida is gone – end of the world – and we look in vain today for a thinker who might be capable of carrying him.

Notes

[1] Jacques Derrida, *Politiques de l'amitié*. Paris: Éditions Galilée, 1994, hereafter *PA*; *Politics of Friendship*, trans. George Collins. London and New York: Verso, 1997, hereafter *PF*. All translations from the French, as also of the German texts, are my own.

[2] See *KSA* 14:144, n. 376.

[3] Diogenes Laertius, *Lives of the Eminent Philosophers*, I, trans. R.D. Hicks. Cambridge, MA and London: Harvard University Press, 1991; Book V, 21, 465.

[4] See Martin Heidegger, "Der Spruch des Anaximander" in *Holzwege*. Frankfurt a. M.: Klostermann, 1980, 319; trans. as "The Anaximander Fragment" by David Farrell Krell and Frank Capuzzi, in Martin Heidegger, *Early Greek Thinking*, 2nd ed. San Francisco: HarperCollins, 1984, 14.

[5] Michael Naas, *Derrida From Now On*. New York: Fordham University Press, 2008.

REVIVING "NATURAL RELIGION": NIETZSCHE AND BERGSON ON RELIGIOUS LIFE

JIM URPETH

The claims advanced in the following discussion both presuppose and elaborate upon the view that the trajectory of the "critique of metaphysics" inaugurated by Kant is only to be regarded as complete in the attempt to articulate a religion of the real. Critique, conceived as the project of the de-anthropomorphisation of thought and feeling, increasingly exposes the human organism to the latent intrinsic divinity of the real and thereby provides an opportunity to participate in reality's auto-apotheosis. This requires, I suggest, a rehabilitation and rethinking (in terms unrecognisable to, for instance, Hume and Kant) of "natural religion". In its post-critical guise "natural religion" is no longer the attempt to construct a "design argument" but the endeavour to articulate, in non-theistic terms, the religious propensities of the real itself without transcendent reference. The conception of the task of philosophy from this perspective is that of placing thought and feeling at the service of intrinsically divine tendencies within and of the real itself and thereby to reintegrate and re-orientate human intellectual and affective capacities to what might be termed (with apologies to Freud) the religious "primary narcissism" of the real. It is an underlying claim of the following reflections on aspects of Nietzsche's and Bergson's thought that it is only through the pursuit of such a trajectory of critique and affirmation that philosophy can reconfirm and revivify its hard-won independence from both theology and natural science and thereby sustain and radicalise its most exacting historical task, namely, the attainment of genuinely "disinterested" thought and a-subjective feeling, in short, metaphysics proper.

Although the focus of this piece are converging features of Nietzsche's and Bergson's thought, the wider project to which this discussion contributes – the articulation of a conception of "natural religion" without reference to "design" – draws upon many thinkers and perspectives. These include key figures in the "phenomenology of religion", particularly

Rudolf Otto and Mircea Eliade, alongside the pioneering work of William James before them. Indeed, I consider the way forward in this respect to consist in something of an "unholy alliance" of philosophical naturalism and phenomenology. However, whilst acknowledging the limited value of such generalisations, I have not found much of relevance to the project in question in the writings of those associated with the "theological turn" within phenomenology. Too many, it seems to me, "shadows of God" fall across the pages of many of those associated with the trend in question and too little by way of genealogical acuity or awareness is evident in relation to the specific religious traditions that tend to be privileged in the texts in question.

A deeper worry arises in this respect concerning the very possibility of the emergence of a "theological turn" in phenomenology. This is the suspicion that a lack of capacity and appetite for genealogical critique was the "Achilles' heel" of phenomenology from the outset, a factor at the source of its constitutional anti-naturalism (or neo-idealism) that always precluded the possibility of a naturalistic ontology of phenomenality or manifestation (in contrast to a phenomenological conception of the natural order). Crudely put, reluctance is often detected within the phenomenological tradition unequivocally to affirm the impersonal nature of the process of presencing as such and to make it the focus of a reorientated reverence. Perhaps a symptom of this reluctance to deify phenomenality *per se* is the dominant pathos of mourning and privation that marks so many writers in this vein as they reflect upon the "absence of the gods", suggesting that in some sense our age, compared to others, is not quite granted full "rights of access" as regards the disclosure of the real. In contrast, the thinkers to whom I am attracted, including Nietzsche and Bergson, embrace unambiguously the historic opportunities afforded to thought and feeling by the "death of God" and do not wish to linger at the wake any longer than propriety demands. They seek to explore and articulate, in a mood of barely concealed celebration, the now "open sea" of full-blown religious atheism aware that, for those of a non-moral disposition, the real presences with equal disclosive force in all epochs[1].

The reconceived "natural religion" advocated in what follows is unequivocally impersonal and atheistic. It proposes that the human organism interpret the "death of God" as the opportunity to explicitly orientate its worship to the now emergent essence of religion as manifest in the self-sufficient order of natural immanence in which the organism is immersed without remainder. The task of philosophy is to guide thought and feeling towards a participation in the primary process of creative becoming as and when this reasserts its ontological primordiality. Hence, in contrast to the secular-transcendental riposte made by Janicaud to the currently rampant "theological" appropriation of phenomenology, I propose that it be challenged from the perspective of a naturalistic and atheistic religious turn already to be found, I suggest, in the thought of Nietzsche and Bergson[2].

I.

Before discussing, in turn, aspects of Nietzsche's and Bergson's thought in relation to an attempt to articulate a notion of "natural religion" in terms of immanence and without reference to design, it is worth recalling and emphasising shared features of their respective philosophical problematics and their pertinence to the broader project sketched here. Arguably Nietzsche and Bergson develop the two most significant philosophical biologies elaborated thus far and, furthermore, both promote the claim that natural life is religious in essence[3]. Both thinkers persistently seek to affirm and prioritise the religious essence of natural life within their respective philosophical naturalisms. They also share a "monistic" (albeit non-reductive and pluralistic in expression) conception of life, Nietzsche in terms of "will to power", Bergson in terms of the "vital impetus" (*élan vital*). On the basis of these primary philosophico-biological principles, both Nietzsche and Bergson reject the presumed primacy of a functional-utilitarian (i.e., adaptative, passive-reactive) conception of life's inherent tendencies. They challenge the presumed primacy of "self-preservation" and endeavour to conceive life as, first and foremost, an active-creative process irreducible to the anthropomorphic categories of either causal determinism or teleology. It is noteworthy that both Nietzsche and Bergson are pioneers in explicitly taking issue, from a naturalistic perspective, with the philosophical and normative presuppositions they identify in Darwin (and historically related figures such as Spencer). Both are keenly aware that, if the underpinnings of Darwin's thought are illegitimately given primary ontological status, then access to the religious tendency of natural life would be blocked. Among the shared critical concerns in this respect are an insistence on life as an active "form-creating" force; the estimation of adaptation as a secondary process; the requirement to undertake a critique of empirical knowledge, including biology, that seeks to reintegrate it within a wider "theory of life"; an instrumentalist conception of the nature and role of empirical science, etc. Furthermore, both Nietzsche and Bergson emphasise the ontological primacy of time, and both the "will to power" and the "vital impulse" implicitly affirm the eternity of becoming. Here we refer, without claiming an equivalence, to the notions of "eternal recurrence" (Nietzsche) and "duration" (Bergson).

More contentiously, I take both Nietzsche and Bergson to be "non-cognitivists". That is to say, both thinkers assert the ontological primacy of affectivity, thereby viewing life as (both chronologically and ontologically) first and foremost "felt" and "lived" before it is conceived and thought. From such a philosophical perspective cognitive content is always derivative of extra-cognitive sources such that it is taken to be philosophically naïve to remain on the level of content and signification. Indeed, from such a philosophical viewpoint it is the ineliminably motivated and "interested" character of the cognitive-perceptual functions of the human organism, nowhere more operative and determining than in its scientific endeavour, which represents the main challenge to critical philosophy in its pursuit of a genuinely "disinterested" thinking. For both Nietzsche and Bergson (although admittedly more obviously so for the former) this "non-cognitivism" entails that the critical evaluation of a body of thought hastens to move beyond the assessment of the truth and consistency of its propositional content and presumed commitments on the order of reference to expose and interrogate the affective economy that constitutes it. Content (i.e., metaphysical structures, categories and propositional claims) is regarded as a symptom of affective essence which requires a psycho-physiological diagnosis rather than a rational-logical refutation.

Indeed, Nietzsche in effect signals an ultimate non-attachment to any specific content or categorical schema insofar as no such adherence necessarily guarantees what he takes to be the ultimate critical issue, namely, the quality of will underlying it[4]. If the decisive arguments in the *Genealogy* concerning the distinctions to be made between origin and purpose, process and meaning are recalled[5], it is clear that, for Nietzsche, no conceptual content comes with an in-built affective correlate (or *vice versa*) but remains, as with all phenomena, subject to the ongoing struggle of appropriating forces. Hence no conceptual-cognitive content is excluded from Nietzsche's most fundamental critical-evaluative question, "is it hunger or superabundance that has become creative here?" (*GSc* sec. 370, *KSA* 3:621, t.m.).

Jim Urpeth 189

Hence, both Nietzsche and Bergson conceive their respective philosophical-biological principles in affective terms. That is to say that both conceive life first and foremost as a qualitative process, an auto-affectivity of and within heterogeneous time without reference to quantification or objectification. Of necessity, due to the exigencies of practical and social existence, life has to be rendered capable of measurement but the magnitudes thereby generated tell us nothing, Nietzsche and Bergson insist, of life's temporal-affective nature.

For the philosophy of religion such "non-cognitivism" has fundamental consequences, not the least of which is an emphasis (appreciated, admittedly, by many phenomenological approaches in this area as well) on the primacy of "religious experience" and its underlying libidinal-affective determinants. For both Nietzsche and Bergson the "deification of existence" (*WP* no. 821) – life's own religious affirmation – is exclusively disclosed in and through the passions[6]. Indeed, it is to be identified *in toto* with such influxes of a-subjective affect. For both thinkers this auto-transfiguration of nature occurs as joy in an unqualified affirmation of all aspects of the real without remainder. It also forms the naturalistic basis of Nietzsche's and Bergson's critical-evaluative approach to specific organised religions, an assessment which focuses not on coherence and validity but on the quality of the sensibility expressed therein. In this regard we can think of Nietzsche's distinction between "healthy" and "sick" forms of religious sensibility and Bergson's contrast between "static" and "dynamic" religion.

Taken together, the broad affinities found between these two pre-eminent philosophical biologies form the basis of a suspicion shared by both Nietzsche and Bergson in relation to both anti-natural religions and (less generally recognised) anti-religious naturalisms. Both thinkers reject the predominant modern functionalist, socio-anthropological interpretation of religion and its implicit assumption that religion can claim no constitutive ontological status, that it is not part of the fabric of natural life itself; in short, that ultimately there is no "reality of the sacred", as religion is taken to have no basis in the nature of things independently of human need and weakness. From such a reductionist perspective, insofar as natural life is credited with any indigenous semiotic capacities at all, it is uncritically assumed that these could not take a religious form, the latter being exclusively a "projection" of an entirely anthropological origin[7]. The only contestable issue from such a viewpoint concerns the value of religion, whether it is an expression of human frailty that ought to be eradicated or, alternatively, the source of a positive framework of purpose and meaning[8]. In contrast to the, admittedly often strong, riposte made by many phenomenologically orientated thinkers to this secular-naturalist, reductionist consensus, Nietzsche and Bergson propound an alternative critique of it from the perspective of a non-reductive naturalism. I shall now turn to each of these thinkers separately to explicate further these general claims.

II.

I shall not rehearse here arguments I have made elsewhere by way of a contribution to the now quite widespread view that, despite superficial appearances to the contrary, Nietzsche is to be conceived as first and foremost a "religious thinker"[9]. Instead I shall address an initial, seemingly difficult *impasse* that strikes many readers of Nietzsche, including those who are otherwise sympathetic to the interpretative perspective sketched here. Taking *The Gay Science* as a prime example, the stumbling block in question concerns the often baffling conjunction within Nietzsche's text of, on the one hand, a supremely joyous affirmative religious celebration of life and, on the other hand, an uncompromising demand, unsurpassed in its radicality, that the project of "de-deification" be pursued to a hitherto unimagined extent (i.e., extended to the constitutive normativities of metaphysics, modern science and the values of secular humanism). It is a requirement of the interpretative stance promoted here that it demonstrate that far from any ultimate incompatibility arising between these two aspects of Nietzsche's text, they mutually support and entail each other and thereby exclude and undermine the credibility of alternative, ostensibly non-religious, responses to the "death of God" (in particular, humanism and scientific atheism).

In simple terms it is clear that, for Nietzsche, the realisation of critique involved in the project of "de-deification" is an essential pre-requisite to the "deification of existence". The former liquidates the transcendent God and its "shadows" (which include any exaggeration of the ontological status of natural science), which are dissolved to allow the auto-deification of the real to display itself. Indeed, the two processes, "de-deification" and the "religious affirmation of life" and the transition between them, are implicit in the first formulation of these themes in *The Gay Science*,

> When will all these shadows of God no longer darken us? When will we
> have completely de-deified [*entgöttlicht*] nature? When may we begin to

naturalize humanity with a pure, newly discovered, newly redeemed nature [*erlösten Natur*]? (*GSc* sec. 109, *KSA* 3:468f., t.m.)

Of course, Nietzsche assists our navigation of this move from "de-deification" to the "deification of existence" in his delimitation of the ontological reach of science[10], sharing with Bergson an instrumentalist conception of it. More significantly, however, is Nietzsche's clear rejection and critique of scientific atheism. Nietzsche seeks to wrest atheism away from science and reclaim it for religion which must also, of course, thereby undergo a process of "de-deification". Both *The Gay Science* and the *Genealogy* seek to establish the genealogical intimacy between Christianity and modern science, the shared constitutive values behind their mutually self-sustaining "opposition", their shared commitment to the "will to truth"[11]. This kinship precludes, for Nietzsche, the claim of science to offer the historically demanded alternative to the "ascetic ideal". This critique of the scientific form of atheism is clear in the following famous formulation,

> ...it is still a *metaphysical faith* upon which our faith in science rests – that even we knowers of today, we godless anti-metaphysicians, still take *our* fire, too, from the flame lit by the thousand-year old faith, the Christian faith... (*GSc* sec. 344, *KSA* 3:577[12])

In a similar vein Nietzsche inveighs against "pale atheists" (See *GM* III, sec. 24, *KSA* 5:398), criticising the self-delusion of their claim to have attained "free spirit" status and exposing their genealogical solidarity with their theistic "opponents" in relation to shared fundamental values (i.e., the "ascetic ideal" in its essence as the "unconditional will to truth"). Indeed, building towards his most audacious claim that modern science is essentially the auto-destructive consummation of Christianity, Nietzsche offers the following critique of atheism's mistaken self-image,

> Everywhere...that the spirit is...at work today...it now does without ideals entirely – the popular expression for this abstinence is 'atheism' – *except for its will to truth*. This will...this *remnant* of an ideal is...not so much its remnant as its *core*. Unconditional honest atheism...is...*not* in opposition to that ideal...it is the awe-inspiring *catastrophe* of a two thousand-year-discipline in truth, which in the end forbids itself the *lie involved in belief in God*. (*GM* III, sec. 27, *KSA* 5:409)

In short, for Nietzsche, scientific atheism is to be understood as a form of hyper-Christian moralism, "Christian morality itself...translated and sublimated into the scientific conscience, into intellectual cleanliness at any price" (*GSc* sec. 357, *KSA* 3:600[13], t.m.). Taken together, the passages cited support the claim that Nietzsche pursues the task of "de-deification" in order to affirm the religious essence of the real. For Nietzsche, scientific atheism pursues, in contrast, a superficial and incomplete form of de-deification as it is the covert "outwork" of Christianity, the last desperate expression of a profoundly anthropomorphic religion in its struggle against the indigenous divinity of the real. Scientific atheism is, for Nietzsche, the latest manifestation and contemporary acceptable face of the evaluative-affective appropriating force that, in defence of its anti-religious commitment to the "ascetic ideal" as the "will to truth", abandons the Church. Such a conception of the trajectory of Nietzsche's critical-affirmative project allows us to hear the genuinely religious fervour behind what can sometimes appear to be rather superficial rhetorical ploys in his struggle with Christianity. An example of this can be identified in Nietzsche's (admittedly somewhat desperate) yearning for the "*redeeming* human of the great love and contempt" who will, "bring home the *redemption* of this reality [*die Erlösung dieser Wirklichkeit*]: its redemption from the curse that the previous ideal placed upon it" (*GM* II, sec. 24, *KSA* 5:336).

A further significant feature of Nietzsche's thought is important to the basic task of locating and excavating the religious core of his critical endeavour. This is Nietzsche's distinctive and persistent rejection of the value of universalism, his questioning of its purported desirability and role as a socio-political and cultural "regulative ideal"[14]. For Nietzsche, universalism harmfully suppresses the reality of radically incommensurable "types of will", which he articulates in terms of the distinction between "nobility" and "slavery", underpinned by a conception of the contrast between "health" and "sickness", in turn conceived as the capacity for "affirmation" rather than "denial" of life. Nietzsche's cultural politics, at its most plausibly modest, simply makes a plea for some cultural breathing-space for the well-constituted, given the suffocating hegemony of moral or "herd" values.

This aspect of Nietzsche's thought is important here on two counts. Firstly, it confirms the possibility of demarcating "healthy" and "sick" forms of religious sensibility rather than identifying religion *per se* as a morbid phenomenon. Secondly, and to reiterate the ontological primacy Nietzsche accords to affectivity, the distinctions in question remind us that Nietzsche orientates all evaluation of religion away from an assessment of its categorical content as concerns its rationality and towards the clarification of the affective-libidinal sensibility that lies at its origin and essence, as well as towards its assessment in terms of the criteria of his philosophical biology. In effect, this concerns the sketching of different affective-libidinal phenomenologies of religious life reflecting contrasting "types of will". In this vein we find the extraordinary accounts given in the *Genealogy* of "sick" religiosity, the description of the libidinal economy of the "feeling of guilt" and account of its origin and historical development, the nature of the "ascetic priest" as the virtuosic, self-interested "physician" to the "sick" and, ultimately, the reflections on the source of the attractiveness to the human will of the "ascetic ideal"[15].

For Nietzsche, the ontological basis of the difference in libidinal-affective types under consideration here lies in the extent to which one's sensibility is claimed either by the interests of the individuated ego or by the transpersonal flow of non-individuated yet self-differentiating natural life within which the human organism is immersed without remainder. Nietzsche's "Dionysianism" simply records that his libidinal-affective economy predominantly belonged to trans-individual, rather than individuated, life and that, ultimately, he was, as determined by such a physiological tendency (within the politics of "his" organism) more invested in the infinite (self-differentiating life) rather than the finite (individuated life)[16]. Both Nietzsche's and Bergson's thought contains and presupposes the recognition of such a difference between, on the one hand, a trans-individual order of self-difference and relation and, on the other hand, a domain of individuation founded upon negation[17]. Only individuated life undergoes "death", as the trans-individual register is characterised by an "eternity" of impersonal self-difference. Both Nietzsche's and Bergson's atheistic religiosity moves within this difference and the experience of it.

A significant, albeit minority, seam of Nietzsche interpretation has always insisted on the importance, when reading Nietzsche, of being attuned to an all-pervasive current within his texts of a very specific "religious feeling" in response to life[18]. An affective register of joy, gratitude and affirmation that celebrates embodied life without transcendent appeal despite, indeed *on the basis of*, its indifference to the fate of the individual and refusal to reduce itself to the categories and principles of the human intellect. Nietzsche's texts have as their tonal-affective centre the expression of a joyously affirmative response to precisely those aspects of existence which, evaluated negatively by those lacking the capacity for their affirmation, lead to that rejection of the real Nietzsche exposes and interrogates relentlessly. This, fundamentally irreligious, denial of the real occurs, for Nietzsche, firstly, in the form of "Platonic-Christian" metaphysics and religion and, subsequently, in the form of modern science. It is the very conceivability of an alternative affective-libidinal religious response to the "negativity" of the real than that which generated the "Platonic-Christian" tradition which renders redundant the overwhelmingly predominant assumptions concerning the origins of religion as these are found in the dominant secular-naturalistic theories of religion – or at least punctures their claim to universality. Nietzsche's religious affirmation of the a-morality of life and its irreducibility to cognition, his celebration of its primary non-egoic violence and his desire to unite with it, requiring as it does, the disconnection from self-preservation and utility[19], are all characteristics of a religious attitude entirely missed by most modern theorists of the sources of religion[20].

Indisputably, Nietzsche's elaboration of a "healthy" religious sensibility is far less developed than his exhaustive exposition and critique of its alternative. Perhaps of necessity Nietzsche's texts are often frustratingly enigmatic and merely suggestive in this respect[21]. An example is Nietzsche's account of the "elevated mood" of the "healthy" type as "a perpetual movement between high and low and the feeling of high and low; a continual sense of ascending stairs and at the same time of resting on clouds" (*GSc* sec. 288, *KSA* 3:529). The general emotional tone is that of an out-pouring of joy in relation to life's inherent dysteleology, jubilation at the irresolvable a-symmetry between life and human cognitive capacities and psycho-physiological needs and weaknesses. This is a feeling of profound gratitude towards the immanent sublimity of life itself[22], and an affirmative response to the ultimate ethical challenge confronting the human will, namely "eternal recurrence", and the overcoming it demands of the will's endemic "revenge against time". These seem to be, for Nietzsche, the hallmarks of a "healthy" religious sensibility. Often Nietzsche evokes and develops a novel conception of "happiness" far removed from that presupposed in both "virtue ethics" and utilitarianism (although significantly closer to the former) and closely related to a feeling of superabundance. This is induced through a becoming one with a primary expenditure Nietzsche identifies within life or "will to power" itself, conceived as a movement of "self-overcoming". He writes in this respect of a "divine happiness full of power and love…a happiness which, like the sun in the evening, continually draws on its inexhaustible riches, giving them away and pouring them into the sea…" (*GSc* sec. 337, *KSA* 3: 565[23]).

III.

Arguably, Bergson pursues such a "de-deification of nature" to the degree demanded by Nietzsche. Furthermore, many of Bergson's texts are pervaded by a "religious" atmosphere, an aspect which becomes thematically explicit in his last major work, *The Two Sources of Morality and Religion*[24]. Taken together, these two key aspects of Bergson's thought indicate that, like Nietzsche's, it moves in the direction of a radically reconfigured conception of "natural religion"[25]. An indication of the shared critical-affirmative trajectory of Nietzsche's and Bergson's thought is evident in the latter's landmark article, "An Introduction to Metaphysics", in which the task of philosophy is identified with the pursuit of the transcendence of the "human" through an affirmative re-engagement with immanent nature towards the attainment of a more originary, non-transcendent, form of transcendence characteristic of natural immanence, a trajectory which is, I suggest, inherently "religious". Thus Bergson famously declares that "philosophy can only be an effort to transcend the human condition" (*IM* 55), which is aligned with the attainment of a "true empiricism" (*IM* 36), which in turn, it is suggested, is to be recognised as the "true metaphysics" (*IM* 37).

In his first major work, *Time and Free Will: An Essay on the Immediate Data of Consciousness*[26], Bergson introduces central themes of his thought which, whilst admittedly still confined to something like a transcendental phenomenology of consciousness, already bespeak an immanent "religious" orientation. Although it surpasses the scope of this piece to discuss this further, I claim that, at least when considered retrospectively from the viewpoint of the subsequent development of Bergson's thought, basic features of *Time and Free Will* are best interpreted as a preliminary attempt to complete both the "de-deification of nature" (i.e., the identification and displacement of anthropomorphic categories and normativities) and to articulate the "deification of existence" (the affirmative recognition of nature's intrinsic self-transcendence) that it precipitates. The remarkable distinction Bergson articulates between "two types of multiplicity"[27], through which a notion of difference prior to negation is recovered, and the elaboration of the notion of "duration" as constitutive of "lived", irreducibly qualitative, inner consciousness can be foregrounded in this respect[28].

Although sufficient argument cannot be provided here, I suggest that Bergson's conception of the ontological primacy of qualitative time, of "perpetual becoming", can be credibly identified with the "deification of existence". In this respect, the "divine" simply is the ontologically constitutive process of "succession without externality" (*TFW* 63). God simply is, from this perspective, an impersonal "confused multiplicity" (*TFW* 54, 73), an ontological process of permeation (*TFW* 59-61). As an intrinsically "lived" process this implicit conception of the "divine" beyond "onto-theology" is inherently elusive and irreducible to the instrumental concerns and orientation of the human intellect driven, as it is, by an "insatiable desire to separate" (*TFW* 72), that culminates in the entirely anthropomorphic notion of a transcendent God. Bergson's early work invites us to contrast the genuinely temporal God of "confused multiplicity" with the (as anthropomorphic) more familiar, ontologically derivative, spatio-geometric God of "discrete multiplicity"[29].

Indisputably the "religious" Bergson posited here only begins to emerge, more or less explicitly, in his *magnum opus*, namely, *Creative Evolution*[30]. This text completes, in effect, the "de-deification of nature" project through the articulation of a radical conception of time as ontological force within the context of a philosophical naturalism in which Bergson offers his conception of enduring life, "a philosophy which sees in duration the very stuff of reality...to show that *a self-sufficient reality is not necessarily a reality foreign to duration*" (*CE* 272, 298). Among the many themes in *Creative Evolution* of relevance to the claims of this piece the following can be highlighted. Firstly, Bergson repeatedly focuses on and endeavours to articulate the interface between the movement of life itself and its utilitarian translation into "human experience"[31]. Bergson refers to this moment of transition and self-surpassing in which the human organism, uniquely it seems, gains access to the nature of the real as the "indistinct fringe" (*une frange indécise*) (*CE* 46). In effect, this is a "religious" theme which marks the advent of an awareness of the impersonal immensity of durational life within which the "human" occurs and from which it is not debarred because, as a living organism itself, it is a part of the real (*CE* xii). It is noteworthy that, in effect, Bergson here credits the human organism with a capacity for "disinterested" thought and feeling[32]. Secondly, by way of a partial justification of the proposed "religious" reading of Bergson suggested here, evidence will be offered of a "poetic" dimension of *Creative Evolution*, in which what Nietzsche refers to as the "religious affirmation of life" wells up, culminating in one of the stranger definitions of "God" in the literature. In contrast, the equivalent in *Creative Evolution* of Nietzsche's motif of the "death of God" is, perhaps, Bergson's persistent attack on the credibility of the notion of a "superhuman intellect" (*CE* 8) for whom "*All is given*" (*CE* 345[33]), such that time is, ultimately, ontologically inconsequential, merely an inconvenient mark of finitude. As if time did not contribute substantively to the being of living things and was not the source of the perpetual creation of new and unforeseeable forms, the font of novelty.

The notion of the "indistinct fringe" marks the point at which Bergson seeks to return evolutionary biology into its forgotten condition of possibility – the ontological order of durational life itself. This is the move from a thinking (evolutionary biology) derived from and limited to the utilitarian concerns of the human species to a disinterested mode of thought reconnected to the generative source of thinking itself. This is a "religious" trajectory that seeks to reintegrate thought and feeling into creative life itself and to allow itself to become a vessel of its more primordial processes. The necessarily half-hearted naturalism of evolutionary biology is surpassed by a more uncompromising affirmation of the natural order, in principle beyond the reach of science. Bergson's direction of travel in *Creative Evolution* here is always only immanent. With Nietzsche he shares the view that thought becomes *more* anthropomorphic the more it aspires to the transcendent and that it becomes religious to the extent it affirms and radicalises its naturalism. The movement of critique within *Creative Evolution* can be conceived as the destruction of two related reductionisms (empirical science and transcendent religion) and the emergence in their place of an anti-reductionist, religious naturalism. This movement seems to be indicated in the following passages,

> We do not *think* real time. But we *live* it, because life transcends intellect. The feeling we have...of the evolution of all things in pure duration is there, forming around the intellectual concept...an indistinct fringe...Mechanism and finalism agree in taking account only of the bright nucleus shining in the centre. They forget that this nucleus has been formed out of the rest by condensation, and that the whole must be used...to grasp the inner movement of life.
> ...if the fringe exists,...it should have more importance for philosophy than the bright nucleus it surrounds.
> ...what can this useless fringe be, if not that part of the evolving principle which has not shrunk to the peculiar form of our organization...? It is there,...that we must look...to expand the intellectual form of our thought; from there shall we derive the impetus necessary to lift us above ourselves. (*CE* 46, 49[34])

A "disinterestedness" is evoked here which, unlike the transcendent orientation of its Kantian predecessor, is aligned with an ever-increasing immersion in immanent nature towards the "coincidence of human consciousness with the living principle whence it emanates" (*CE* 369f). I shall conclude this brief identification of relevant themes from *Creative Evolution* by citing some passages in which the renaturalisation of the human organism into the durational whole of life assumes a decidedly religious tone,

> Like eddies of dust raised by the wind as it passes, the living turn upon themselves, borne up by the great blast of life. They...counterfeit immobility so well that we treat each of them as a *thing* rather than as a *progress*, forgetting that the very permanence of their form is only the outline of a movement. At times, however, in a fleeting vision, the invisible breath that bears them is materialized before our eyes...a glimpse of the fact that the living being is above all a thoroughfare, and that the essence of life is in the movement by which life is transmitted. (*CE* 128)

In a similar vein,

> Yet a beneficent fluid bathes us, whence we draw the very force to labor and to live. From this ocean of life, in which we are immersed, we are continually drawing something, and we feel that our being, or at least the intellect that guides it, has been formed therein by a kind of local concentration. Philosophy can only be an effort to dissolve again into the Whole...by expanding the humanity in us and making us even transcend it. (*CE* 191f.)

Here we see, I would suggest, the same movement of critical-affirmative thought as that undertaken by Nietzsche, an overcoming of the human conceived as the critique of the transcendent or "moral" (i.e., unmasked as merely utilitarian) conception of transcendence in favour of its immanent form, a "this-worldly", naturalistic transcendence in which nature intensifies rather than escapes itself. Nature, conceived as creative evolution, is an incessant becoming or self-transcendence, "what is admirable *in itself*, what really deserves to provoke wonder, is the ever-renewed creation which reality, whole and undivided, accomplishes in advancing" (*CE* 217). On this basis, Bergson offers the following conception of "God",

> I speak of a centre from which worlds shoot out like rockets in a fire-works display – provided, however, that I do not present this centre as a *thing*, but as a continuity of shooting out. God thus defined, has nothing of the already made; He is unceasing life, action, freedom. (*CE* 248)

God is here the term for an impersonal "power of creation" (*CE* 217). Bergson does not, like many of those within the "theological turn" school of phenomenology, offer to theology the resources of a radical temporal ontology of natural life to enable the development of a more sophisticated conception of a transcendent deity. Instead, Bergson proposes that we reorientate our devotional feelings towards the deification of duration itself, the creative passage of impersonal time.

IV.

Bergson's *The Two Sources of Morality and Religion* contains many themes relevant to the concerns of this discussion. The non-reductive character of Bergson's discussion of morality and religion in his final major work follows from the fact that it represents an extension to the moral, religious and socio-political domains of the naturalistic ontology of *Creative Evolution*. Bergson introduces contrasts between "open" and "closed" forms of morality and "dynamic" and "static" forms of religion, with the second of each pair referring to the biological formation and maintenance of stable societies, the first of each pair to their growth and progress. These distinctions recall Nietzsche's contrast between "species-preserving and species-enhancing" (*GSc* sec. 318, *KSA* 3:550) values and forces, where the ontological primacy of the latter is asserted.

Minimally, Nietzsche and Bergson share a conception of the biologically-grounded nature of religion in a primary sense. Neither thinker pursues (at least not in relation to "healthy" or "dynamic" religion, respectively) a reductionist explanation of it in non-religious terms. Neither Nietzsche nor Bergson assumes the primacy of a merely "survivalist" or "functionalist" tendency within nature and thus they reject the reductionist explanations of the origin and role of religion (*per se*) that often characterise accounts of it offered by evolutionary biologists. Rather, both thinkers seek to identify a becoming-religious of the real itself, a self-affirmation which takes place as a specific type of autonomous, ontological affectivity implanted in exceptional members of one of its creative experiments – the human organism.

This perspective presupposes the credibility of an order of emotion that has ontological status and is thus not a merely subjective feeling arising in response to, and therefore dependent on and subsidiary to, an object. This possibility (doubtless initiated in its modern form in Kant's insistence on an order of transcendental affectivity) is implicit in Nietzsche's and

Bergson's shared conception of the real as, in essence, a qualitative becoming. Bergson offers an extended and impressive theory and phenomenology of ontological emotion in *Two Sources*[35]. A shared conception of "God" can be detected here as both thinkers identify the divine as a specific type (rather than merely a product) of a-subjective "desire flow" through and as which the "will to power" or "élan vital", respectively, manifest and reaffirm themselves. As Bergson states, "divine love is not a thing of God: it is God Himself" (*TSMR* 252[36]).

In this context, in which God is identified as natural life's *Grundstimmug*, both Nietzsche and Bergson accord "mysticism" pride of place[37]. Bergson seeks to conceive mysticism in "relation to the vital impulse…it is this impulse itself, communicated to exceptional individuals who in turn would fain impart it to all humanity" (*TSMR* 213). This further underlines Bergson's view of the intrinsically religious nature of reality. As he states, "the ultimate end of mysticism is the establishment of a contact…a partial coincidence, with the creative effort which life itself manifests. This effort is of God, if it is not God himself" (*TSMR* 220[38]). Indeed, in the following passage, Bergson offers a formulation of the trajectory of his thought, culminating in the discussion of mysticism,

> For this intuition was turned inward; and if, in a first intensification, beyond which most of us did not go, it made us realise the continuity of our inner life, a deeper intensification might carry it to the roots of our being, and thus to the principle of life in general. Now is not this the privilege of the mystic soul? (*TSMR* 250[39])

As for Nietzsche, for Bergson, the ontological affect in question here is joy[40], and he offers a sustained phenomenology of its development[41] towards the attainment of the condition of "complete mysticism" (*TSMR* 231), characterised as "an unmixed joy, lying beyond pleasure and pain" (*TSMR* 261). The watchwords in this non-reductive renaturalisation of mysticism are "energy" and "vitality". For Bergson, mystics "represent a vast expenditure of energy…the superabundance of vitality…flows from a spring which is the very source of life…God, Who is this energy itself" (*TSMR* 237, 257[42]). Again it is apparent that, for Bergson, "God" is not simply the supreme object of the mystic's desire but is rather, *in toto*, the very inundation of a-subjective energy and affectivity itself[43]. This conception of mysticism as the very creative becoming of life itself, and particularly Bergson's privileging of Christian mysticism[44] raises, in comparison with Nietzsche, the diagnostic question concerning the aetiology of mystical states and "religious experience" more generally.

Whilst admittedly Bergson does not explore this issue with anything like Nietzsche's tenacity and suspicion, he does address the issue and indicates due critical restraint[45]. However, like Nietzsche, Bergson insists on demarcating a non-morbid form of mysticism in which "there is an exceptional, deep-rooted mental healthiness" (*TSMR* 228[46]).

It is important to note the extent to which Bergson implicitly reasserts throughout *Two Sources* an essential feature of the reconceived "natural religion" suggested throughout this discussion. This is the claim that there is a universal origin and source of religion intrinsic to natural life, in principle available to all independently of organised religion, which specific religions affirm to varying degrees. Bergson formulates this point thus,

> ...an original content, drawn straight from the very well-spring of religion, independent of all that religion owes to tradition, to theology, to the Churches...philosophy...must confine itself to experience and inference... it would suffice to take mysticism unalloyed, apart from the visions, the allegories, the theological language which express it, to make it a powerful helpmeet to philosophical research...We must then find out in what measure mystic experience is a continuation of the experience which led us to the doctrine of the vital impetus. All the information with which it would furnish philosophy, philosophy would repay in the shape of confirmation. (*TSMR* 250f.[47])

Bergson concludes his text with a very striking formulation, again implicitly radicalising the notion of "natural religion" that inverts the trajectory of the "design argument" and underlines the extent to which his thinking, like Nietzsche's before him, surpasses the banal terms of the debates between "intelligent design" and evolutionary biology. Both thinkers enable us to recognise such an "opposition" as essentially a dispute between two forms of neurosis concerning nature's primal religious dysteleology. As Bergson states, "...the essential function of the universe...a machine for the making of gods" (*TSMR* 317[48]).

Notes

[1] These comments evoke themes in Nietzsche's *The Gay Science* sec.s 343, 374.

[2] I refer here to Dominic Janicaud, "The Theological Turn of French Phenomenology" in *Phenomenology and the 'Theological Turn'*. New York: Fordham University Press, 2000, 16-103.

[3] By "philosophical biologies" I am referring to the prominent role in both Nietzsche's and Bergson's thought of the notion of ☐life and to the sense in which,

for both, this is not to be read as a contribution to an empirical natural science but as a philosophical reflection able to include the categories and implicit values of any empirical biological theory within its critical evaluation of all cultural phenomena.
[4] For a clear statement of Nietzsche's ultimate indifference to cognitive content, extended even to the prioritisation of becoming over being, see *GSc* sec. 370.
[5] See Friedrich Nietzsche, *On the Genealogy of Morality*, trans. Maudemarie Clark and Alan Swenson. Indianapolis: Hackett, 1998, hereafter *GM* II, sec.s 12f.
[6] These comments draw upon *WP* no. 1052.
[7] The philosophical perspective elaborated here presupposes the overcoming of the "fact/value" and "meaning/meaningless-ness" distinctions and all idealist proprietorial claims to the source of meaning.
[8] This issue could be said to circumscribe the parameters of the critical debate concerning the nature and value of religion as found in Hume, Feuerbach, Marx, James and Freud.
[9] For a statement of how I interpret this interpretative stance see, Jim Urpeth, "'Health' and 'Sickness' in Religious Affectivity: Nietzsche, Otto and Bataille" in John Lippitt and Jim Urpeth (eds.), *Nietzsche and the Divine*. Manchester: Clinamen Press, 2000, 226-51. Other examples of the trend in question, offering a range of alternative conceptions of it, include Bruce Ellis Benson, *Pious Nietzsche: Decadence and Dionysian Faith*. Indiana: Indiana University Press, 2008; Giles Fraser, *Redeeming Nietzsche: On the Piety of Unbelief*. London: Routledge, 2002; Tim Murphy, *Nietzsche, Metaphor, Religion*. Albany, NY: SUNY Press, 2001; and Tyler Roberts, *Contesting Spirit: Nietzsche, Affirmation, Religion*. Princeton: Princeton University Press, 1998.
[10] See *GSc* sec.s 112, 373.
[11] See *GSc* sec.s 344, 347, 357; *GM*, III, sec.s 23-25, 27.
[12] Cited in *GM* III, sec. 24, *KSA* 5:400f.
[13] Cited *GM* III, sec. 27, *KSA* 5:409f.
[14] *In extremis*, Nietzsche sometimes (e.g., *GM* III, sec. 14) seems to be drawn towards a policy of strict segregation in order to ensure the future viability of the "health" of the human species.
[15] See *GM* II and III *passim*.
[16] Appeal is hereby made to the introduction ("Finite and Infinite Life in the Greek Language") of Carl Kerényi's seminal study, *Dionysus: Archetypal Image of Indestructible Life*. Princeton: Princeton University Press, 1976, xxxi-xxxvii. Kerényi reflects upon the significance of there being two different words for "life" in Greek. On the basis of Kerényi's argument it might be possible to suggest a "vitalogical difference" (perhaps as an alternative to more familiar varieties, "ontological", "différance" etc.) concerning the co-dependent relation between, on the one hand, life (*zoë*) as non-individuated self-difference and, on the other hand, life as individuated or "characterised" (*bios*). This is an irresolvable relation within which non-individuated life maintains a finite priority over all individuated organisms.

[17] For evidence of this in Bergson see Henri Bergson, *An Introduction to Metaphysics*, trans. Thomas Ernest Hulme. Indianapolis: Hackett, 1999, 49, hereafter *IM*.
[18] Examples of the interpretative strand in question include Henri Birault, "Beatitude in Nietzsche" in David B. Allison (ed.), *The New Nietzsche*. Cambridge, MA: MIT Press, 1985, 219-31; and Clement Rosset, *Joyful Cruelty: Towards a Philosophy of the Real*. Oxford: Oxford University Press, 1993. Whilst Rosset's text as a whole is highly recommended, the chapter "Notes on Nietzsche" (*ibid.*, 22-69) is of particular relevance here.
[19] See *GSc* sec. 318. A further important statement of the basic contrast between affective-libidinal types and their respective religious sensibilities concerns Nietzsche's distinction between "romantic" and "Dionysian" forms of pessimism as formulated in *GSc* sec. 370.
[20] A notable exception is, of course, Georges Bataille, who articulates a fundamentally "Nietzschean" religious sensibility and elaborates a critique of religion that recognises the affirmation/denial distinction (both between and within specific religions) in numerous works, but perhaps most notably in *Inner Experience*, trans. Leslie Anne Boldt. Albany, NY: SUNY Press, 1988; *Theory of Religion*, trans. Robert Hurley. New York: Zone Books, 1992; and *Eroticism*, trans. Mary Dalwood. London: Marion Boyars, 1987.
[21] See *GSc* sec. 346.
[22] See *GSc* sec.s 343, 382.
[23] See also *GSc* sec.s 338, 382.
[24] Henri Bergson, *The Two Sources of Morality and Religion*, trans. R. Ashley Audra and Cloudesley Brereton. Notre Dame, IN: University of Notre Dame Press, 1977, hereafter *TSMR*.
[25] Bergson explicitly expresses an affinity with the notion of "natural religion" but decides against its positive incorporation (at least in relation to "static" religion) into his vocabulary given the burden of its received meaning (see *TSMR* 205, 207, 222). For Bergson's avowal of the empiricist philosophical ethos underpinning the notion of "natural religion", see *TSMR* 250.
[26] Henri Bergson, *Time and Free Will: An Essay on the Immediate Data of Consciousness*, trans. Frank Lubecki Pogson. New York: Dover Publications, 2001, hereafter *TFW*.
[27] See *TFW*, 53, 69, 72.
[28] For statements of Bergson's conception of temporal consciousness as inherently processional and qualitative, see also *TFW* 13, 61, 63, 69, 73.
[29] We shall not include here a discussion of how the "religious" interpretative perspective I am proposing for Bergson's thought applies to his second major work, *Matter and Memory*, trans. N.M. Paul and W.S. Palmer. New York: Zone Books, 1991, hereafter *MM*. This work is of course crucial in the overall development of Bergson's thought in terms of its "ontologising" of the notions from *TFW* discussed above. This is apparent in the notion of the "continuity of the real" (*MM* 165) and claim concerning a "continuity of becoming which is reality itself" (*MM* 139).

[30] Henri Bergson, *Creative Evolution*, trans. Arthur Mitchell. Mineola, NY: Dover Publications, 1998, hereafter *CE*.

[31] See *CE* 237f. This aspect of *CE* deepens the reflection on what in *MM* had been referred to as the "turn of experience" (*MM* 184). This, and other topics discussed in this section, would ultimately require an account of Bergson's key notion of "intuition" and the "method" he associates with it. This task cannot be undertaken here.

[32] See *CE* 159, 176ff., 255, 274, 343. At one point Bergson identifies such a capacity with the "duty of philosophy" (*CE* 196).

[33] See also *CE* 37, 196.

[34] See also *CE* xiif.

[35] See *TSMR* 38-54.

[36] See also *TSMR* 53, 253, 268f.

[37] In this respect it worth noting the pioneering, and still very stimulating, sympathetic discussion of this aspect of Nietzsche's and Bergson's thought offered by Evelyn Underhill in her seminal 1911 study, *Mysticism: The Nature and Development of Spiritual Consciousness*. Oxford: One World Publishers, 1993. See especially, ch. II, "Mysticism and Vitalism", *ibid.*, 26-43. Underhill underlines (*ibid.*, "Note to the Twelfth Edition", 43) the reservations expressed in her earlier discussion (*ibid.*, 37) concerning the ultimate plausibility of a "vitalist" account of mysticism and distances herself from Bergson's thought in particular. Underhill's statement of her revised views precede by a couple of years the publication of *TSMR* in which Bergson expresses his admiration for her "remarkable works" (see *TSMR* 227, n.3), clearly unaware of her recent reconsiderations.

[38] See also *TSMR* 179, 186.

[39] See also *TSMR* 256.

[40] *TSMR* 212, 230, 317.

[41] *TSMR* 227-40.

[42] These formulations invite a comparison with Georges Bataille's remarkable, often very similarly articulated, discussion of mysticism in "Mysticism and Sensuality", *Eroticism, op. cit*, 221-51.

[43] For a stunning elaboration of the conception of mysticism suggested here see, Jill Marsden, *After Nietzsche: Notes Towards a Philosophy of Ecstasy*. Basingstoke: Palgrave, 2002, especially ch. 6, "The Night of Unknowing", 123-47, and see also 160-70. Marsden's remarkable book – surely one of the most original and significant contributions to Nietzsche studies in recent years – includes stimulating and profound discussions of many of the topics and thinkers considered here, including extended reflections on the Nietzsche/Bergson relation.

[44] See *TSMR*, 216-27. Bergson underpins his valorisation of Christian mysticism through an extended and detailed evaluation of many other Western and Eastern alternatives.

[45] See *TSMR*, 228ff., 245f., 250; and 228ff., 245f., 250.

[46] However, Bergson and Nietzsche disagree in their assessments of individual cases, most notably St. Paul and St. Theresa of Avila. The topic of distinguishing between "healthy" and "sick" types of "religious feeling" calls to mind James's seminal discussion of the issue, see William James, *The Varieties of Religious*

Experience. Harmondsworth: Penguin, 1985, especially Lectures IV-VIII, XVI-XVII, 78-188; 378-429. See also Marsden, *op. cit.*, 96-109, 118-22.
[47] See also *TSMR* 262.
[48] As will have been noted, the emphasis in this discussion has been on drawing attention to the very considerable common ground between Nietzsche and Bergson in relation to the task of revivifying and reconfiguring the notion of "natural religion". Obviously, however, there are also many fault lines between them which would need to be addressed in a longer study, albeit in terms of a hermeneutic of mutual radicalisation. Some prominent issues here would include: the interrogation, from a genealogical perspective, of the normativities endorsed in *TSMR* and, reciprocally, a critical evaluation of Nietzsche's notion of the "future" (and what it makes possible in his thinking) from the point of view of Bergson's conception of the nature of time. For a valuable discussion of aspects of the Nietzsche/Bergson relation with reference to *TSMR* see, Len Lawlor, *The Challenge of Bergsonism*. London and New York: Continuum, 2003, "Appendix I: The Point where Memory Turns Back into Life: An Investigation of Bergson's *Two Sources of Morality and Religion*", 85-111.

CONTRIBUTORS

Douglas Burnham – is the author of *Kant's* Critique of Pure Reason, *An Introduction to Kant's* Critique of Judgment, *Kant's Philosophies of Judgement*, *Reading Nietzsche: An Analysis of* Beyond Good and Evil, (with Enrico Giaccherini*) The Poetics Of Transubstantiation: From Theology To Metaphor*, and (with Martin Jesinghausen) *Nietzsche's* The Birth of Tragedy. He is Professor of Philosophy at Staffordshire University.

Ullrich Haase – is co-author (with Will Large) of *Maurice Blanchot*. He published *Starting With Nietzsche* in 2008. He has written articles and book chapters on Nietzsche and Phenomenology. He is the Editor of the *Journal of the British Society for Phenomenology*. Ullrich Haase is Senior Lecturer in Philosophy at Manchester Metropolitan University.

Martin Jesinghausen – has published in the areas of Art, Literature and Culture, on the political implications of theories of the novel, and on Benjamin and Foucault. He is co-author (with Douglas Burnham) of a series of readings of Nietzsche's works. He is Senior Lecturer in English at Staffordshire University.

Sean Kirkland – is the author of *The Ontology and Socratic Questioning in Plato's Early Dialogues*, and he has published broadly in the areas of Ancient Greek philosophy and contemporary continental philosophy. He is Associate Professor of Philosophy at DePaul University, Chicago.

David Farrell Krell – has written books on Heidegger and Nietzsche, including *Postponements: Woman, Sensuality, and Death in Nietzsche, Intimations of Mortality: Time, Truth, and Finitude in Heidegger's Thinking of Being, Daimon Life: Heidegger and Life Philosophy, The Good European: Nietzsche's Work Sites in Word and Image*, and *Infectious Nietzsche*. Additionally, Krell has written extensively on German Idealism. His books in this area include *The Tragic Absolute: German Idealism and the Languishing of God*, and *Contagion: Sexuality, Disease, and Death in German Idealism and Romanticism*. He also translated Heidegger's lectures and essays on Nietzsche and on the early

Greek thinkers, and was the editor of Heidegger's *Basic Writings*. His most recent translation is of Friedrich Hölderlin's *The Death of Empedocles: A Mourning-Play*. He is Emeritus Professor of Philosophy at DePaul University, Chicago.

Jill Marsden – is the author of *After Nietzsche: Notes Towards a Philosophy of Ecstasy*, as well as articles on Nietzsche, Freud, Schreber, Bataille, Deleuze, and Feminism. Jill Marsden is Senior Lecturer in Philosophy and English at the University of Bolton.

William McNeill – is the author of *The Time of Life: Heidegger and Ethos*, and *The Glance of the Eye: Heidegger, Aristotle, and the Ends of Theory*, as well as numerous articles on Heidegger. He is the translator of *Pathmarks*, *Hölderlin's Hymn "The Ister"* (with Julia Davis), *The Fundamental Concepts of Metaphysics: World, Finitude, Solitude* (with Nicholas Walker), and *The Concept of Time*. William McNeill is Professor of Philosophy at DePaul University, Chicago.

Graham Parkes – Graham Parkes is the author of *Composing the Soul: Reaches of Nietzsche's Psychology* and editor of *Nietzsche and Asian Thought*, and he published a new translation of *Also sprach Zarathustra* in 2005. He is Professor of Philosophy and Head of the School of Philosophy and Sociology at University College Cork, Ireland.

Andrea Rehberg – co-edited (with Rachel Jones) *The Matter of Critique – Readings in Kant's Philosophy*. She has written articles and book chapters on Kant, Nietzsche, and Heidegger. She teaches in the Philosophy Department at Middle East Technical University, Ankara, Turkey.

John Sallis – is the author of more than twenty books. These include two systematic works on the imagination (*Force of Imagination* and *Logic of Imagination*), several works on ancient philosophy (*Being and Logos*, *Chorology*, and *Platonic Legacies*), and several studies of 19th- and 20th-century European philosophers (*Crossings:Nietzsche and the Space of Tragedy*, *Echoes: After Heidegger*, and *Transfigurements: On the True Sense of Art*). He is the founding editor of the journal *Research in Phenomenology*. He is the Frederick J. Adelmann Professor of Philosophy at Boston College.

Jim Urpeth – co-edited (with John Lippitt) *Nietzsche and the Divine*. He has written articles on Kant, Nietzsche, Heidegger, Foucault, Focillon,

Otto, Bataille, and Deleuze/Guattari. His main research interests are Philosophical Naturalism and the Philosophy of Religion. He is Senior Lecturer in Philosophy at the University of Greenwich.

INDEX

212 Index